商务英语报刊选读

马 宾 编著

苏州大学出版社

图书在版编目(CIP)数据

商务英语报刊选读 / 马宾编著. —苏州：苏州大学出版社，2020.12（2024.7重印）
ISBN 978-7-5672-3399-7

Ⅰ.①商… Ⅱ.①马… Ⅲ.①商务-英语-阅读教学-自学参考资料 Ⅳ.①F7

中国版本图书馆 CIP 数据核字（2020）第 226505 号

书　　名：	商务英语报刊选读
编　　著：	马　宾
责任编辑：	汤定军
策划编辑：	汤定军
封面设计：	刘　俊
出版发行：	苏州大学出版社（Soochow University Press）
社　　址：	苏州市十梓街1号　邮编：215006
印　　装：	广东虎彩云印刷有限公司
网　　址：	www.sudapress.com
邮　　箱：	sdcbs@suda.edu.cn
邮购热线：	0512-67480030
销售热线：	0512-67481020
开　　本：	787 mm×1092 mm　1/16　印张：18.75　字数：399千
版　　次：	2020年12月第1版
印　　次：	2024年 7月第4次印刷
书　　号：	ISBN 978-7-5672-3399-7
定　　价：	68.00元

凡购本社图书发现印装错误，请与本社联系调换。服务热线：0512-67481020

序言

一、必要性和重要意义

"经济"一词系指"经世济民",即治理国家以及提高人民生活水平。对于国家和民众而言,发展经济可以说是头等大事。经济生活构成我们生存和发展的基本层面,商品生产和贸易是人类社会得以继续存在和进一步发展的前提条件和物质基础。经济发展对于提高人们的物质生活水平和精神生活水平、推动社会进步起到至关重要的基础性的作用,是社会、历史和文化发展的物质基础,也是人民群众生活幸福的物质保障。早在《国语》当中就有记载"轻关易道,通商宽农",可以说发展贸易、减轻赋税一直以来就是社会经济发展的必然要求。这也是为何当今各个国家和地区都在做出种种努力来克服贸易保护主义,尽量消除贸易壁垒,提倡公平竞争和自由贸易,增强核心竞争力,力求提升经济发展动力。

当代英语专业大学生不仅要学习英语语言知识,也要关注现实生活、放眼全世界。如何实现经济地位平等、企业和个人的全面充分发展、区域经济与全球经济的协调发展等,这些都涉及国家和世界经济全局及国计民生诸多方面的重大问题。阅读商务英语报刊,可以帮助我们了解当今世界经济发展的新动态、扩展知识面、开拓学术视野、养成科学思维方式。在此基础上,我们可以更加全面和深入地学习英语,掌握必要的经济和贸易类专业知识,成为符合当今社会发展需要的复合型人才。阅读商务英语报刊原文,可以让我们接触到现代经济学的最新理论和观点,了解到世界经济的最新动态,将中国经济置于全球经济中来考察,自觉地将中国和其他国家和地区经济的发展道路和所取得的成就进行比较分析。这有助于我们树立正确的世界观,增强我们的道路自信、理论自信、制度自信和文化自信,更加坚定走中国特色社会主义道路的信心。

二、内容提要

本书包括15个单元,涵盖了中国经济、美国经济、世界经济、国际金融、国际投资、全球化、企业发展战略、企业并购、企业创新、发展平等、职业生涯、市场营销、产品营销等方面。将宏观与微观视角结合起来,全面反映当今世界经济发展动态、规律和未来展望。

三、本书特点

选材新颖,客观全面:所选材料基本来自2017年以来的《哈佛商业评论》《金融时报》《经济学人》《中国日报》等,力求反映世界经济的最新动态。编著者对材料进行仔细甄别,所选文章篇幅长短适宜,内容难易适中,观点翔实深刻,客观反映了中国及其他国家和地区的经济发展形势,能够激发读者的阅读兴趣,兼顾学术性和趣味性。编著者将相同主题的文章从不同报刊当中选取出来,将不同的视角和观点呈现给读者,旨在帮助大家进行深度且全面的阅读,在此过程中着重培养辩证思维方式,养成独立自主思考问题的习惯。

主题突出,覆盖面广:本书每个单元的主题都不相同,内容重点突出,详略得当。所选材料既有宏观全面地介绍中国、美国及世界经济,也有微观而深入地分析税收政策、男女平等、管理方法、思维方式等方面,力图能够反映商务英语报刊面向专业读者、覆盖范围广的特点。

专业性强,注释详尽:商务英语报刊中的生词量特别大,非经济贸易类专业的读者缺乏相关专业知识,这导致了大部分读者对商务英语报刊望而生畏。编著者将生词尽可能详尽地列出并且注释,必要时则附上专业背景知识及延伸阅读材料。此举目的在于帮助读者克服文字障碍并且拓展知识面,从而让读者在阅读英文报刊过程当中感到轻松而且能够享受到乐趣。

形式多样,适合教学:本书包含15个单元,便于安排授课计划;文章的形式包括简报、深度报道及名人访谈;每个单元都编排了不同难易程度的文章,考虑到学生之间存在的语言和专业知识储备方面的客观差异,满足不同层次学生的需求。教师可以根据学生的语言基础、知识水平、学习能力、学习兴趣及情感需求来灵活机动地选择和安排每个单元的课堂教学内容,有利于实现课堂讲授和课外自主阅读的有机结合。

Contents

Unit	Title	Subtitle	Page
One	Chinese Economy	Foreign Trade Prospects Stay Upbeat	1
		China Leads New Energy Vehicle Development	4
		Chinese Investors Buy Kyoto Sportscar Maker	7
		Top China Beer Brands Hammered as Tastes Shift	10
		Chinese Private Security Goes Global	16
Two	US Economy	Trump's Tough Talk on Jobs Reshoring Puts Banks to Test	24
		President Proves Comedy Gold for US Television Networks' Late-Night Satire	30
Three	World Economy	Zimbabwe Is Staring at Currency Chaos Again	33
		German Business Chiefs Prepare to Defend Free Trade in US	39
		Delusional Lawyering Won't Save European Bonds	42
		Fiscal Rules and Fiscal Cryogenics	46
		Thailand's Economy: The Dangers of Farsightedness	50
		Tata Saga Shows Corporate India Must Change Its Ways	56
Four	International Finance	Our Financial Standards Benefit Everyone	62
		Foreign Exchange: A Losing Battle	67
		Not Passing the Buck: Global Capital Flows Have Slowed Down	71
		European Insurers Feeling Squeezed	76
Five	International Investment	Defending a Good Company from Bad Investors	80
		UK Workplace Pension Invests in UBS Climate Fund	87
		Fund Houses Turn Against Investment Consultants	93
		The Surprising Behaviors That Can Make a Difference	99
Six	Globalization	Saving Globalisation: The Reset Button	106
		Deregulation and Competition: A Lapse in Concentration	112

Unit	Title	Subtitle	Page
Seven	Enterprise Development Strategy	The Data: Where Long-Termism Pays Off	121
		Why High Potentials Struggle and How They Can Grow through It	124
		Don't Try to Protect the Past	135
Eight	Merger and Acquisition	Aldo Ernesto Belloni Lured from Retirement to Tackle $65bn Chemical Tie-Up Challenge	147
		EU Vetos Deutsche Boerse-London Stock Exchange Merger Deal	151
		Unilever's Best Option May Be to Do Nothing	155
Nine	Innovation	Sometimes, Less Innovation Is Better	160
		What's Your Best Innovation Bet?	167
Ten	Economic Equality	Gain and Pain	181
		A Field Day for America's One Per Cent	189
		Miners Warn ANC Over Black Ownership Plan	193
		The Board View: Directors Must Balance All Interests	196
Eleven	Payment	Decoding CEO Pay	200
		Some Lenders Demand $10,000 for Single Phone Call with Most Senior Analysts	210
		Infighting Hobbles Efforts to Curb Bumper Bonuses	214
		Shareholders Demand Right to Cap Bosses' Pay	217
		The Clintons' Financial Affairs Bill and Hillary Inc.	221
Twelve	Career Development	Millennial Women See No Glass Ceiling	227
		Long Lives Mean Demand for Endless Coaching	233
		Neurodiversity as a Competitive Advantage	237
Thirteen	CMO	The Evolution of the CMO	250
		The Power Partnership: CMO & CIO	256
Fourteen	Product Promotion	Finding the Platform in Your Product	259
		The Science of Pep Talks	269
		Grading a Sales Leader's Pep Talk	276
Fifteen	Enterprise Data Management	What's Your Data Strategy?	279

Unit One

Chinese Economy

Foreign Trade Prospects Stay Upbeat

Zheng Xin
July 14, 2017, *China Daily*

China's foreign trade prospects are set to remain upbeat during the upcoming six months, after expanding at the fastest pace since the second half of 2011.

The General Administration of Customs said on Thursday that China's foreign trade was 13.14 trillion yuan ($1.94 trillion) from January to June, an year-on-year increase of 19.6 percent.

The exports amounted to 7.21 trillion yuan during the same period, up by 15 percent, while the imports increased by 25.7 percent to 5.93 trillion yuan, leading to a 1.28 trillion yuan trade surplus, down 17.7 percent year-on-year, it said.

"The brisk growth was bolstered by a lower comparison basis, government support and healing global demand," GAC spokesman Huang Songping told a media briefing.

Considering a higher comparison basis, uncertainties in the global environment and deep-seated problems in the domestic economy, Huang emphasized a tough stance on foreign trade in the second half of this year.

"With China's trade structure optimized, and its quality and benefits improved, it's believed the economic prospects will remain good, whereas unstable and uncertain factors will still affect the foreign trade environment, and some deep-seated problems and difficulties will continue to exist in the long term," he said.

Tu Xinquan, a professor of foreign trade at the China Institute for WTO Studies at the University of International Business and Economics in Beijing, said China's overall foreign trade remained sound and steady.

"The trade volume has expanded and witnessed positive changes since the second half of last year, buffering the economy from a slowdown amid headwinds at home and abroad," said Tu.

"Trade prospects are expected to remain stable during the next six months, thanks to the current macroeconomic stimulus, structural reforms and economic recovery in the US and European countries."

Against the backdrop of global economic recovery, the international market demand growth has boosted China's export volume by 8.9 percent, while the continuous optimization of the foreign commodities trade structure also led to the increase, which is in line with the stabilizing and positive trend since 2016, said Huang.

The rising external demand has led to an increase in exports during the past six months, while the increasing import volume and price of major bulk commodities including iron ore, crude oil and natural gas also contributed to the boost, according to the administration.

During the first six months, the imports of iron ore, crude oil, soybean and natural gas hit 539 million tons, 212 million tons, 44.81 million tons and 31.09 million metric tons, which increased 9.3 percent, 13.8 percent, 14.2 percent and 15.9 percent respectively.

The imports of crude oil and copper reached 15.03 million tons and 2.23 million tons, a respective increase of 2.8 percent and 18.4 percent, and China's import prices have witnessed an overall growth of 12.7 percent, said the administration.

Huang said the rising import-and-export proportion of private businesses will ensure trade prospects remain stable during the next six months.

The imports and exports of private enterprises grew by 20.6 percent to 5.02 trillion yuan, accounting for 38.2 percent of the total national figure, 0.3 percent higher than the previous year.

The exports by private businesses increased 17.8 percent to 3.37 trillion yuan, 46.7 percent of the total export value, according to the administration.

While the imports and exports to traditional markets witnessed a full recovery, those to the economies participating in the Belt and Road Initiative have also registered growth.

In the past six months, China's trade with the European Union, the United States and ASEAN members increased by 17.4 percent, 21.3 percent and 21.9 percent respectively, altogether accounting for 41.4 percent of China's total import and export value.

Over the same period, the imports and exports to Russia, Pakistan, Poland and Kazakhstan increased by 33.1 percent, 14.5 percent, 24.6 percent and 46.8 percent respectively, according to the figures from the administration.

Unit One　Chinese Economy

Words and Expressions

prospect	n.	前景,期望,景象,(竞赛中的)有望获胜者
	vi.	找矿,勘探,勘察
be set to		准备,开始
upbeat	adj.	积极乐观的,愉快的,高兴的
brisk	adj.	轻快的,快的,爽快而清新的,兴隆的
	vi.	活跃起来,变得轻快
	vt.	使……活泼,使……轻快
bolster	vt.	支持,支撑,鼓励,援助
	n.	垫枕,长枕,衬垫,支持物
healing	adj.	康复的,复原的
deep-seated	adj.	根深蒂固的,深层的,牢固的
stance	n.	态度,立场,站姿,被放置的姿势,位置
optimize	vt.	使最优化,使尽可能有效
buffer	vt.	缓冲
	n.	缓冲器,起缓冲作用的人(或物)
headwind	n.	逆风,顶头风
backdrop	n.	背景
bulk commodities		大宗商品
ore	n.	矿,矿石
register	vt.	显示(读数),记录,登记,注册
	n.	登记表,注册簿

Notes to the Text

1. Association of Southeast Asian Nations：东南亚国家联盟,简称东盟(ASEAN)。成员国有马来西亚、印度尼西亚、泰国、菲律宾、新加坡、文莱、越南、老挝、缅甸和柬埔寨。东盟成为东南亚地区以经济合作为基础的政治、经济、安全一体化合作组织,并建立起一系列合作机制。总部位于印度尼西亚的雅加达。

China Leads New Energy Vehicle Development

July 16, 2017, *China Daily*

BEIJING — China now leads the world in new energy vehicle (NEV) development, according to a survey ranking China top in its global electric vehicle development index for the first time in the second quarter of 2017.

The results of the survey, the E-Mobility Index (2Q/2017), were jointly released by German consultancy Roland Berger and automobile study institute Forschungsgesellschaft Kraftfahrwesen Aachen on Tuesday.

Starting in 2009, China's new energy auto industry experienced a robust expansion and it has become the world's largest market since 2015, according to a statement from the Ministry of Industry and Information Technology (MIIT).

The German consultancy's report said that China will play a leading role in the future development of the global NEV industry thanks to its strong market growth.

The sales of electric cars in China grew rapidly, from less than 5,000 in 2011 to around 510,000 in 2016.

Production and sales were particularly robust in June of this year, with 59,000 units sold and 65,000 produced, up 33 percent and 43.4 percent respectively from a year earlier.

The China Association of Automobile Manufacturers estimated that the domestic NEV sales could hit 800,000 units at the end of this year.

The industry insiders attributed the impressive progress of the Chinese market the government support and simpler licensing procedures.

"The output, sales and ownership of NEVs in China all accounted for more than half of global levels last year," said Chinese Vice Premier Ma Kai at a meeting in early July, adding more research should be carried out in batteries, charging technology and the construction of charging facilities.

In April, the "Guideline on China's Medium and Long-term Car Industry Development" was jointly published by the MIIT, the National Development and Reform Commission and the Ministry of Science and Technology.

The document said that new energy cars were expected to be a key area in building China from a "big" auto power to a "strong" one.

Besides the government support, the market demand and efforts by auto makers also prompted the domestic industry's trend, according to the survey.

Beijing Automotive Industry Corp (BAIC), a leading domestic auto manufacturer, recorded the year-on-year sales growth of NEVs as high as 159 percent in 2016 and 99 percent in the first half of 2017.

The Chinese auto companies including BYD, BAIC and Geely ranked among the top brands worldwide in terms of electric car sales last year, according to the China Passenger Car Association.

The international cooperation on NEV production is also gearing up.

In June, German car giant Daimler signed a framework agreement in Berlin with China's BAIC to produce Mercedes-Benz-branded electric cars via their joint venture, Beijing Benz Automotive.

In accordance with the agreement, both enterprises are preparing to produce electric vehicles in China by 2020 and to provide the necessary infrastructure for battery localization using Chinese cells, as well as to expand the research and development capacity.

Volkswagen plans to offer Chinese consumers about 400,000 NEVs by 2020 and over 1.5 million by 2025, which has been an important part of the company's ambition in the Chinese market, according to Jochem Heizmann, CEO of Volkswagen Group China.

As downward economic pressure becomes more intensive and the domestic market continues to expand, the deep-rooted challenges facing the industry need to be addressed.

"The cost of batteries is the issue of most concern for current development," said Ouyang Minggao from China EV100, a domestic industry group.

"The industrial foundation is not solid and we have not achieved breakthroughs in the core technology of NEV batteries, so the competitiveness of the industry should be further sharpened," said Qu Guochun, deputy director-general of the machinery industry department at the MIIT.

To further promote the healthy and sustainable development of the industry, more efforts should be made in improving the innovation system, advancing the industrial transformation and upgrading, and strengthening the application of NEVs, Qu said.

Words and Expressions

attribute to		把……归因于……
license	n.	许可证,执照,特许
	vt.	同意,发许可证
account for		导致,引起,(在数量、比例上)占,对……负责

charge	vi.	充电,索价,向前冲,记在账上
prompt	v.	提示,促使,导致,鼓励
	adj.	迅速的,敏捷的,立刻的,准时的
	n.	提示,提示符,激励
	adv.	准时地
gear up		换高速挡,改进……以适应提高生产的需要,使做好行动准备
infrastructure	n.	(国家或机构的)基础设施,基础建设

Notes to the Text

1. MIIT（Ministry of Industry and Information Technology）：中华人民共和国工业和信息化部（简称：工业和信息化部或工信部），是根据 2008 年 3 月 11 日公布的国务院机构改革方案组建的国务院直属部门。

2. Beijing Automotive Industry Corp：北汽集团,是原"北京汽车工业集团总公司"的简称,总部在北京,是中国五大汽车集团之一,由北京汽车集团有限公司、北京首钢股份有限公司、北京市国有资产经营有限责任公司、现代创新控股有限公司、北京国有资产经营管理中心和北京能源投资（集团）有限公司共同发起组成,公司注册资本 56 亿元。主要从事整车制造、零部件制造、汽车服务贸易、研发、教育、投融资等业务,是北京汽车工业的发展规划中心、资本运营中心、产品开发中心和人才中心。

3. BYD：比亚迪,是中国一家高新技术的民营企业,总部位于深圳坪山。2002 年,比亚迪在香港主板发行上市,创下了 H 股最高发行价纪录。2003 年,比亚迪正式收购西安秦川汽车有限责任公司,进入汽车制造与销售领域,开始民族自主品牌汽车的发展征程。发展至今,比亚迪已建成西安、北京、深圳、上海四大汽车产业基地,汽车产品包括各种高、中、低端系列燃油轿车,以及汽车模具、汽车零部件、双模电动汽车、纯电动汽车等。作为电动车领域的领跑者和全球二次电池产业的领先者,比亚迪将利用技术优势,不断制造清洁能源的汽车产品。

4. GEELY：浙江吉利控股集团有限公司,始建于 1986 年,是中国国内汽车行业十强中唯一民营轿车生产经营企业,经过三十多年的建设与发展,在汽车、摩托车、汽车发动机、变速器、汽车电子电气及汽车零部件方面取得辉煌业绩。特别是 1997 年进入轿车领域以来,凭借灵活的经营机制和持续的自主创新,取得了快速的发展,现资产总值超过千亿元,连续四年进入全国企业 500 强。

5. localization：本地化,是指企业在国际化过程中,为了提高市场竞争力,同时降低成本,将产品的生产、销售等环节按特定国家、地区或语言市场的需要进行组织,使之符合特定区域市场的组织变革过程。

6. Daimler AG：戴姆勒股份公司，总部位于德国斯图加特，是全球最大的商用车制造商，全球第一大豪华车生产商、第二大卡车生产商。公司旗下包括梅赛德斯-奔驰汽车、梅赛德斯-奔驰轻型商用车、戴姆勒载重车、戴姆勒金融服务四大业务单元。旗下品牌包括迈巴赫、奔驰、Smart、AMG、乌尼莫克。20世纪80年代，戴姆勒公司和中国北方工业公司合作，向中国转让奔驰重型汽车的生产技术。2005年，戴姆勒与北京汽车工业控股有限责任公司成立了北京奔驰-戴姆勒·克莱斯勒汽车有限公司，生产梅赛德斯-奔驰C级和E级轿车，以及GLA级运动型多功能汽车。2007年，戴姆勒与福建省汽车工业集团有限公司共同合资组建福建戴姆勒汽车工业有限公司，生产梅赛德斯-奔驰威霆、唯雅诺和凌特轻型商用车。2012年，北京福田戴姆勒汽车有限公司在京隆重成立。戴姆勒和福田汽车喜结连理。2010年，德国汽车企业戴姆勒与比亚迪正式签署合资协议，成立深圳比亚迪·戴姆勒新技术有限公司，在中国开发电动汽车，比亚迪将提供电动车的核心技术。2018年，戴姆勒发布两款电动卡车，并且将其中一款直接定位成特斯拉Semi电动卡车的竞争对手。

7. Volkswagen：大众汽车，是一家总部位于德国沃尔夫斯堡的汽车制造公司，也是世界四大汽车生产商之一的大众集团的核心企业。Volks在德语中意思为"国民"，Wagen在德语中意思为"汽车"，全名的意思即"国民的汽车"，故又常简称为VW。集团的乘用车业务分为两大品牌。在集团之下，奥迪和大众各自独立管理其品牌群，并负责从中创造利润。各个品牌均有其自己的标识，自主经营。奥迪品牌群包括奥迪（Audi）、西亚特（Seat）、兰博基尼（Lamborghini）、杜卡迪（DUCATI）4个品牌。大众品牌群包括大众商用车、大众乘用车、斯柯达（SKODA）、宾利（Bentley）、布加迪（Bugatti）、保时捷（Porsche）、斯堪尼亚（SCANIA）等共8个品牌。

Chinese Investors Buy Kyoto Sportscar Maker

July 17, 2017, *China Daily*

　China's drive to dominate the electric vehicle market has claimed another overseas target.

　When Japanese electric vehicle startup GLM needed more funding to put its high-end sports car into production, domestic backers couldn't muster the financing.

　The search for an investor ended last week, when a Hong Kong-based investment company called O Luxe Holdings agreed to purchase the firm for 12.8 billion yen ($113 million).

　O Luxe will fund the deal by issuing new shares to stockholders, which include Chinese

TV maker TCL. With the backing of its new owner, GLM gets access to global money for research and development, founder and CEO Hiroyasu Koma said in an interview at his Kyoto headquarters after the sale.

"Electric vehicles are catching on, and China is the leader," Koma said. "But Japanese technology will maintain an edge for the next five years and we want to take a share of the market."

The Chinese government is pouring subsidies into the domestic market for new energy vehicles and Chinese companies are snapping up foreign battery and electric vehicle makers like GLM in order to beef up their technology.

In a filing to the Hong Kong Stock Exchange, O Luxe said the acquisition represents an opportunity to tap into the fast growing electric vehicle industry.

Under its new owner, GLM plans to start production of its G4 ultra-luxury sports car—which has a planned price tag of 40 million yen—in the second half of 2019.

There are also plans, he said, to introduce an electric mini-bus and a seven-seater family car, adapting the G4's power train and other key electrical components.

Founded in 2010 by seven engineers who defected from Toyota Motor and other Japanese automakers, GLM's first model was a lightweight two-door sports car called the Tommykaira ZZ, which debuted in Japan in 2014 for about 8 million yen. Fewer than 100 have been sold, according to the company.

While GLM will count on sales of its vehicles to keep the business going in the short term, Koma said the emphasis will shift toward supplying other carmakers with customized engineering solutions and components like chassis platforms, power systems and control units.

The company is close to signing several contracts to supply carmakers mostly in China, he said, without naming the firms.

Wang Jianfeng, chairman of Ningbo Joyson Electronic, whose United States subsidiary last month agreed to buy bankrupt Japanese airbag maker Takata, in April said the country's auto industry can't compete globally without absorbing more foreign engineering knowhow.

The deal for GLM follows a series of global electric vehicle investments for Chinese firms.

In the last five years, autoparts maker Wanxiang Group bought the Karma electric car business operated by US startup Fisker Automotive, along with Karma's battery supplier, A123 Systems.

Jia Yueting, the founder of Chinese technology company LeEco, is an investor in Faraday Future, the Los Angeles-based maker of electric sports cars that hopes one day to compete with Tesla.

Chinese private equity firm GSR Capital is reportedly close to a deal to buy a battery venture owned by Nissan Motor.

Words and Expressions

drive	n.	有组织的努力,运动,车道,冲劲,干劲,精力,计算机的磁盘驱动器
claim	n./vt.	索要,索取,获得,赢得,取得,(灾难、事故等)夺走,夺去(生命)
startup	n.	启动,新兴公司
backer	n.	支持者,资助者
muster	vt.	聚集,召集
edge	n.	优势,边缘
	vi.	缓慢地移动,挪动
snap up		抢购
beef up		改善,加强,改进,提高
filing	n.	档案,卷宗
tap into		利用,开发
seven-seater	n.	七座小客车
power train		动力传动系统
defect	vi.	倒戈,叛逃
	n.	缺点,缺陷
debut	n.	初次露面,初次表演,首次出场,处女秀
	v.	初次表演,初次登台
	adj.	首张的,首场的,首次的
count on		指望,依靠
customized	adj.	客户指定的,订制的
chassis	n.	(车辆的)底盘
bankrupt	adj.	破产的,倒闭的
airbag	n.	安全气囊(遇车祸时充气保护车内的人)
knowhow	n.	专项技术,诀窍
close to a deal		达成一项协议,完成一项交易

Notes to the Text

1. Kyoto：京都的字面意思为"首都"，它位于日本本州岛的中部，在历史上有一千多年的时间，曾经作为日本的首都，现在是位于关西地区的京都府的府厅所在地。京都市也是京都、大阪、神户都会区的重要组成部分。

2. GLM：它的全称是 Green Lord Motors，2010 年，七名从丰田等日本大型汽车制造商辞职的工程师创立了 GLM，致力于打造顶级纯电动超跑车型。GLM 的首款车型是名为 Tommykaira ZZ 的轻型双门电动跑车，该车于 2014 年在日本首次推出。该公司在巴黎车展上亮相的纯电动超跑车型 G4 博得了众人的眼球，可以说这是一款速度与时尚的艺术品。

3. subsidy：补贴，是指一成员方政府或任何公共机构向某些企业提供的财政捐助以及对价格或收入的支持，以直接或间接增加从其领土输出某种产品或减少向其领土内输入某种产品，或者对其他成员方利益形成损害的政府性措施。

4. FF（Faraday Future）：法拉第未来，是一家有着美国硅谷背景的智能互联电动车新兴企业，成立于 2014 年，FF 因与中国乐视集团的合作而备受关注，其全球总部位于美国拉斯维加斯，研发中心在洛杉矶。据悉，FF 与乐视的合作涉及汽车、技术、互联网、云、娱乐内容等多个方面。

5. PE（Private Equity）：私募股权投资，从投资方式角度看，是指通过私募形式对私有企业，即非上市企业进行的权益性投资，在交易实施过程中附带考虑了将来的退出机制，即通过上市、并购或管理层回购等方式，出售持股获利。

Top China Beer Brands Hammered as Tastes Shift

Snow, Tsingtao and Yanjing sales volumes fall while imports and craft brews gain ground

Tom Hancock — Shanghai

February 27, 2017, *Financial Times*

Ignoring the cheap beer on tap in a smoky Beijing bar, Cheer Qiu reaches into a fridge bursting with craft ales and pulls out a bottle of locally made Panda Brew, flavoured with honey. "I'm interested in brewing culture," Ms Qiu says.

She is not alone in shunning cheaper beers for more distinct brews. The volume sales in China at Carlsberg, the Danish brewer, fell 6 per cent last year while Panda says its sales trebled.

Kurt Xia founded Panda in 2013 and is selling his products in 60 cities across the country. He has drawn venture capital investment of RMB 20m ($2.9m). "Consumers are not only satisfied with lager but want to have something unique and which makes them look cool," he says.

The brewers' contrasting fortunes underline the challenge of China's more than $70bn-a-year beer market. Volumes have been falling about 5 per cent annually for the past three years.

The drop has been driven by the rising popularity of wine and other alternatives, and a decline in the working-age population that consumes most of the cheap lager, which is priced at less than $1 per bottle and accounts for more than 90 per cent of volumes.

At the same time, the value of Chinese beer sales has risen slightly as younger and more affluent consumers switch to premium drinks, especially craft beers.

Many of these are from abroad. The home consumption of imported beer rose 40 per cent last year, according to Kantar Worldpanel, to comprise 3.6 per cent of the market.

That has been a boost for small European brewers.

Premium brands have experienced rapid growth, says Antoine Bolly, China marketing manager for Vandergeeten & EG DistriSelecta, which distributes Chimay beer and Huyghe Brewery's flagship Delirium Tremens beer in China. "The consumer goes more and more for premium instead of value."

Brand recognition and loyalty for beers such as Chimay, brewed by Trappist monks in Belgium, are rising, Mr Bolly says, with consumers "asking for the brand in Chinese".

Dutch brewer Heineken said this month that its sales volumes in China increased slightly last year on the strength of its more expensive offerings.

"We are totally super premium with the Heineken brand in China," says Jean-François van Boxmeer, chairman. "It's a promise for the future."

Scottish "punk" brand BrewDog has also expanded in China. "It seems to have a following," says Gary Brown, managing director for Topshelf Asia, which distributes the beer. "They are serious about the market here. There's only a few big markets that haven't been tapped."

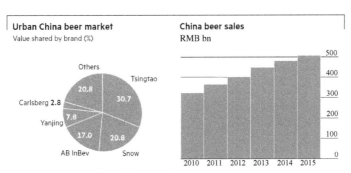

Sources: Kantar Worldpanel; Euromonitor

Carlsberg says sales of its premium Tuborg and 1664 Blanc brands are strong in China. "The gain is not volume but value and premiumisation, and we are well placed for that and in that respect optimistic for China," says Cees't Hart, chief executive.

But China beer groups appear to be struggling with the shift to premium drinks. The urban sales volumes of Snow, Tsingtao and Yanjing, the biggest domestic brands, contracted 3, 7 and 8 per cent respectively last year, according to Kantar.

The revenues at China Resources Snow Breweries—the world's biggest beer group by sales volume — fell 2 per cent to RMB 15bn in the first half of last year. China Resources Beer acquired SABMiller's 49 per cent stake in Snow for $1.6bn last year.

Yanjing's 2016 sales were down more than 10 per cent to RMB 6.3bn and profits fell one-quarter compared with the previous year to RMB 451m.

The group is "heavily indebted, and the market believes they are looking for a strategic investor to bail them out," Gordon Orr of McKinsey writes. "However much they try, their brands aren't premiumising well. Consumers view them as the cheap brew that their parents and grandparents turned to. They want something different."

Tsingtao posted an 8 per cent fall in revenues to RMB 14.7bn in its most recent report, with profits down 6 per cent. Japan's Asahi is considering selling its 20 per cent stake.

But the China market is not all smooth sailing for premium brands. A lack of refrigeration in bars and distribution vehicles can spoil the taste, and distributors say "parallel" imports of foreign beer brands that avoid paying customs duties are a challenge.

"When Heineken is sold in Europe under promotion, some containers are shipped to China—it's very difficult to control," Mr van Boxmeer says.

Ceinwen Michael, a sales manager in China for Vandergeeten, says the problem of parallel imports is extensive: "All big popular beers are getting bought in through other methods."

Lax enforcement of rules against unofficial vendors has exacerbated the problem. "We've given up reporting [parallel imports] to the authorities," Mr Brown says.

Words and Expressions

hammer	vt.	轻易打败(对方)
brew	vt.	酿造,酝酿
	vi.	酿酒,被冲泡,即将发生
	n.	啤酒,质地
craft beer		精酿啤酒

draft beer		生啤酒
on tap		随时调用的,现成的
burst with		充满
ale	n.	浓啤酒,(英国产)麦芽酒
flavor	n.	香味,滋味
	vt.	给……调味,给……增添风趣
distinct	adj.	明显的,独特的,清楚的,有区别的
treble	vt. & vi.	使成为三倍,增加两倍
	adj.	高音的,三倍的,三重的,最高声部的,尖锐刺耳的
	n.	三倍,最高音部,高音
venture	vt.	敢于
	vi.	冒险,投机
	n.	企业,风险,冒险
lager	n.	(浅颜色的、有许多泡沫的)淡啤酒
communicate	vt.	传达,表达,显示,清晰地揭示,表明,传染,扩散
	vi.	通信,交际,相连,相通
underline	vt.	强调,在……下面画线,预告
	n.	下划线,下期节目预告
affluent	adj.	富裕的,丰富的,流畅的
	n.	支流,富人
switch to		切换到,转到,转变成
premium	adj.	优质的,高端的
comprise	vt.	包含,由……组成
flagship	n.	旗舰,(作定语)一流,佼佼者
executive	adj.	行政的,经营的,执行的,经营管理的
	n.	经理,执行委员会,执行者,经理主管人员
respectively	adv.	分别地,各自地,独自地
compare with		与……相比较
indebted	adj.	负债的,感激的,受惠的
	v.	(indebt 的过去分词)使负债,使受恩惠
bail out		(常通过提供资金)帮助……摆脱困境
refrigeration	n.	制冷,冷藏,冷却
lax	adj.	松懈的,松弛的

vendor	n.	卖主,小贩,自动售货机
exacerbate	vt.	使加剧,使恶化,激怒

Notes to the Text

1. panda beer：熊猫王啤酒,与专业的酿酒师团队合作,打造国内前沿酿酒工艺 Lager & Ale 混合型酿造技术的精酿啤酒,以高品质、持续创新、打造国内高端品牌为目标。保留 Lager 与 Ale 各自酵母发酵的特点,醇香与酯香混合交融。

2. Gary Brown：一名影视演员,其主要作品有《今日剧》等。

3. Carlsberg：嘉士伯,是世界第五大酿酒集团,于 1847 年创立,总部位于丹麦哥本哈根,同时嘉士伯也是该公司主要的啤酒品牌。

4. Tuborg：乐堡啤酒,是全球第四大酿酒集团嘉士伯旗下的品牌,于 2012 年进入中国,是目前国内唯一拥有创新易拉啤酒瓶盖设计的啤酒品牌。始于 1880 年哥本哈根的乐堡啤酒,是丹麦第一款淡味型啤酒。拥有清爽顺口的口感和淡雅适中苦度的乐堡被誉为"全球十大高档啤酒品牌之一",并被打造为一款为全球年轻消费者的时尚啤酒品牌。

5. Chimay：智美,是著名比利时修道院啤酒(Trappist)品牌。离著名的智美镇 10 千米的斯高蒙特圣母玛利亚修道院有一家特拉比斯特啤酒厂在商业运作上非常成功。修道院 1850 年在尔吉斯建立,最终由于农庄缺乏足够的粮食,无法资助修道院而变卖,到 1862 年就重新开了这家啤酒厂。看起来生活枯燥的僧侣却酿造了堪称杰作的啤酒。1862 年,智美的僧侣们生产出第一批啤酒,完全按照古代僧侣传统的自然酿造、发酵和瓶中的再次发酵。今天,这座酿酒厂已经发展成为现代酿酒艺术的典范,在这里现代科技依然尊重僧侣们的宝贵酿酒知识。

6. Delirium Tremens beer：浅粉象,属于比利时风格的烈性淡爱尔啤酒(Belgian Strong Pale Ale),具有泡沫丰富细腻、酒体呈金黄色、酒精浓度高、口味丰富而口感厚重的特点。浅粉象在酿造的不同时段使用了三种不同的酵母,搭配大麦芽和小麦经过多次发酵酿造而成,所以造就了它出众的味道。

7. Heineken [ˈhaɪnɪkən]：全称 Heineken Brouwerijen,中文译名为"喜力",是世界著名的荷兰啤酒品牌,于 1864 年杰拉德·阿德里安·海尼根(Gerard Adriaan Heineken)于阿姆斯特丹创立。

8. BrewDog：直译过来是"酿酒狗"。没错,这家苏格兰啤酒生产商连名字都这么标新立异,其生产的啤酒更是荒诞不断、花样百出。酿酒狗这个在 2007 年由两个苏格兰年轻人无聊时突发奇想创造出来的啤酒厂现在几乎已经主宰了英国精酿啤酒市场,不断创造新的啤酒风格,广受年轻人追捧。

9. 1664 Blanc：该啤酒属于经典风格白啤酒,是典型的小麦酿造上发酵啤酒,它在口味和口感上十分接近比利时风格白啤酒,而与德国风格白啤酒有着很大区别。

10. AB InBev:百威英博,是全球领先的酿酒制造商,总部位于比利时鲁汶,成立于1876年。百威英博旗下经营着300多个品牌,其中包括百威、哈尔滨啤酒、科罗娜等。

11. China Resources Snow Breweries:华润雪花啤酒(中国)有限公司,成立于1994年,是一家生产、经营啤酒、饮料的央企控股企业。总部设于中国北京。其股东是华润创业有限公司。目前华润雪花啤酒在中国大陆经营几十家啤酒厂。旗下拥有30多个区域品牌,在中国众多的市场中处于区域优势。

12. SABMiller:世界上最大的啤酒公司之一,在伦敦和约翰内斯堡股票市场分别上市,总部设在英国伦敦。SABMiller从事着大规模的啤酒和其他饮料的生产和销售,业务遍及世界五大洲,在40多个国家拥有100多个啤酒厂、150多个啤酒品牌。

13. Yanjing:燕京啤酒,成立于1980年,总部位于北京,是一家啤酒生产企业。燕京已经成为中国最大啤酒企业集团之一。

14. Tsingtao:青岛啤酒,产自青岛啤酒股份有限公司,公司的前身是国营青岛啤酒厂,1903年由英、德两国商人合资开办,是最早的啤酒生产企业之一。2008年北京奥运会官方赞助商,跻身世界品牌500强。

15. Asahi:朝日啤酒,是由一家酿制啤酒和生产软性饮品的公司共同研制的。朝日啤酒株式会社成立于1889年,朝日啤酒是日本最著名的啤酒制造厂商之一。

16. McKinsey&Company:麦肯锡公司,是由美国芝加哥大学商学院教授詹姆斯·麦肯锡(James O'McKinsey)于1926年在美国创建的,现在麦肯锡公司已经成为全球著名的管理咨询公司。麦肯锡目前拥有近万名咨询人员,均具有世界著名学府的高等学位。

17. Parallel Imports:平行进口,一般是指未经相关知识产权权利人授权的进口商将由权利人自己或经其同意在其他国家或地区投放市场的产品,向知识产权人或独占被许可人所在国或地区的进口。

18. Venture Capital investment:风险投资,也被称为"创业投资",是以权益资本(equity capital)的方式存在的一种私募股权投资(private equity investment)形式,其投资运作方式是投资公司(investor)投资于创业企业(venture companies)或高成长型企业(growth orientated enterprises),占有被投资公司(investee)的股份,并在恰当的时候增值套现(cash out)。

Chinese Private Security Goes Global

Charles Clover
February 26, 2017, *Financial Times*

It was illegal until 2010 but Beijing's overseas expansion has given birth to a protection industry that looks after state-owned companies and workers in some of the most dangerous places on earth.

On the evening of July 8, the streets of the South Sudanese capital of Juba were raked with gunfire as an uneasy truce between warring political factions broke down. Inside the offices of DeWe Security, a Chinese private security firm, phones started ringing.

Panicked Chinese oil workers employed by the China National Petroleum Corp, the main client of DeWe (pronounced "DeWei") in South Sudan, were calling an emergency number to say they were in arm's way and awaiting instructions.

For Kong Wei, head of DeWe's Juba office and a veteran of the People's Liberation Army who retired five years ago, it was the start of a 50-hour-marathon without sleep as he and his colleagues executed an evacuation plan. "Bullets and shells flew over our compound all day and night," says Mr Kong.

The contractors soon realized that their tin-roofed cinder-block building couldn't stop bullets—just one of the many lessons they would learn. In all, 330 Chinese civilians, stranded at 10 locations across the city, were instructed to hunker down until the airport could reopen. Some moved into shrapnel-proof metal containers. It was only on the fourth day of the fighting, once the government had blasted the rebels out of Juba, that the trapped workers were evacuated to Nairobi, the capital of Kenya.

Details of the operation last year, revealed here for the first time, point to the greater role being played by China's fledgling private security industry. Its growth has echoes of the prominent and often controversial part played by Western contractors such as Blackwater, now known as Academi, and DynCorp in Iraq and Afghanistan after the September 11, 2001 attacks. The logic is the same: contractors are convenient and deniable. But they and the military are in reality two sides of the same coin.

"The intermingling between PLA and private security contractors often staffed by 'former PLA' is a blurry line," says Andrew Davenport, chief operating officer of RWR Advisory Group, a risk consultancy. Though private, few doubt the groups are solidly under the control of China's national security bureaucracy. They represent "a parallel security strategy", as Mr Davenport puts it.

Foreign policy shift

China has been reluctant to get involved in politics abroad, part of a decades-old doctrine of "non-interference". That caution is being tested by its rapid economic growth and the boldness of some state-owned companies, which routinely work in environments that Western counterparts avoid. Chinese companies service power stations in Iraq and a telecommunications network in Syria; they mine copper in Afghanistan and pump oil in South Sudan. SIA Energy, a Beijing consultancy, estimates that 7m tonnes a year of oil produced by Chinese state companies are routinely shut in worldwide due to violence in the likes of Iraq and South Sudan.

The job of protecting China's ever expanding commercial interests and the more than 1 m Chinese living abroad has led to shifts in the country's traditionally cautious foreign policy. Its navy has fended off pirates in the Gulf of Aden since 2012 and rescued civilians trapped in Yemen in 2015. Its combat troops are being deployed under UN peacekeeping mandates in countries where China has investments, such as South Sudan and the Democratic Republic of Congo. And last year Beijing established its first foreign military base in Djibouti.

The growth in the use of Chinese security contractors is part of this trend as Beijing looks for ways to protect its assets abroad without resorting to an imperialistic foreign policy that could play badly, both at home and abroad.

"The need for security protection overseas is quite significant and the army is clearly not suitable for this job due to the potential problems it might cause for foreign relations," says Yue Gang, a retired PLA officer.

About 3,200 Chinese employees of private security groups were based abroad last year, says Liu Xinping, deputy director of the China Overseas Security and Defense Research Centre. That compares with 2,600 Chinese troops deployed under UN mandates—China's only foreign military deployments in conflict zones.

Yet with a few exceptions the security contractors are usually unarmed. DeWe's Chinese staff did not carry weapons during the fighting in Juba but led teams of armed locals.

Beijing is extremely cautious about the industry, partly due to the abuses of the type that have periodically plunged US occupations of Afghanistan and Iraq into crisis. In 2010, supervisors at a Chinese-owned coal mine in Zambia fired into a crowd of workers demanding higher pay, injuring 11 and triggering an anti-China backlash. Two years later, a supervisor was killed at the site during a dispute over wages.

One security company manager, who asked to remain anonymous, says all contracts they sign with Chinese state companies prohibit employees from carrying weapons.

Preventing "diplomatic incidents"

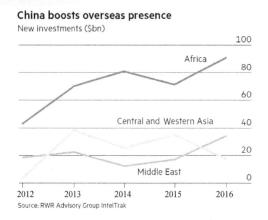
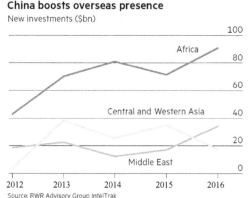

According to a study by the Watson Institute for International and Public Affairs, 7,071 US contractors have lost their lives in Iraq, Afghanistan and Pakistan since October 2001, slightly more than the 6,860 losses of the US military. "Private security contractors allow politicians to move some of their military activities off the books in terms of oversight and political responsibility," says John-Clark Levin, a private maritime security expert based in the US.

The difference between stationing troops and contractors was further blurred after DeWe announced plans to build two "security camps" in South Sudan and the land locked Central African Republic. These appear to be the first private security facilities of this type to be used by Chinese companies, heralding a more permanent security presence.

Li Xiaopeng, DeWe's chief executive, told a Beijing forum on overseas security in October that "our next step is to mass-produce [safety camps] in countries with Chinese investments as well as [those] within stability factors".

Government backing

Based near Beijing airport, DeWe's compound has a converted warehouse featuring a mock-up of a Middle East town. The model's facades are used to practise evasion tactics and hostage rescues.

Hao Gang, a former police official who is DeWe's general manager for Beijing, says the group's biggest revenue generator is to provide what he calls "integrated solutions" for Chinese companies going abroad, including training, on-site security and risk assessment.

The group was founded in 2011 by a number of former military and police officers who had first worked together during the 2008 Beijing Olympics. Since 2013, 86,000 Chinese civilian employees have been trained, says Mr Hao.

"It depends where they are going. If they are going to Paris, we teach them how not to have their passport stolen. If they are going to Kabul, we teach them how to evade kidnappers," says Mr Hao.

Private security firms were only made legal in China in 2010, by legislation that allowed companies to provide armed services to domestic businesses like banks and factories. Now, DeWe has 352 Chinese employees based abroad, as well as 3,000 locally hired staff working for companies such as China Road and Bridge Corporation building the Nairobi-Mombasa railway, as well as defending CNPC in Sudan.

Chinese security companies are still finding their feet, says Frauke Renz, a researcher who specializes in the private security industry. "The big international contractors are more experienced in those environments," she says. "If you take Iraq or Nigeria, for instance, most international companies have been operating in those countries for years."

Yet many Chinese contractors are benefiting from government pressure to use only domestic security firms. CNPC, for example, used to employ Control Risks, a UK company, to guard fields in Iraq, but in 2010 began to employ Guanan, a Chinese company with close links to ZhenHua Oil, China's fifth-largest oil company.

DeWe's profile rose dramatically last summer when Chinese Poly-GCL Petroleum Group Holdings hired it to manage security at a $4bn LNG project in Ethiopia—the largest project that the Chinese private security industry has been asked to protect.

Some other companies appear to have friends in high places. HXZA, for example, has a near-monopoly on security for Cosco Holding and China Shipping Container Lines, China's two largest state-owned shipping groups. "They clearly have very solid relations to the state, considering how loyal their customer base is. And they are not that cheap," says one foreign private contractor. HXZA declined to be interviewed.

A handful of other companies such as Shandong Huawei, Veterans Security Services and Dingtai Anyuan, have similar profiles and recruit from the same pool of veterans, providing guard services abroad and training state company employees. Aside from the language advantage, they are cheaper than their foreign counterparts—a team of 12 Chinese guards costs about $700 – $1,000 a day, the same as one British or US guard, say contractors.

The legal basis for permitting Chinese companies to deploy guards abroad is still vague, admits DeWe's Mr Hao: "We obey all local laws in the countries in which we work."

"Private contractors are sometimes the least bad option for security," says Edward Allen of ViennEast, a risk consultancy and former security analyst in Iraq, "that is the reason they are there."

New market Blackwater founder looks to China for business

The boom in private security services for Chinese companies has attracted a number of entrepreneurs including Erik Prince, the founder of Blackwater, the US private military company that achieved notoriety following a series of shootings in Iraq.

He is executive chairman of Hong Kong-based Frontier Services Group, which specializes in what it describes as "securing supply chains" in Africa. China International Trust and Investment Corporation, a major Chinese state investment company, owns a 20 per cent stake in the group. Aside from this link to the Chinese government, Mr Prince brings political connections from the US—he is the brother of Betsy DeVos, Donald Trump's education secretary.

The company raised eyebrows in December when it announced it would establish two "forward operating bases" in China, one in Yunnan Province to service Southeast Asia, and the second in the restive western region of Xinjiang, which abuts central Asia. FSG said the strategy is to take advantage of China's "One Belt, One Road" programme for trade and investment expansion.

Despite its militaristic terminology FSG insists it will not provide armed guard services and weapons training—which are heavily restricted in China. The company says the bases will provide "training, communications, risk mitigation, risk assessments, information gathering, medical evacuation and joint operations centres that co-ordinate security, logistics and aviation services".

Mr Prince objects to the suggestion that FSG is a "Chinese Blackwater" and says that while many Chinese companies approach him for armed guard services, "I quickly try to disabuse them of the notion that it would be a good idea or that it would be permitted".

Words and Expressions

rake	vt.	扫射,耙,梳理
truce	n.	停战协议,休战,停战期
panicked	adj.	惊慌失措的
cinder-block	n.	渣煤(空心)砖
strand	vt.	使滞留,使搁浅,使陷于困境
hunker	vi.	盘坐
hunker down		沉潜待发,蹲下,盘坐,保持低调,放低姿态
shrapnel	n.	飞溅的弹片
blast	vt.	击毁,摧毁
evacuation	n.	疏散,撤离
fledgling	adj.	刚开始的,无经验的

intermingle	vt.	使混合,使掺和
	vi.	混合,掺杂
staff	vt.	在……工作,为……配备职员,任职于
blurry	adj.	模糊的
state-owned companies		国有公司
service	vt.	检修,维修,向……提供服务,保养,满足需要
power station		发电厂,发电站
shut in		锁封在里边
combat troops		战斗部队
deploy	vt.	部署,调度(军队或武器)
mandate	n.	授权,命令,委任,任期
resort to		诉诸,采取
plunge	vt.	使陷入
trigger	vt.	引发,引起,触发
backlash	n.	强烈抵制
instructive	adj.	有益的,教育性的
lethal	adj.	致命的,致死的
	n.	致死因子
escort	n.	陪同,护航舰,护卫队,护送者
	vt.	护送,陪同,为……护航
station	vt.	安置,派驻(士兵或官员),使驻扎
blur	vt.	涂污,使……模糊不清,使暗淡,玷污
	vi.	沾上污迹,变模糊
	n.	污迹,模糊不清的事物
herald	n.	预兆,征兆,先驱,传令官,报信者
	vt.	通报,预示……的来临
mock-up	n.	伪装工事,实物模型
facade	n.	(建筑物的)正面,立面,(虚假的)表面,外表
recruit	n.	招聘,新兵
	vt.	补充,聘用,征募,使……恢复
	vi.	复原,征募新兵,得到补充,恢复健康
deploy	vt.	部署,调度(军队或武器),有效地利用
vague	adj.	不清楚的,含糊的
prodigious	adj.	异常的,惊人的,巨大的,庞大的
notoriety	n.	恶名,丑名,臭名昭著

raise eyebrows		引起惊奇或轻微的不满,使不满,使不快
restive		难驾驭的,焦躁不安的,不耐烦的
abut	v.	紧邻,毗邻
mitigation	n.	减轻,缓解
disabuse	vt.	去除……的错误想法,使醒悟

Notes to the Text

1. The Republic of South Sudan：南苏丹共和国,简称"南苏丹",是东非的一个内陆国家。首都为朱巴(南苏丹总统基尔于2011年9月发布命令,决定把拉姆塞尔定为该国新首都,并计划在5至8年内完成迁都)。南苏丹原是英埃共管苏丹的一部分,1956年后成为苏丹共和国的一部分。2011年,南苏丹独立公投通过,南苏丹共和国遂于2011年7月9日宣告独立,成为非洲大陆第54个国家。

2. Central African Republic：中非共和国,简称"中非",是非洲大陆中部的内陆国家。中非国土面积为62.3万平方千米。

3. Poly Technologies Inc.：中国保利集团公司与协鑫(集团)控股有限公司是长期合作伙伴,共同组建保利协鑫天然气集团控股有限公司(POLY-GCLPetroleum Group Holdings Limited,以下简称"保利协鑫集团"),投资开发埃塞俄比亚石油天然气项目。

4. CSCL (China Shipping Container Lines)：中远海运集装箱运输有限公司(中远海运集运),隶属中国远洋海运集团有限公司,由原中远集团旗下"中远集运"整合原中海集团旗下"中海集运"的集装箱业务及其服务网络组建而成。

5. China International Trust and Investment Corporation：中国中信集团有限公司(前称"中国国际信托投资公司",简称"中信集团",英文为CITIC Group),主要业务集中在金融、实业和其他服务业领域。2018年,《财富》世界500强排行榜中国中信集团有限公司排名第149位。

6. Gulf of Aden ['eidn]：亚丁湾,是位于也门和索马里之间的一片阿拉伯海水域,它通过曼德海峡与北方的红海相连,并以也门的海港亚丁为名。亚丁湾是船只快捷往来地中海和印度洋的必经站,又是波斯湾石油输往欧洲和北美洲的重要水路。由于该地区海盗猖獗,所以亚丁湾又被叫作"海盗巷"。水域面积53万平方千米。亚丁湾西侧有北岸亚丁港、南岸吉布提港,是印度洋通向地中海、大西洋航线的重要燃料港和贸易中转港,具有重要的战略地位。

7. Yemen Republic：也门共和国,位于阿拉伯半岛西南端,与沙特、阿曼相邻,濒红海、亚丁湾和阿拉伯海。1990年5月由阿拉伯也门共和国(北也门)和也门民主人民共和国(南也门)合并组成。2015年3月,也门总统阿卜杜勒-拉布·曼苏尔·哈迪宣布,因其首都萨那被胡塞武装分子占领,亚丁为临时首都。

8. Djibouti:吉布提共和国,简称"吉布提",是一个位于非洲东北部亚丁湾西岸的国家,北与厄立特里亚为邻,西部、西南及南部与埃塞俄比亚毗连,东南同索马里接壤,东北隔着红海的曼德海峡和也门相望。其东临红海进入印度洋的要冲曼德海峡,因此战略位置十分重要,国内有美军在非洲最大的军事基地和法军在海外最大的军事基地,另外中国也在此地建设有保障基地。但其国内自然资源贫乏,工农业基础薄弱,加上政局不稳,所以是世界上最不发达国家之一。

9. DeWe Security:北京德威保安服务有限公司,成立于2011年,是中国国内能够成体系开展海外安保业务、具有为中资企业境外项目提供专业服务成功经验的专业海外安保服务企业。德威安保人员在2012年至2015年的一些非洲国家内战等事件中协助中国驻当地使馆和中资企业正确决策、妥善处置、有序撤离,有关客户单位不仅发来感谢信,主要领导还专程登门致谢。特别是在2015年7月北京申办2022年冬奥会工作中,公司派出安全专家组织协调马来西亚警方、安保公司等安保力量,圆满完成了申办代表团、中央和北京市主要领导在吉隆坡活动的安全保卫任务,受到了中央和北京市的表彰。

Unit Two

US Economy

Trump's Tough Talk on Jobs Reshoring Puts Banks to Test

Ben Mclannahan—New York; Laura Noonan—Dublin

February 27, 2017, *Financial Times*

On the day that Donald Trump won the presidential election, partly on a promise to bring back jobs for US workers, Goldman Sachs posted a job advertisement for a derivatives analyst in Bangalore.

In the three months since then, the Wall Street bank has put up ads for another 180 or so jobs based in the *Incendiary*. Goldman is not alone in relying on staff in outposts in Asia and cheaper parts of Europe: all its peers employ significant numbers of overseas staff to support their global banking operations.

Gary Cohn, Goldman's former president and chief operating officer, made a staunch defence of the need for operations in Bangalore at an event in Naples, Florida, in November. "We hire people there because they work for cents on the dollar versus what people work for in the United States," he said.

But Mr Cohn could have such convictions put to the test after entering government as the top economic adviser to Mr Trump. The president has made it clear he wants to see an end to the decades-long trend of US companies hiring workers overseas—to the point of threatening to tax companies that offshore US jobs.

Such a heavy-handed approach could cause tensions as US banks seek to run their global businesses as efficiently as possible, under pressure to cut costs and deal with a welter of new regulations.

"We see offshoring to peak soon, much due to Trump," says John Boyd of the Boyd Consultancy based in Princeton, New Jersey. He notes automation and a "continued rush to quality customer service" are also restricting the flow.

But banks may struggle to reverse the tide of jobs that have been leaving US shores for years. As banks' revenues have languished, dragged down by low interest rates and falling commissions from trading, many have tried to preserve margins by shifting more back office processes to cheaper locations all over the world.

In India, for example, total support staff employed by four top US investment banks—Morgan Stanley, JPMorgan Chase, Bank of America and Citigroup—rose 50 per cent between 2008 and 2015 to more than 12,500, say figures compiled for the Financial Times by McLagan, a pay consulting firm.

Almost 9,500 of these are in IT and operations, but so-called "control function" jobs have been growing more quickly as banks look for cheaper ways to comply with the deluge of regulations that followed the financial crisis.

Executives also say the strategy is more complex than mere cost-cutting. Some stress their hiring overseas is primarily to support day-to-day operations worldwide.

JPMorgan, for example, which runs the world's biggest investment bank, has what it calls a "follow-the-sun" strategy, using 14 technology hubs in cities including Glasgow, Mumbai, Bangalore, Hyderabad and Singapore. That approach is unlikely to change, whatever Mr Trump says, according to a person familiar with the bank's strategy.

At Goldman, a person familiar with its staffing says it has always had a high rate of attrition at its Bangalore operation, which it opened in 2004 on the Embassy Golf Links campus on the outskirts of the city. Despite the flurries of job ads, net headcount has been falling for the past year to about 5,000, the person says.

Meanwhile, banks have already been making efforts to spread jobs around the US.

As many have struggled to hit profit targets outlined to shareholders, they have uprooted back- and middle-office jobs from expensive cities such as New York, San Francisco and Boston to cheaper places like Nashville, Boise and Des Moines. Smaller cities such as Henderson in Nevada, Scranton in Pennsylvania and Billings in Montana have also benefited.

JPMorgan recently added its eighth US hub in Chicago to a list that includes Brooklyn, Columbus, Dallas, Houston, Jersey City, Tampa and Wilmington. Morgan Stanley has opened offices in Jacksonville, Columbus and Baltimore.

Goldman, for its part, expects to expand in its two main US hubs of Salt Lake City and Irving, west of Dallas, where it has about 3,000 staff across compliance, finance, research, human resources, investment management and technology.

According to McLagan, the six big US banks together employ about 85,000 people in US support centers, which are defined as locations where there are more than two support workers for every revenue-producing employee or manager.

Those figures rose almost 8 per cent in the three years to the end of 2015, with control functions growing at almost three times the rate of IT and operations staff, which still account for almost 85 per cent of total employees.

Some big banks are still willing to boost staffing outside the US. David Warfield, associate partner at McLagan's performance practice, says that global banks still have an "appetite to look at what else can be done" in Asia, particularly in the area of control functions, where hiring has been growing most quickly in the past few years.

However, Johan Gott, partner at AT Kearney in Washington, DC, says that financial services companies have broadly "hit the pause button" since Mr Trump won the election. His company is recommending clients undergo "war-gaming" scenarios to understand the impact of different levers the administration could use—more aggressive enforcement of existing rules, or more drastic options such as tariffs on goods or services.

For now, clients are freezing offshoring initiatives, says Mr Gott, or at least not announcing investments outside the US.

"What we're all looking at is an incredibly high level of uncertainty around this issue, larger than in many decades," he says.

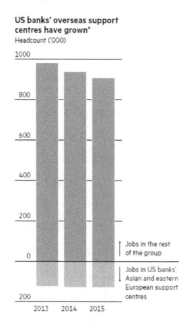

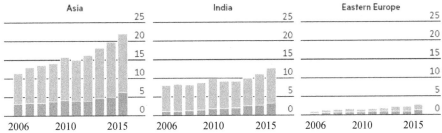

Source: McLagan *JPMorgan Chase, Bank of America, Goldman Sachs, Wells Fargo, Morgan Stanley and Citigroup

** Excludes all McLagan defined high-cost US locations and medium-cost locations

*** JPMorgan, Bank of America Merrill Lynch and Morgan Stanley

 Words and Expressions

reshoring	n.	（商品生产）回流（到国内）
presidential	adj.	总统（总裁、议长、董事长、校长等）的
derivative	n.	衍生性金融商品，派生物
Bangalore	n.	（英国）班加罗尔
outpost	n.	边区村落，前哨
staunch	adj.	坚定的，忠诚的，坚固的
on the dollar		以美元计
conviction	n.	确信
heavy-handed	adj.	高压的，缺乏同情心的，冷酷的
welter	n.	混乱，杂乱，混合，大杂烩
revenue	n.	税收，国家的收入，收益

languish	vi.	变得衰弱,衰落,未能取得进展,被迫滞留,长期受苦,受煎熬
commission	n.	服务费,手续费,佣金,回扣
margin	n.	利润,盈余
back office		后台(公司中不直接与外界接触的部门)
deluge	n.	涌现的事物,蜂拥而至的事物
Glasgow	n.	(英国)格拉斯哥
attrition	n.	消耗,磨损
outskirt	n.	郊区,市郊
flurry	n.	一阵轰动,骚动,一阵风、雨或雪
headcount	n.	人数统计,统计出的人数
uproot	vt.	根除,连根拔起,把……赶出家园,使无家可归
	vi.	迁离,改变生活方式,根除,灭绝
Boise	n.	(美国爱达荷州首府)博伊西
Des Moines		(美国艾奥瓦州首府)得梅因
hub	n.	中心
compliance	n.	顺从,服从,承诺
operations staff		操作人员
war-gaming	n.	军事演习
scenario	n.	方案,情节,剧本
lever	n.	杠杆,手段,方法
aggressive	adj.	侵略的,侵犯的,攻势的,有进取心的,好争斗的,积极行动的
enforcement	n.	执行,实施,强制
drastic	adj.	(法律等)严厉的,激烈的,猛烈的
initiative	n.	积极的行动,倡议,主动权,首创精神
	adj.	主动的,自发的,起始的

Notes to the Text

1. JPMorgan:摩根大通集团(JPMorgan Chase & Co),业界称之为"西摩"或"小摩",总部在美国纽约,分行有6000多家,是美国最大金融服务机构之一。

摩根大通于2000年由大通曼哈顿银行及J. P. 摩根公司合并而成,并分别收购芝加哥第一银行和贝尔斯登银行和华盛顿互惠银行。摩根大通是一家跨国金融服务机构及美国最大的银行之一,业务遍及60多个国家,包括投资银行、金融交易处理、投资管理、商业金融服务、个人银行业务等。摩根大通的总部设于曼哈顿区的第一大通曼哈顿广场（One Chase Manhattan Plaza），部分银行业务则转移到得克萨斯州休斯敦的摩根大通大厦（JPMorgan Chase Tower）。

2. Goldman Sachs ['gəʊldmən sæks]：高盛集团，一家国际领先的投资银行，向全球提供广泛的投资、咨询和金融服务，拥有大量的多行业客户，包括私营公司、金融企业、政府机构及个人。

高盛集团成立于1869年，是全世界历史最悠久及规模最大的投资银行之一，总部位于纽约，并在东京、伦敦和香港设有分部。其所有运作都建立于紧密一体的全球基础上，由优秀的专家为客户提供服务，同时拥有丰富的地区市场知识和国际运作能力。

高盛公司在中国证券经纪公司高盛高华中持有股份，它还为三家中国企业经办了首次公开募股（Initial Public Offerings，IPO）事宜，这三家公司是中国石油、平安保险和中国银行，它们的募股规模在中国股市均排在前几位。

3. Gary Cohn：加里·科恩，高盛总裁兼首席运营官，此前在大宗商品部门工作。2016年12月，美国当选总统特朗普邀请加里担任美国全国经济委员会的主席及特朗普的经济政策顾问。美国全国经济委员会主要负责协调国内、国外的政策制定以及追踪总统经济政策的实施。

北京时间2018年3月8日消息，据美国知名财经网站CNBC报道，周三在唐纳德·特朗普总统的首席经济顾问加里·科恩辞职后，使用钢铁、铝等金属的公司股价下跌。在特朗普宣布对钢铁和铝进口征收关税的5天之后，反对实施关税的自由贸易倡导者科恩周二晚间辞职。辞职标志着特朗普实施关税的可能性增加。自特朗普宣布以来，金属类的股价一直面临压力。科恩辞职的消息令美国股指纷纷下跌，原因是人们对一场贸易战的担忧日益加剧。道琼斯工业平均指数下跌超过130点。科恩被华尔街认为是白宫的理性声音，而白宫似乎正处于持续的动荡之中。考虑到他在华尔街的声誉，他在白宫的表现也受到了投资者的青睐。

4. Morgan Stanley：摩根士丹利，是一家成立于美国纽约的国际金融服务公司，提供包括证券、资产管理、企业合并重组和信用卡等多种金融服务。

5. Naples ['neɪplz]：那不勒斯，坐落于佛罗里达西南部的墨西哥湾沿岸，以高端购物、世界一流的文化和精致的饮食而闻名。逛街购物必去的Fifth Avenue South 和Third Street South 有许多艺术画廊和服装精品店。

6. compliance officer：是一个新词，在中文里还没有一个官方的统一的译法。compliance指的是企业对法律或政府命令、政策的遵守和执行。Compliance Officer 是企业内的职位，她/他的职责就是审查企业的制度和运作，确保企业遵守、执行各种法律条例和政府命令，因为企业一旦因不合规而被政府调查或起诉，将要付出很大的名誉和经济的代价。例如，一个美国的金融企业要确保遵守反洗钱法、客户隐私保护方面的法律，以及有关人事聘用中的反歧视和机会均等的法律。

President Proves Comedy Gold for US Television Networks' Late-Night Satire

Shannon Bond—New York
February 27, 2017, *Financial Times*

Donald Trump is turning out to be a gold mine for his comic foes on late-night television, lifting ratings and advertising revenues for shows that deliver the sharpest criticism of the US president.

On CBS's *Late Show*, Stephen Colbert has homed in on politics, helping him unseat NBC's *Tonight Show* with Jimmy Fallon as the most-watched nightly chat show for three straight weeks.

Late-night television is an important source of profit and cultural cachet for US broadcasters. NBC has long dominated the networks' rivalry, but Mr Colbert has widened his lead to nearly 300,000 viewers in the week ending February 17, the most since he debuted on CBS in 2015.

Across the TV dial, audiences are flocking to a brand of biting political satire that largely originated with Jon Stewart at Comedy Central's *The Daily Show*, but which has now spread to the television mainstream. *The Daily Show* alumni include Mr Colbert on CBS, John Oliver on HBO and Samantha Bee on TBS.

Mr Colbert had suffered declining ratings at CBS since he succeeded David Letterman at the *Late Show* desk. He struggled to win over viewers after dropping the blustery rightwing pundit character that made him a star on Comedy Central. In August 2016, his audience dipped below 2m for the first time.

But Mr Trump's ascendancy appears to have sharpened the focus of Mr Colbert and his writers on the frenetic Washington news cycle, and the ratings trend is now in reverse. Viewership grew 3 per cent in January from a year ago; it is now 3m, 30 per cent above last summer's lows, say Nielsen data.

On CBS's earnings call last week, Les Moonves, chief executive, talked up Mr Colbert's contribution to the network's "great story in late night". CBS said ad revenue for the network's nightly line-up rose 10 per cent in 2016.

"Colbert's show has become more aggressively political. That's probably responsible for his numbers going up," said Robert Thompson, director of Syracuse University's Bleier

Center for Television and Popular Culture.

 Words and Expressions

gold mine		财源,宝库
foe	n.	敌人,仇敌,危害物,反对者
rating	n.	收听率,收视率,等级,评估,评价,极限
nightly	adj.	每晚的
homed in		将注意力集中(于)
unseat	vt.	降级,撤职,革除(职位),使失去资格
straight	adj.	连续的,直的
cachet	n.	威信,声望
rivalry	n.	竞争,对抗,竞赛
debut	n.	初次露面,初次表演,首次出场,处女秀
	v.	初次表演,初次登台
	adj.	首张的,首场的,首次的
dial	n.	遥控器
flock	n.	兽群,鸟群,群众,棉束,大堆,大量
	vi.	群集,成群结队而行
	vt.	用棉束填
biting	adj.	尖锐刺人的,刺痛的,辛辣的,嘲讽的
alumni	n.	(统称)校友,毕业生(alumnus 的复数),前成员
desk	n.	(报社、电视台等的)办公处,部,室,组
win over		争取,赢得……的支持
blustery	adj.	跋扈的,盛气凌人的,狂风大作的
pundit	n.	行家,权威,专家,有学问的人
ascendancy	n.	支配地位,优势,影响
sharpen	vt.	加重,加强,使更加明显
frenetic	adj.	狂热的,发狂似的,狂乱的
reverse	n.	相反的情况(或事物)
viewership	n.	(电视节目或频道的)观众人数,观众类型
talk up		吹捧夸大,过分夸奖,说服……提高出价,抬高……的价格
line-up	n.	节目安排,项目安排,阵容,阵式

Notes to the Text

1. NBC（National Broadcasting Company）：美国全国广播公司，总部设于纽约，成立于1926年，是美国历史最久、实力最强的商业广播电视公司。

2. CBS（Columbia Broadcasting System）：哥伦比亚广播公司，1927年成立，总部设在纽约。

3. ABC（American Broadcasting Corporation, Inc）：美国广播公司，1945年成立。目前的最大股东是华特迪士尼公司，为迪士尼-ABC电视集团的成员。

4. Comedy Central：美国喜剧中心频道，主要播放各种幽默喜剧节目，包括脱口秀、幽默动画片、喜剧短片集等。在出色成熟的幽默表演的同时，大多数喜剧节目更加注重严肃时事的深刻讨论。很多节目是以恶搞讽刺为主调，使观众在开怀大笑的同时能够思考更加深层次的东西。

5. Nielsen：尼尔森，全球著名的市场监测和数据分析公司，1923年由现代市场研究行业的奠基人之一的阿瑟·查尔斯·尼尔森先生创立，总部位于英国牛津。

6. earnings call：收益报告，上市公司以多方通话的方式发布和讨论一个报告期内财务成绩。

7. Syracuse［ˈsɪrəkjuːs］University：美国雪城大学。雪城（又名"锡拉丘兹"，Syracuse）居纽约州中部，绰号"盐城"（The Salt City），素有Central New York之称，是纽约州第四大城市，是一座中型城市。

Unit Three

World Economy

Zimbabwe Is Staring at Currency Chaos Again

Tony Hawkins
February 27, 2017, *Financial Times*

Celebrating his 93rd birthday on Saturday at a lavish party in the Matopos Hills near Bulawayo, resident Robert Mugabe made it clear: he is going nowhere and intends to fight next year's presidential election.

The front runner to succeed him, vice president Emmerson Mnangagwa, promised his continuing support, pledging that the Zanu-PF party "will rule forever".

Many Zimbabweans, especially business people, hoped but did not expect that after 37 years in office the president would signal his intention to step down. They fear the economic consequences of a continued leaderless drift as the country faces its most severe economic challenges since dollarisation in 2009, which put an end to a decade during which per capital incomes halved.

Now, Zimbabwe is again staring down the barrel of currency chaos. One set of numbers says it all: at the end of 2016, the country's commercial banks were holding $1.35 bn in treasury bills—equivalent to 180 per cent of bank capital—issued by a government unable to pay its way either at home or abroad. The country appears to be facing another economic meltdown, scarily reminiscent of the lost decade to 2008.

Today, bank lending to government and its agencies totals 42 per cent of domestic credit—up from just 13 per cent when the ruling Zanu-PF party returned to monopoly control after the dissolution of the shortlived government of national unity in mid-2013. The central bank, which has no deposits of its own to speak of, virtually trebled its lending to the state to

$970m last year.

The difference a decade ago was that the exchange rate for the defunct Zimbabwe dollar took the strain until its ultimate collapse in 2008. Inflation is not the problem now. After four years of deflation, consumer prices in 2016 were just one per cent above their 2011 level, partly due to the overvalued currency.

Since dollarisation, the currency has floated upwards with the US dollar, while that of South Africa, its main trading partner, has depreciated substantially.

This, combined with weak international commodity prices and two years of drought, resulted in a trade deficit, averaging $3 bn a year.

A large part of this gap has been closed by diaspora remittances ($750m annually), foreign aid and reckless short-term offshore borrowing. So much liquidity drained out of the economy last year that the authorities were forced to resume printing their own bank notes—bond notes, of which about $100 m are in circulation.

The authorities insist that their bond notes and the electronic dollars locked into the banking system are identical in value to US dollars. They are not. Depositors are denied ready access to their money with banks dispensing daily amounts of $50 to $100, half in US notes and the balance in bond notes. On the Zimbabwe Stock Exchange a gap of 25 per cent has opened up between the Harare and Johannesburg valuations of dual-listed Old Mutual shares, meaning that the US dollar in Zimbabwe is seriously overvalued. Adjusting for inflation differentials, it could be as much as 75 per cent.

Business leaders and some bankers see a switch of the country's currency from the dollar to the rand as a possible solution. Given the debt overhang of $5.2 bn in international arrears, however, a shift to the endemically weak rand seems an unpromising solution. The government hopes that the "Lima Agreement" of 2015 for the clearance of $1.7 bn of arrears to the Bretton Woods institutions and the African Development Bank, will come to its rescue. This agreement has the backing of some Western governments, notably the UK and Brussels, as well as multilateral lenders, but Zimbabwe has been unable to source the required bridging finance.

Economists and opposition politicians question the viability of still more international and domestic borrowing by a country already deemed by the IMF to be in debt distress.

Yet it seems that Western governments—with the exception of the US—and the Bretton Woods institutions have learnt little from past fruitless interactions with the Mugabe government.

Words and Expressions

lavish	adj.	耗资巨大的,慷慨的,大量的,给人印象深刻的
front runner		一路领先的人
succeed	vt.	继承,继任,随……之后
pledge	vt. & vi.	使发誓,保证,典当,抵押
	n.	保证,誓言,抵押权,誓约
drift	n.	流动,趋势,(尤指向坏的方面)逐渐变化
halve	vt.	对分,把……分成两半,把……减半
stare down		盯视或仿佛盯视而导致动摇或屈服
treasury bill		短期国库券
pay its way		支付
meltdown	n.	彻底垮台,(核反应堆的)堆芯熔毁
scarily	adv.	可怕地
reminiscent	vt.	使回忆起(人或事)
monopoly	n.	垄断,专卖,垄断者,专利品
dissolution	n.	溶解,融化,(社团等)解散,离婚,腐朽,崩溃
shortlived	adj.	短暂的,短命的
deposit	n.	保证金,储蓄,存款,沉淀物,寄存,寄存品
virtually	adv.	无形中,实际上,实质上,事实上,几乎
treble	vt. & vi.	使成为三倍,增加两倍
defunct	adj.	不再起作用的,不再使用的
take the strain		承担压力
overvalued currency		汇率过高的货币
substantially	adv.	大体上,本质上,实质上,充分地,相当多地
drought	n.	旱灾,干旱
diaspora	n.	移民社群
remittance	n.	汇款,汇款额
reckless	adj.	鲁莽的,不计后果的,无所顾忌的
offshore borrowing		海外借款
drain out		流失,流出,失掉,停止
bank note		钞票,纸币
bond note		债券
identical	adj.	同一的,完全同样的,相同的

depositor	n.	储户
ready access		迅速存取
dispense	vt.	分配,分给
balance	n.	账户余额,等额
	vt.	使(在某物上)保持平衡,立稳,相抵,抵消,同等重视(相对的两个事物或方面)
valuation	n.	估价,评价,定价
dual-listed	adj.	双重上市的
adjust for		调整,扣除
differential	n.	(经济学中的)差价,差额
rand	n.	(南非共和国货币单位)兰特
debt overhang		快到偿还期的债务
arrear	n.	欠款
endemically	adv.	地方性地
unpromising	adj.	无前途的,没有希望的
clearance	n.	(支票的)兑现,偿还
notably	adv.	尤其,显著地
Brussels	n.	(比利时首都)布鲁塞尔
source	vt.	寻求(尤指供货)的来源
viability	n.	生存能力
debt distress		债务困境

Notes to the Text

1. Harare [həˈrɑːreɪ]：哈拉雷,津巴布韦的首都和最大城市,津巴布韦政治、经济、文化中心,位于国境东北高原上。

2. Bulawayo：布拉瓦约,津巴布韦第二大城市,在西部高原上,海拔1365米,以工业著称,为全国最大的制造业中心。

3. Johannesburg [dʒəʊˈhænɪsbɜːg]：约翰内斯堡,南非共和国最大的城市。南非拥有三个首都,即行政首都(中央政府所在地)为茨瓦内,立法首都(议会所在地)为开普敦,司法首都(最高法院所在地)为布隆方丹。南非是非洲的第二大经济体,国民拥有较高的生活水平,经济相比其他非洲国家相对稳定。

4. Lima：利马,秘鲁共和国首都。秘鲁(The Republic of Peru)是一个总统制议会民主共和国,全国划分为25个地区。安第斯山脉纵贯国土南北,西部沿海地区则为干旱的平原,东部又有亚马孙盆地的热带雨林。秘鲁经济主要依赖农业、渔业、矿业及制造业(如纺织品)。

Unit Three　World Economy

5. Robert Gabriel Mugabe：罗伯特·加布里埃尔·穆加贝，1924年出生于南罗得西亚索尔兹伯里市（现为津巴布韦首都哈拉雷），毕业于南非赫尔堡大学，获文学学士和教育学学士学位。1980年津巴布韦独立后，穆加贝出任总理。他从1987年开始直到2017年连续担任总统。2017年11月21日，津巴布韦议会宣布，穆加贝辞去总统职务。2019年9月6日，罗伯特·穆加贝去世，享年95岁。

6. liquidity：资产流动性，资产折现力。一种资产或证券在不影响资产价值的情况下被买入或卖出的可能性，交易活动多是流通性高的指标；一种资产转换成为现金的能力。

7. dollarisation：美元化，是指一国居民在其资产中持有相当大一部分外币资产（主要是美元），即指一国或经济体的政府让美元取代自己的货币并最终自动放弃货币或金融主权的行动。

8. the lost decade：失去的十年，指的是一个国家或地区陷入长期的经济不景气并持续达10年左右才逐渐转好的情况。曾经出现过这种情况的国家和地区包括：英国第二次世界大战后的1945—1955年期间；拉丁美洲在20世纪80年代长期经济低迷；日本在泡沫经济崩溃后自1991年开始到2000年初期的长期经济不景气。

9. inflation：通货膨胀。在货币流通条件下，因货币供给大于货币实际需求，即现实购买力大于产出供给，导致货币贬值，而引起一段时间内物价持续而普遍上涨现象。其实质是社会总需求大于社会总供给（供远小于求）。

在凯恩斯主义经济学中，其产生原因为经济体中总供给与总需求的变化导致物价水平的移动。在货币主义经济学中，其产生原因为：当市场上货币发行量超过流通中所需要的货币量，就会出现纸币贬值，物价上涨，导致购买力下降，这就是通货膨胀。该理论被总结为一个非常著名的方程：$MV=PT$。其中，M是货币的总量，V是货币的流通速度，P是物价水平（也就是通货膨胀的量度），T是总交换量（也就是该经济体内的总产出）。货币主义的创始人、诺贝尔经济学奖得主弥尔顿·弗里德曼认为这个方程是一个由左至右的方程，也就是说，当货币总量增加并且货币的流通速度因此上升时，右边的两个参数的积会增加。如果P增长的百分比比T更多，物价水平就比产出上升得快，从而通货膨胀产生。

10. deflation：通货紧缩。市场上流通货币减少，人民的货币所得减少，购买力下降，影响物价至下跌，这就造成了通货紧缩。长期的货币紧缩会抑制投资与生产，导致失业率升高及经济衰退。对于其概念的理解，仍然存在争议。但经济学者普遍认为，当消费者价格指数（CPI）连跌三个月，即表示已出现通货紧缩。通货紧缩就是产能过剩或需求不足导致物价、工资、利率、粮食、能源等各类价格持续下跌。

11. CPI（consumer price index）：居民消费价格指数，是一个反映居民家庭一般购买的消费品和服务项目价格水平变动情况的宏观经济指标。它是在特定时段内度量一组代表性消费商品及服务项目的价格水平随时间而变动的相对数，是用来反映居民家庭购买消费商品及服务的价格水平的变动情况。

居民消费价格统计调查的是社会产品和服务项目的最终价格，同人民群众的生活密切相关,同时在整个国民经济价格体系中具有重要的地位。它是进行经济分析和决策、价格总水平监测和调控及国民经济核算的重要指标。其变动率在一定程度上反映了通货膨胀或紧缩的程度。

12. Old Mutual Plc:英国耆卫保险公司,成立于1845年,是全球财富500强公司之一,也是被列入英国《金融时报》100指数的金融服务集团之一。

13. Bretton Woods System:布雷顿森林体系,是指第二次世界大战后以美元为中心的国际货币体系协定。布雷顿森林体系是该协定对各国对货币的兑换、国际收支的调节、国际储备资产的构成等问题共同做出的安排所确定的规则、采取的措施及相应的组织机构形式的总和。在布雷顿森林体系以前两次世界大战之间的20年中,国际货币体系分裂成几个相互竞争的货币集团,各国货币竞相贬值,动荡不定,以牺牲他人利益为代价,解决自身的国际收支和就业问题,呈现出无政府状态。

1944年7月,在美国新罕布什尔州的布雷顿森林召开有44个国家参加的联合国与联盟国家国际货币金融会议,通过了"布雷顿森林协定"。建立了金本位制崩溃后的人类第二个国际货币体系。在这一体系中美元与黄金挂钩,美国承担以官价兑换黄金的义务。各国货币与美元挂钩,美元处于中心地位,起世界货币的作用。实际是一种新金汇兑本位制,在布雷顿货币体制中,黄金无论是在流通还是在国际储备方面的作用都有所降低,而美元成为这一体系中的主角。

14. African Development Bank:非洲开发银行,是在联合国"非洲经济委员会"支持下由非洲国家合办的互助性、区域性国际金融机构。1964年9月正式成立,1966年7月开始营业。宗旨为:向成员国的经济和社会发展提供资金,协助非洲大陆制定发展的总体战略,协调各国的发展计划,以便逐步实现"非洲经济一体化"。

15. bridging finance:过渡性筹款,过渡性融资。过渡性筹款是筹款人在以银团贷款或发行债券筹措资金的过程中,由于银团的筹组(如编制贷款协议、资料备忘条)和债券发行准备尚需一个时间,而筹款人又需要在银团贷款协议生效前或债券款项收到以前使用一定数额的资金,这时可以筹措一笔过渡性贷款以应急需。

16. IMF(International Monetary Fund):国际货币基金组织,是根据1944年7月在布雷顿森林会议上签订的《国际货币基金协定》,于1945年12月27日在华盛顿成立。与世界银行同时成立,并列为世界两大金融机构之一,其职责是监察货币汇率和各国贸易情况,提供技术和资金协助,确保全球金融制度运作正常。其总部设在华盛顿。

German Business Chiefs Prepare to Defend Free Trade in US

Stefan Wagstyl—Berlin
February 27, 2017, *Financial Times*

German business leaders are preparing for a campaign in the US to push the benefits of free trade as fears grow that President Donald Trump's administration is embracing protectionism.

Executives are worried that ideas put forward by the White House, such as possible import taxes, restrictions on foreign workers and a rethink on trade agreements, could damage German business and hurt economic ties worldwide.

They are particularly concerned about recent comments by Peter Navarro, Mr Trump's top trade adviser, who has accused Germany of exploiting the Low euro to boost exports and run huge trade surpluses. "There are conversations about how we can explain in Washington how important the role of foreign trade investment, including German trade and investment, is in the US," said a spokesman for BDI, the main German industry association.

Some 4,000 German companies have together invested a total of $224 bn in the US and employ 700,000 workers, according to US government data. Some 40 per cent of all jobs created by German companies in the US are in manufacturing, compared with 9 per cent in the economy as a whole.

"If Trump has a project to reindustrialise America, then Germany is a good partner," Jürgen Hardt, the government's coordinator for transatlantic co-operation, told the FT. While no final decisions have been taken, industry representatives say any campaign would probably be led and funded by companies, with the BDI and other business bodies and Chancellor Angela Merkel's government giving political support. "I would back a public offensive by German companies to set out head vantages of trade," Mr Hardt said. "We must do the utmost in trying to convince people in Washington of our case. Chief executives must do this ... because the administration takes chief executives seriously. They must go to Washington, not only to sign contracts but to persuade people."

Executives have indicated they are considering a multilevel approach in which high-level lobbying in Washington and in US states with big German investments could be accompanied by publicity aimed at workers at German plants, their suppliers and buyers of German goods.

Some companies have already started lobbying, notably in the car industry.

Mr Trump has singled out the sector for attack, saying the vehicle trade was "a one-way street" in Germany's favour. He was particularly critical of BMW for constructing an export-oriented plant in Mexico, saying the company is wasting "its time and money" as vehicles imported into the US will face import duties of 35 per cent.

BMW responded by highlighting to US officials and journalists its strong role in the country, where it has its largest plant and is the biggest vehicle exporter. "We are explaining our position," said a spokesman. "I would not call it a campaign but we are talking to all government departments and agencies."

Mr Trump has yet to spell out his policies, and German business leaders and politicians do not want to risk making a potentially difficult situation worse by provoking the president. Participants at the Munich Security Conference this month were struck by the contrast between Mr Trump's isolationist language and the more conciliatory tones of US officials who attended the event, led by the vice president, Michael Pence.

German industry groups would be unlikely to set targets for future investment or job creation, an industry representative said, but companies could highlight their future plans. BMW, for example, is investing 1 bn in South Carolina to increase capacity at its Spartanburg factory, already its largest anywhere, from 411,000 vehicles last year to 450,000. Meanwhile, discount retailer Lidl is entering the US market, investing 1 bn to open around 100 stores in the next year, with more planned.

Words and Expressions

embrace	vt.	拥抱,欣然接受,乐意采纳(思想、建议等),信奉(宗教),包含
	n.	拥抱
rethink	vt. & vi.	重新考虑或再想(尤其是准备改变原来的想法)
	n.	重新考虑,反思,新想法
exploit	vt.	开拓,剥削,开采,利用(为自己谋利)
offensive	n.	进攻,攻势
multilevel	adj.	多级的,多层的
lobby	vi.	游说
	n.	(公共建筑物进口处的)门厅,前厅,(英国议会的)民众接待厅,(就某问题企图影响从政者的)游说团体,游说
publicity	n.	宣传,公众信息,宣传效用

single out		单独挑出
one-way street		单行道,单方面
critical	*adj.*	关键的,批评的,爱挑剔的
spell out		解释明白,讲清楚,用字母拼
provoke	*vt.*	激起,引起,挑衅,激怒
isolationist	*n.*	孤立主义者
conciliatory	*adj.*	调解的,抚慰的,和解的
Spartanburg	*n.*	(美国城市)斯巴达堡

Notes to the Text

1. trade surplus:贸易顺差,贸易盈余,出超。所谓贸易顺差,是指在特定年度一国出口贸易总额大于进口贸易总额,又称"出超"。贸易顺差就是在一定的单位时间里(通常按年度计算),贸易的双方互相买卖各种货物,互相进口与出口,甲方的出口金额大过乙方的出口金额,或甲方的进口金额少于乙方的进口金额,其中的差额对甲方来说就叫作"贸易顺差",反之,对乙方来说,就叫作"贸易逆差"。贸易顺差越多并不一定好,过高的贸易顺差是一件危险的事情,意味着经济的增长对外依存度过高。

2. Bayerische Motoren Werke AG:宝马汽车公司,简称BMW,生产的汽车主要以生产豪华轿车、摩托车和高性能发动机而闻名于世。创建于1916年,总部设在德国慕尼黑,职工5万余人。

3. Munich [ˈmjuːnɪk] Security Conference:慕尼黑安全会议,自1963年以来召开至今,是有关国际安全政策的年度会议。第46届慕尼黑安全政策会议开幕现场是由非官方机构承办的高规格安全政策论坛,与会者多为各国国防官员以及安全领域的专家,故有"防务领域的达沃斯论坛"之称。

5. Lidl:历德,是德国发展迅猛的一家零售商,食品日用品和小家电销售量比较大。Aldi和Lidl作为德国第一和第二的零售企业,甚至联手将世界零售巨头沃尔玛赶出了德国。随着沃尔玛在欧洲的势微,Aldi和Lidl不仅在整个欧盟地区迅速扩张,甚至扩张到了沃尔玛的总部美国。2017年Lidl在中国的天猫开出了旗舰店,取名"历德"。同年,Aldi在中国取名"奥乐齐",也正式在天猫开设旗舰店。

Delusional Lawyering Won't Save European Bonds

John Dizard
February 24, 2017, *Financial Times*

Mocking the delusions of US populism has been easy work for journalists. Now it is time to do the same for European elite opinion. Lately, I have been coping with the sheer tonnage of bank and law firm research on re-denomination risk.

This refers to how European sovereign bond investors should prepare for the risk of one or more euro zone countries readopting national currencies. Would another paragraph of lawyer do the trick?

To me, this seems like preparing for a giant meteor strike by packing another pair of socks. Yet we are seeing just that sort of thinking in the market's pricing of European bonds.

The magic lawyer in European sovereign bonds is supposedly provided by the Model CAC, for Collective Action Clause, that has been incorporated in all euro-zone sovereign bonds since January 2013.

The Model CAC was a post-Greek crisis bit of language that says any hypothetical restructuring of bond payments can be agreed by a super majority of 75 percent of bondholders.

At the time, this was considered a way to avoid allowing a few evil New York hedge funds to profit by refusing to take a haircut like nice regulated Europeans wanted. Not that any other European countries would ever "do a Greece".

Except that now leading national candidates in France and Italy are openly proposing a return to the franc and the lira, at least for paying foreigners and distant institutions. Nothing would happen to voters' savings, those candidates tell us, just as their counterparts in Argentina told that country's voters over the years.

Some of the bond market's lawyers believe that if such a candidate is elected in either France or Italy, they will not be able to pay the national debt in depreciated francs or lire, at least for those bonds that incorporate Model CAC's.

The assumption is that more than three-quarters of bondholders would vote against confiscation and the new populist government would have no choice but to pay in full in euros.

The problem with this logic is that most of the older French and Italian bonds were issued without CACs, and the post-2013 bond issues that include these clauses are all governed by national law.

Any French or Italian government that chose to switch the national currency could also just retroactively change the bond issues to either remove the Model CAC language or otherwise render it ineffective.

Despite offering only evanescent protection from a populist re-denomination, French and Italian bonds incorporating Model CACs have been outperforming comparable older bonds, at least for shorter maturities.

According to the economics group at ABN Amro, the Dutch lender: "The outperformance of [French] Model CAC bonds started in the autumn of last year, in which the French elections moved more to the headlines and radar of investors."

Similarly, in Italy, the ABN Amro researchers added: "The outperformance of Model CAC bonds is also found in Italian sovereign bonds ... as also here the Eurosceptic party M5S has signalled [it will] possibly convert the euro into a new currency."

But this is delusional. All of Europe would be a mess.

Lee Buchheit, the eminent sovereign debt lawyer, says that with or without these clauses, "an abrupt redenomination would risk chaos". Look at Argentina in 2002.

"Were a large eurozone country to re-denominate unilaterally, it would shake the foundations of the monetary union," he says.

Leading national candidates in France and Italy are openly proposing a return to the franc and the lira —Lorenzo16VDreamstime

The key legal point is not which clauses are in the euro sovereign bonds, but whether the bonds are governed by "local law".

In the case of an Italian exit from the euro, Mr Buchheit says the collateral value of bonds governed by Italian law would collapse. This would prompt the European Central Bank to tell the banks to top up their collateral, but they would not be able to.

Mr Buchheit says: "The Italian legislature may have the power to redenominate the currency of bonds governed by Italian law. But exercising that power abruptly would have many unintended consequences. For example, the value of Italian government bonds pledged as collateral could collapse, resulting in margin calls that Italian banks would struggle to meet.

"A simple reprofiling, with no haircut to the principal of the debt, might give the banking system a fighting chance of survival."

Even if Italy's unsustainable debt burden is magicked away for a few years, the country still has a competitiveness and growth problem. Any "reform" programme requires a rapidly ageing population to remake itself like the characters in a vitamin-supplement advert.

Or Italy could devalue its way into competitiveness and full employment. Would France follow? I do not know, but I do know that the market's fixation on fine points of bond language is pointless.

Words and Expressions

mock	vt.	嘲笑,(模仿)嘲弄
delusion	n.	妄想
populism	n.	平民主义,平民论
tonnage	n.	吨位
sovereign	adj.	有主权的
	n.	君主,独立国,最高统治者
do the trick		获得成功
meteor strike		陨石撞击
pack	vt.	包装,打包,收拾(行李),装(箱)
another pair of socks		完全是另一回事,两码事
hypothetical	adj.	假设的
restructure	vt.	调整,重建,更改结构
take a haircut		接受损失
confiscation	n.	没收,征用,充公
populist	n.	民粹主义者,平民主义者
	adj.	平民主义的,平民化的
bond issues		债券发行
retroactively	adv.	追溯地,逆动地
render	vt.	使成为,使变得,使处于某状态
evanescent	adj.	瞬息即逝的,迅速遗忘的
outperform	vt.	做得比……更好,胜过
maturity	n.	(票据等的)到期

Eurosceptic	n.	欧洲统一怀疑论者,反对英国亲近欧盟的人
convert	vt.	使转变,转换,使……改变信仰
	vi.	转变,变换,皈依,改变信仰
	n.	皈依者,改变宗教信仰者
eminent	adj.	杰出的,有名的,明显的
top up		给……加满
collateral	n.	抵押品,担保品,旁系亲属
	adj.	并行的,旁系的,附属的
legislature	n.	立法机关,立法机构
abruptly	adv.	突然地,意外地,(言谈举止)唐突地
margin	n.	边缘,利润,余裕,页边的空白
	vt.	加边于,加旁注于
margin call		追加保证金的通知
principal	n.	本金,首长,负责人,主要演员,主角,委托人,当事人
	adj.	本金的,资本的,主要的,最重要的
fighting chance		成败均有可能的公平机会
unsustainable	adj.	不能持续的,无法维持的
magic away		使……像变魔术一样消失
competitiveness	n.	竞争性,竞争
vitamin-supplement	n.	维生素补充剂
advert	n.	〈英口〉广告
fixation	n.	固定
fine point		要点
pointless	adj.	无谓的,无意义的,不得要领的

Notes to the Text

1. Sovereign Bond:主权债券,指由政府支持的机构发行的债券。各国政府(多为发展中国家)在国际市场以外币(如美元、欧元等主要货币)发行的政府债券。主权债券的发行主体是政府。它是指政府财政部门或其他代理机构为筹集资金,以政府名义发行的债券,主要包括国库券和公债两大类。一般国库券是由财政部发行,用以弥补财政收支不平衡;公债是指为筹集建设资金而发行的一种债券。有时也将两者统称为公债。中央政府发行的被称为"中央主权债券"(国家公债),地方政府发行的被称为"地方主权债券"(地方公债)。美国联邦政府发行的各种债券包括国库券(treasury bills)、国库本票(treasury notes)和联邦政府公债(treasury bonds)。

2. hedge fund：采用对冲交易手段的基金，被称为"对冲基金"，也被称为"避险基金"或"套期保值基金"，是指金融期货-金融期权等金融衍生工具与金融工具结合后以营利为目的的金融基金。它是投资基金的一种形式，意为"风险对冲过的基金"。对冲基金采用各种交易手段进行对冲、换位、套头、套期来赚取巨额利润。这些概念已经超出了传统的防止风险、保障收益操作范畴。加之发起和设立对冲基金的法律门槛远低于互惠基金，使之风险进一步加大。社会学家、作家、财经记者 Alfred W. Jones 创造了"对冲基金"一词，1949 年，他还第一次确立了对冲基金的结构，为此广受赞誉。为了中和市场总体的波动，Jones 采用买入看涨资产、卖空看跌资产的手法来避险，他把这种管理市场总体波动的风险敞口的操作称为"对冲"。对冲（hedging）是一种旨在降低风险的行为或策略。套期保值常见的形式是在一个市场或资产上做交易，以对冲在另一个市场或资产上的风险，如某公司购买一份外汇期权以对冲即期汇率的波动对其经营带来的风险。进行套期保值的人被称为"套期者"或"对冲者"（hedger）。

3. ABN AMRO：1991 年由两家荷兰银行 Algemene Bank Nederland（ABN）和 the Amsterdamsche-Rotterdamsche Bank（AMRO）合并而成，到 2005 年 9 月为止，它在欧洲银行中排名第 11 位，资产额世界排名第 20 位，在全世界 60 多个国家建有 3000 多个网点，总资产达 8993 亿元。

4. debt reprofiling：债务重新安排，债务国一方不能按期偿还债务本金和利息时，与债权国一方重新协商并达成对到期债务或拖延债务重新安排的协议。

5. debt restructuring：债务重组，在债务人发生财务困难的情况下，债权人按照其与债务人达成的协议或法院的裁定做出让步的事项。

Fiscal Rules and Fiscal Cryogenics

Hong Kong and São Paulo
December 15, 2016, *The Economist*

Freezing the size of government

From its headquarters in Brasília, a sterile, technocratic city, Brazil's federal government doles out money for health, education, generous pensions and artistic awards, among other things. Over the past two decades, this spending has grown by more than 185% in real terms. Over the next 20 years, its growth will be zero.

That, at least, is the intention of a constitutional amendment passed this week by Brazil's Senate. The measure, which allows federal spending (excluding interest payments and transfers to states and municipalities) to grow no faster than inflation, is an unusually ambitious example of a fiscal rule: a quantitative limit on budget-making, which lasts beyond a single year and perhaps beyond a single government.

The best known, and least loved, fiscal rule is the euro area's stability and growth pact. But such rules are also now common among emerging economies. According to the IMF's latest count, 56 developing countries in 2014 had rules of some kind, including 15, like Brazil, that impose limits on the growth of public spending.

The reasons so many emerging-market governments choose to limit their fiscal choices vary. Some recognize that it is better to abide by their own limits than test the markets'. By cutting the scope fiscal mischief in the future, a credible fiscal rule can make a government's bonds more appealing today. The risk of profligacy goes hand in hand with the danger of "pro-cyclicality". Governments in emerging economies tend to overspend in good times and cut back in bad times, adding to economic instability rather than dampening it.

Do fiscal rules help? A famous example is Chile's 15-year-old rule, which requires fiscal tightening when economic growth, copper prices and the price of molybdenum (a metal used in steel alloys) rise above their long-term trends, and permits fiscal easing in the opposite case. Several numbers—such as the trend rate of growth or long-term copper price—can only be guessed, not observed. But the guesses are made by an independent expert committee, so the government cannot make its own fiscally convenient estimates.

Other countries, including Peru and Colombia, have tried to implement similarly sophisticated rules. But it is not easy. They work best in countries with a reasonably stable tax base and a well-understood macroeconomic rhythm. Elsewhere, simpler rules can be easier to monitor and enforce. One simplification is to set rules for spending alone, rather than the overall budget balance, thus escaping the need to project revenues. Emerging economies comply with their spending rules about two-thirds of the time, according to a 2015 IMF working paper, whereas their compliance rate for budget-balance rules is less than 40%. Despite their simplicity, spending rules can make fiscal policy more counter cyclical. In upswings, they deter overspending; in downturns, they permit government revenues to fall of their own accord, without requiring demand-sapping tax hikes.

Spending rules do, however, pose a philosophical riddle: they require policymakers to settle the age-old question of the proper size of government. Georgia's rule makers, for example, think government should not exceed 30% of GDP. Brazil's think it should not exceed 1.24trn reais ($373bn) in today's money. Rules on deficits or debt, in contrast, are compatible with government of all sizes, provided that taxes are kept in line with spending.

The appropriate size of fiscal deficits, given the stage of the business cycle, is a technocratic question, which can yield a bipartisan answer, as Chile shows. Such a consensus can be formalised in a politically robust fiscal rule, capable of surviving a change of government, as Chile's has also done. It is harder to imagine all parties agreeing on the appropriate size of government. Debate on that question is, after all, one reason why multiple parties exist.

Words and Expressions

cryogenics	n.	低温学
sterile	adj.	贫瘠的
technocratic	adj.	受技术专家官员影响的,由技术专家官员组成的
dole out		少量地发放(食物、救济金等)
pension	n.	退休金,养老金
in real terms		扣除物价因素,按实质计算实际,不变价,实值
constitutional amendment		宪法修正案
senate	n.	参议院
municipality	n.	自治市,市(或区)政当局
quantitative	adj.	定量的,数量(上)的
count	n.	计算(或清点)总数
abide by		遵守,信守
cut scope		缩小范围
mischief	n.	损害,危害,祸根,恶作剧
credible	adj.	可信的,可靠的
appealing	adj.	吸引人的,令人心动的
profligacy	n.	肆意挥霍,放荡,不检点
instability	n.	不稳定,不稳固
dampen	vt.	抑制,控制,减弱
copper	n.	铜
molybdenum	n.	钼
alloy	n.	合金
fiscal easing		财政宽松
trend rate of growth		趋势增长率
convenient	adj.	实用的,便利的
sophisticated	adj.	复杂的,精致的,富有经验的
rhythm	n.	规律性变化,节奏

budget balance		预算余额,预算平衡
project	vt.	预测,预计,推想,规划,计划,拟订方案
comply with		顺应,服从,遵从
working paper		研究报告
compliance	n.	服从,听从
simplicity	n.	简单(性),容易(性)
upswing	n.	上升,改进,进步,提高
deter	vt.	阻止,制止
downturn	n.	(价格或活动)开始下降,衰退,低迷时期
of their own accord		自愿地,主动地
sap	vt.	逐渐削弱(某人/某事物的力量、活力等)
tax hike		赋税增加
hike		提高,涨价
riddle	n.	谜语,猜不透的难题
reais	n.	雷亚尔(又音译为"里奥"或"黑奥",巴西现在通用的货币)
compatible	adj.	兼容的,相容的,和谐的
keep in line with		与……保持一致
business cycle		商业周期
yield	vt.	产生(收益、效益等),提供
bipartisan	adj.	两派的
consensus	n.	一致的意见,共识
formalise	vt.	使(协议、计划等)成书面文字形式,使成为正式,使具有一定形式
robust	adj.	强劲的,富有活力的
capable of		有……能力(或技能)的,能……的
survive	vi.	幸存,活下来

Notes to the Text

1. Brasilia:巴西利亚,巴西联邦共和国首都,巴西第四大城市。1960年4月21日,巴西为了加快内陆的开发,将当时首都由里约热内卢迁至巴西利亚。

2. pro-cyclicality:亲周期性,是指金融部门与实体经济之间动态的相互作用(正向反馈机制)。这种互相依存的作用关系会扩大经济周期性的波动程度,并造成或加剧金融部门的不稳定性。从金融理论上讲,金融系统本身就具有内在的亲周期性。在经济上升时期,由于抵押资产升值,市场前景看好,银行将增大信贷供给,刺激经济进一步扩张。然而,这一时期发放的许多贷款很可能转化成经济衰退期的不良贷款;当经济出现衰退时,由于借款人财务状况恶化,抵押物价值下降以及贷款风险得以暴露,银行在发放贷款时更加谨慎,提高了贷款条件、担保要求、信贷审查的要求,提取更多的风险拨备、核销了坏账,银行贷款增长速度放缓、贷款规模减少。信贷的急剧减少对经济冲击很大,导致经济进一步衰退,经济复苏举步维艰。

3. Stability and Growth Pact:《稳定与增长公约》,是为了保证欧元的稳定,防止欧元区通货膨胀而制定的。1997年6月17日在阿姆斯特丹首脑会议上通过的欧盟《稳定与增长公约》规定,欧元区各国政府的财政赤字不得超过当年国内生产总值(GDP)的3%、公共债务不得超过GDP的60%。按照该公约,一国财政赤字若连续3年超过该国GDP的3%,该国将被处以最高相当于其GDP之0.5%的罚款。

Thailand's Economy: The Dangers of Farsightedness

Khon Kaen
October 1, 2016, *The Economist*

**The junta lavishes attention on the economy's future
but neglects the poor of today**

In planning for the future, democratic politicians dare not look far beyond the next election, lest they lose power before the future arrives. Thailand's military rulers have no such qualms. They have rewritten the constitution to guarantee themselves a guiding hand over future governments even after elections resume. That has given them the confidence to draw up a 20-year plan for the economy. In a speech in Bangkok on September 28th, Prayuth Chan-ocha, coup leader and prime minister, promised to turn Thailand into a developed country by 2036.

The junta sees Thailand climbing to a fourth stage of economic development ("Thailand 4.0") beyond agriculture, light manufacturing and heavy industry. This next stage will feature new "growth engines", such as biotechnology, the Internet of things and "mechatronics" (a fusion of mechanics and electronics).

In pursuit of this vision, some welcome structural reforms are underway. The junta has passed an inheritance tax; one on land and property will follow. It has also begun to reform the corporate governance of the country's 56 state-owned enterprises, hoping to free them from political interference, even if not from public ownership. To bind the country closer together, the government is contemplating big outlays on infrastructure, including $51 billion to be spent on railways, roads and airports.

Much remains to be done. Thailand's service sector is the most protected in South-East Asia. Neither America nor the European Union is willing to negotiate a free-trade deal with the junta, even as they talk to such regional rivals as Indonesia, the Philippines and Vietnam.

Nonetheless, the regime's economic plan has left it open to an unusual charge: it is holding too many seminars on the long term and neglecting the short term, says Suradech Taweesa engsakulthai, a businessman in Khon Kaen, a north-eastern provincial capital. The junta's efforts to advance structural reform are more impressive than its efforts to revive demand. That is not something that can be said about most of the world's governments.

A revival of domestic demand is necessary. Thailand's economy is operating well below capacity. Inflation is far less than the central bank's target; the current-account surplus is strikingly high (about 10% of GDP); private credit is subdued (growing by 5% in the first quarter) and sovereign debt is modest (44% of GDP in 2015). Public investment, thanks to the junta's big plans, is growing at a double-digit pace, but Thailand's indebted consumers remain cautious and private investment is stagnant (see the chart).

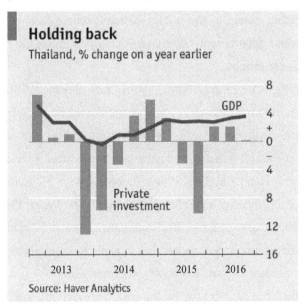

The overall shortfall in demand will amount to about 1.4% of GDP this year, according to the IMF. Strip out spending by foreign tourists and the gap is even larger, as the current-account surplus attests. This lack of spending is manifest in the inflation figures: consumer prices fell for 15 straight months last year and this. They rose by only 0.3% in the year to August.

Stagnant demand is especially visible in the provinces. The rural economy has contracted for seven quarters in a row. Nongpetch Khunnasarn, a used-cardealer outside Khon Kaen city, the political heartland of the government ousted by the junta, has not made a sale for two months. Under Yingluck Shinawatra, the deposed prime minister, she sold one a week.

In Ban Phue, an hour's drive from Khon Kaen, two years of drought and falling agricultural prices have led to a collapse in farm incomes. Last year Bangkok ordered farmers not to plant a second crop, because of poor rains. This year farmers are running a lottery to determine who can draw stored rain water.

Thailand's farmers used to rely on ballots, not lottery tickets, to get what they needed. When Thaksin Shinawatra, Yingluck's brother, became prime minister in 2001 he aimed to bolster the income of the poor who voted for him. He introduced cheap medical care, accessible rural credit, higher minimum wages and generous price floors for agricultural goods. At one point in his sister's tenure, a tonne of rice brought in as much as 20,000 baht ($625). It now fetches 8,000 baht, thanks to the fall in global prices and the removal of the government's price floor. "If the government does not pay more, what can we do?" asks Anong Wannasupring, a farmer.

For all of its waste and corruption, the Shinawatra style of clientilistic mass politics helped to spread spending power to the poorer regions, where local bigwigs doled out funds disbursed from the central government. All that has changed under the junta, which has kept a firmer grip on the purse-strings.

The National Village Community Fund, which has allocated 500,000 baht each to almost 80,000 villages for rural projects, is now administered by the ministry of interior. The state's Special Financial Institutions, which provide rural credit, are now regulated by the central bank, having previously been the playthings of provincial politicians. These days, if you wait for money from Bangkok, "you'll wait forever," says Mr Suradech.

His complaint is confirmed by a startling calculation. The World Bank reckons that over 70% of Thailand's public expenditure in 2010 benefited Greater Bangkok, home to 17% of the country's population. In no other economy with a comparable level of income is government spending as skewed, say the bank's economists.

Rather than lift the shopping power of the rural masses, the junta has aimed to boost spending by tourists and urbanites. It has cut taxes markedly for the relatively few businesses and people that pay them. It has also succeeded in doubling the number of visitors from China to 10m a year.

Bangkok's efforts to clawback fiscal decision-making may curb clientelism. But this reconcentration of power may also result in a reconcentration of prosperity. The renewed centrality of "one man in Bangkok", says Ms Nongpetch, the used-car dealer, has been bad for business.

 Words and Expressions

junta	n.	军人集团,军政府
lavish	v.	过分给予,滥施
	adj.	大量的,给人印象深刻的,耗资巨大的,慷慨的
qualm	n.	(对自己行为的)顾虑,不安
coup	n.	政变,了不起的成就
mechatronics	n.	机电一体化
underway	adj.	起步的,在进行中的
inheritance	n.	继承,遗传,遗产
interference	n.	干涉,干扰
bind	vt.	捆绑,约束,使紧密联系,使关系密切
contemplate	vt.	注视,凝视,盘算,计议,周密考虑
	vi.	沉思,深思熟虑
outlay	n.	费用,花费
	vt.	花费
infrastructure	n.	基础设施,基础建设
negotiate	vi.	谈判,协商,交涉
	vt.	谈判达成,成功越过,议价出售
rival	n.	对手,竞争者
	vt.	与……竞争,比得上某人
	vi.	竞争
regime	n.	政治制度,政权,政体
seminar	n.	研讨会,研讨班,讲习会
revival	n.	复兴,复活
private credit		私人信贷
subdue	vt.	制服,征服,克制
indebted	adj.	负债的
shortfall	n.	亏空,缺少,不足之数
strip out		剥除
attest	vt.	作证,宣称……为真实的,证明,证实
manifest	adj.	明白的,明显的
straight	adj.	连续的,直的

stagnant	adj.	停滞的,不发展的,无变化的
in a row		接连
oust	vt.	剥夺,罢免,革职
depose	vt.	罢免,废黜
under		用,以(某一名字)
drought	n.	旱灾,干旱
collapse	vi.	崩溃,倒塌,折叠,(尤指工作劳累后)坐下
	vt.	使倒塌,使坍塌,使瓦解
	n.	垮台,(身体的)衰弱
second crop		第二茬作物,第二次收成
run a lottery		开奖
draw water		汲水
ballot	n.	投票,投票权,投票用纸
bolster	vt.	支持,支撑,鼓励,援助
	n.	垫枕,长枕,衬垫,支持物
accessible	adj.	易使用的,易得到的
rural credit		农村信贷
generous		(尤指在钱财上)慷慨的,大方的,宽松的
price floor		最低限价
tenure	n.	(尤指重要政治职务的)任期,任职
baht	n.	铢(泰国货币单位)
fetch	vt.	售得,卖得(某价)
clientilistic	adj.	侍从型的
bigwig	n.	〈口〉放(食物、救济金等)
disburse	vt. & vi.	支出,付出
purse-string	n.	(字面意思)系钱包的绳子,财政资源
allocate	vt.	分配,分派,把……拨给
administer	vt.	管理,执行
regulate	vt.	(用规则条例)约束,控制,管理
plaything	n.	玩物,供消遣的东西
complaint	n.	抱怨,控诉
confirm	vt.	证实,确认,批准
startling	adj.	令人吃惊的

reckon	vt.	认为,评定,断定,计算,测算,估计
expenditure	n.	花费,支出,费用,经费,(尤指金钱的)支出额
comparable	adj.	可比较的,比得上的
skewed	adj.	偏的,斜的,歪的
urbanite	n.	都市人
markedly	adv.	显著地,引人注目地
clientelism	n.	庇护主义
reconcentration	n.	再集中
renewed	adj.	更新的,重建的,复兴的
centrality	n.	中心,向心性,中央,集中性

Notes to the Text

1. Bangkok:曼谷,是泰国首都和最大城市,别名"天使之城",东南亚第二大城市,经济占泰国总量的44%,曼谷港承担着泰国90%的外贸。

2. Khon Kaen:孔敬,是泰国依善地区的一个城市,也是孔敬府和孔敬郡(孔敬府的下辖地区)的首府,孔敬是泰国东北部的中心以及政府机构所在地。

3. Private Credit:私募债,是指通过非银行和公开债券市场进行的融资活动。私募债的形式是多种多样的,可以是直接融资(direct lending),也可以通过辛迪加贷款(syndication)的形式进行融资。私募债的收益一般根据风险而定。通常情况下,私募债的收益会高于公开上市的债券,但略低于私募股权。优先级私募债的年化收益率在5%和10%之间,夹层债或劣后级私募债的年化收益率在10%和15%之间,而不良私募债的收益率可以达到20%。当然,不良私募债的投资风险也是最高的。

4. Yingluck Shinawatra:英拉·西那瓦,泰国前总理,国防部前部长,著名企业家。1967年6月21日出生于泰国清迈府,第四代泰国华裔,祖籍广东省梅州市丰顺县塔下村,梅州客家人后裔,是泰国前总理他信·西那瓦最小的妹妹,比他信小18岁。英拉先后在泰国清迈大学和美国肯塔基州立大学取得政治学学士和政治学硕士学位。2011年8月5日,在第24届国会下议院第二次会议上当选为泰国第28位总理,成为泰国历史上首位女性政府首脑。

5. Thaksin Shinawatra:他信·西那瓦,1949年7月26日出生于泰国清迈,知名政治家和企业家,2001年2月9日当选为泰国第23任总理,成为泰国史上第一位任期满四年的总理,也是第一位通过选举连任的总理。2006年9月19日,泰国军方发动政变,他信被迫下台,并于2008年流亡海外,此后一直遭泰当局通缉。

6. mass politics:群众政治,大众政治。所谓大众政治,就是政策和法规的制定代表民意,是由民众的意见来决定的,不是由少数人来决定的。这样制定出来的政策和法规未必科学或合理,但代表着大多数民众的意见。

与大众政治相反,精英政治是指政策和法规的制定是由(少数)社会精英来制定的。从理论上讲,精英政治会比大众政治更有效率(没有很多人的参与)、更科学(决策者有很好的专业知识)。从世界各国的具体实践经验来看,精英政治确实效率很高,但是所制定的政策往往是以牺牲大多数人的利益为代价的。

Tata Saga Shows Corporate India Must Change Its Ways

February 26, 2017, *Financial Times*

Stand in the lobby of Tata Consultancy Services' head office in Mumbai and you could be visiting any multinational professional services group. Walk to nearby Bombay House, home of ancestral holding company Tata Sons, and you could only be in India—from the busts of founder Jamsetji Tata and former chairman JRD Tata, to the stray dogs allowed to laze in the entry hall.

Last Tuesday, Natarajan Chandrasekaran, formally promoted from head of the consulting group to chairman of Tata Sons, the holding company for TCS and 13 other listed subsidiaries, garlanded the statues of Tata's former leaders and promised to "do everything we need to do to delight all the people who are proud of the group".

Delight is a long way from the sentiment that has enveloped Tata since Cyrus Mistry's dismissal as chairman last October, when tension between him and Ratan Tata, the group's patriarch, boiled over. As Simon Mundy of the *Financial Times* has reported, the fallout risks hurting Indian business as a whole.

When I visited India just before Mr Mistry's departure, many of the people I met were still holding up Tata as a model. The best-known group in India's "promoter" system, where strategy is overseen by a powerful individual or holding company, its benevolent influence was summed up by one Tata executive, later swept away in a post-Mistry purge. He said Tata applied "different models of parenting" to its many companies, from Tata Steel to the UK's Jaguar Land Rover.

I applauded Tata's long-term approach when Mr Mistry was named chairman in 2011. It was a relatively conservative choice (Mr Mistry was a board member, part of a family linked to the Tatas that still owns 18 per cent of Tata Sons), but justified by the group's long success and laudable devotion to important values.

That seems a long time ago. In a public campaign against the Tata Sons board, Mr Mistry and his supporters have implied he was subject to a parenting style more reminiscent of King Lear, as Ratan Tata took issue with changes and sought to maintain control.

The crisis may encourage family owners and promoters to tighten their grip over professional managers. On the other hand, it could—and I think should—accelerate the professionalisation of Indian companies by demonstrating to the next generation of founder-entrepreneurs how an overly dynastic approach can lead to infighting and stasis.

The seeds for this next phase are already sown. The mix of companies operating in India is broader than it has ever been—and they can all learn from one another. AM Naik, who heads Larsen & Toubro, an engineering and construction conglomerate, points out that owner promoters coexist with Indian-born information technology groups, such as Wipro and Infosys, foreign multinationals and start-ups. Mr Naik shares plenty of Mr Tata's paternalistic characteristics: L&T visitors are treated to a lengthy video praising his philanthropic and management virtues. But, as head of a broadly owned listed group, he will carry out a smooth handover to a successor later this year.

The other cause for optimism comes from the new generation of founders. "Three years ago, people said they looked down on me for being an entrepreneur ... They said I wouldn't [be able to] get married," says Sangeeta Devni, deputy manager of a Bangalore start-up incubator run by Nasscom, the technology trade body. But now, she says, "Entrepreneurship is worshipped."

The temptation for founders to influence their companies after they have left will always be strong, even outside the promoter system. Narayana Murthy, one of the men who launched Infosys, recently criticised the group's governance, putting him at odds with the managers who run the company.

Sandeep Murthy, a partner with Lightbox, a Mumbai-based venture capital group, says he sets out to fund start-ups with the "definitive view [they] aren't trying to start a dynasty", obliging founders to sign an employment agreement underlining that they serve at the pleasure of the board. "I tell them, 'Your son and grandson won't be the ones running this business; that's not why we're building it," he says.

But he concedes such efforts will not change the wider corporate system. That will require a concerted effort by professional managers such as Mr Chandrasekaran to rebalance the relationship with the influencers who still tug on the reins of India's best-established companies.

At the same time, patriarchs, individual promoters and founders will need to cede some power to allow their companies to delight their admirers—and advance.

Words and Expressions

saga	n.	萨迦(尤指古代挪威或冰岛讲述冒险经历和英雄业绩的长篇故事),(讲述许多年间发生的事情的)长篇故事,传说,冒险故事,英雄事迹
corporate	adj.	法人的,团体的,社团的,公司的
lobby	n.	门厅,大厅,投票厅,休息室,游说团
	vi.	为了支持或抵制某项特定目标游说
	vt.	对……进行游说,陈情
ancestral	adj.	祖先的,与祖先有关的,祖宗传下的
holding company		控股公司
bust	n.	半身雕塑像,胸围
	vt. & vi.	打破,打碎
stray dog		流浪狗
laze	vi.	懒散,闲散,混日子,闲散地打发时间
subsidiary	n.	附属事物,附属机构,子公司,附属者,附属品
	adj.	附带的,附属的,次要的,帮助的,补足的
garland	v.	戴花环,把……做成花环,给……饰以花环
	n.	花环,花冠,花圈,华饰,诗歌选集,胜利和荣誉的象征
sentiment	n.	情操,感情,情绪,意见,观点,感伤
envelope	vt.	包住,盖住,围绕
dismissal	n.	解雇,免职
tension	n.	紧张,不安,紧张气氛,张力,拉力,矛盾
	vt.	紧张,使紧张
patriarch	n.	家长,族长,元老,创始人
boil over		沸腾,溢出,到了爆发点,〈非正〉发怒
promoter	n.	筹办人,发起者,赞助者,助长者,发起人,促进者
oversee	vt.	监督,监视,俯瞰
benevolent	adj.	慈善的,仁慈的,乐善好施的
sweep away		扫除,清除,冲走,刮走
purge	n.	净化,整肃,泻药
	vt.	肃清,清除,(使)净化,(使)通便
parenting	n.	养育,教养,抚养
conservative	adj.	保守的,(英国)保守党的,(式样等)不时新的

Unit Three World Economy

	n.	保守的人,(英国)保守党党员,保守党支持者
justify	*vt.*	证明……有理,为……辩护,对……做出解释
laudable	*adj.*	应受赞扬的,值得赞美的
devotion	*n.*	忠诚,热爱,献身,奉献,信仰,祈祷
public campaign		公开活动
imply	*vt. & vi.*	暗示,意味,隐含,说明,表明
subject to		使服从,使遭受,受……管制
reminiscent	*adj.*	使回忆起(人或事)
take issue		采取反对立场,持反对意见,不同意
temptation	*n.*	诱惑,引诱,诱惑物
grip	*n.*	控制力,影响力,握力,紧握,掌握,理解,能力,胜任
accelerate	*vt.*	促进,(使)加快
professionalization	*n.*	职业化,专业化
demonstrate	*vt.*	论证,证明,证实,显示,展示,演示,说明
	vi.	示威游行
overly	*adv.*	过度地,极度地
dynastic	*adj.*	朝代的,王朝的
infighting	*n.*	内讧,内部纠纷,钩心斗角
stasis	*n.*	停滞,静止
conglomerate	*n.*	联合大企业,砾岩,合成物,组合物
coexist	*vi.*	同时共存,和平共处
multinational	*n.*	跨国公司
	adj.	跨国的,多国的
start-up	*n.*	刚成立的公司,新企业
	adj.	[only before noun] (新企业或工程)开办阶段的,启动时期的
paternalistic	*adj.*	家长式作风的
treat to		款待,招待
lengthy	*adj.*	啰唆的,(演说、文章等)冗长的,长的,漫长的
philanthropic	*adj.*	博爱的,慈善的
listed company		股票上市的公司
handover	*n.*	交接,移交
successor	*n.*	继承人,继任者,接替的人或事物
optimism	*n.*	乐观,乐观主义
founder	*n.*	(组织、机构等的)创建者,创办者,发起人

entrepreneur	n.	企业家,主办人,承包人
incubator	n.	孵化器
trade body		贸易组织
entrepreneurship	n.	企业家能力,职能,企业家(主办人等)的身份(地位、职权、能力)
worship	vt.	崇拜,尊崇,爱慕
	vi.	做礼拜,热爱,爱慕,崇拜(尤指达到看不到缺点的地步)
	n.	崇拜,礼拜
launch	vt.	开始从事,发起,发动(尤指有组织的活动)
criticise (criticize)	vt. & vi.	评论,批评
governance	n.	管理,统治,支配,统治方式
at odds with		与……不和,与……争吵
venture capital group		风险投资集团
set out to		打算,着手
fund	vt.	积存,为……提供资金,提供资金偿付(债款等)的本息
	n.	基金,储备,现款,特别基金管理机构
definitive	adj.	最后的,确定的,决定性的,限定的,明确的
	n.	限定词
oblige	vt.	(以法律、义务等)强迫,迫使
underline	vt.	在……下面画线,加强,强调
concede	vt.	承认,退让,给予,容许
	vi.	让步
concerted	adj.	协调的,协定的,协商好的,合拍调的
rebalance	n./vt.	再平衡
influencer	n.	影响者
tug	n.	(两人或双方的)激烈争夺,(突然的)猛拉,猛拽
rein	n.	支配权,控制权,缰绳,驾驭(法),统治手段
patriarch	n.	家长,族长,元老
cede	vt.	放弃,让给,割让
delight	vt.	使高兴,使欣喜
	vi.	感到高兴
	n.	快乐,高兴
admirer	n.	崇拜者,赞赏者,羡慕者,(女子的)爱慕者

Unit Three　World Economy

Notes to the Text

1. Tata Consultancy Services Limited（TCS）：塔塔集团,由詹姆谢特吉·塔塔（Jamsetji Tata）于1868年创立,集团的早期发展深受民族主义精神的鼓舞。塔塔集团在印度开辟了数个对国家具有重要意义的行业:钢铁、电力、酒店和航空业。近年,塔塔集团的开拓精神在其旗下的公司中得到了体现。这些公司包括塔塔咨询服务公司——该公司是印度第一家软件公司;塔塔汽车公司——该公司于1998年生产出印度第一辆本土研制汽车Indica,并于2008年推出了世界上最经济小型车Nano。

塔塔集团是印度最大的集团公司,总部位于印度孟买。塔塔集团的商业运营涉及七个领域:通信和信息技术、工程、材料、服务、能源、消费产品和化工产品。

贾姆谢吉的继任者R.D.塔塔推行新的规则,将劳动时间削减为8小时,并为职工提供免费医疗服务,即便是在公司最艰难的时期也依然坚持这样的制度。

2. Jaguar Land Rover:捷豹路虎(英文简称JLR),是一家拥有两个顶级奢华品牌的英国汽车制造商,属于印度塔塔汽车旗下,研发、生产、销售捷豹品牌和路虎品牌的全部汽车。公司主要业务是开发、生产和销售捷豹和路虎汽车。其中拥有辉煌历史的捷豹是世界上生产豪华运动轿车和跑车的主要制造商,而路虎则是全球生产顶级奢华的全地形4×4汽车制造商。

3. Infosy:印孚瑟斯技术有限公司(Infosys Technologies Ltd),1999年通过了CMMI5级(软件工程规范最高级别)认证,2000年位列全球20强,2008年《福布斯》全球最具声望排行榜位列第14位,2008年国际外包专业组织发布全球软件出口100强中,Infosys和埃森哲、IBM名列全球前三名。

4. NASSCOM（National Association of Software and Service Companies）:全国软件及服务公司协会。NASSCOM是印度软件和服务业企业行业协会,是印度信息技术和软件业最具有影响力的组织,拥有1100家会员单位,其中200家是全球性公司。作为印度IT服务产业的"市场部",NASSCOM在印度乃至全球服务外包领域的地位举足轻重,对政策推动、对行业咨询以及协调作用非常明显,保证了印度在全球离岸服务外包中的领导地位。

Unit Four

International Finance

Our Financial Standards Benefit Everyone

Sam Woods
February 27, 2017, *Financial Times*
(The writer is deputy governor for prudential regulation at the Bank of England)

The UK banking system is large and concentrated. The first job of the Prudential Regulation Authority is to keep it safe and sound.

Parliament has also given the PRA a secondary objective: to facilitate effective competition both in banking and insurance. Competition is good for consumers and should help the system renew itself for a more resilient future. Last week, the PRA announced an important step to promote competition in the capital framework for banks and building societies.

It has authorised 23 new banks since the current regulatory framework came into effect in 2013, during which time challenger banks have continued to compete with the bigger players. These banks have brought new technology, innovative business models and valuable services to many types of customers.

The PRA has sought to facilitate new comers' entry to the market, setting up a dedicated supervisory unit to support them. However, they do face some difficulties competing with the large incumbents, which came out of the global financial crisis with a greater market share than when they went in.

Regulators around the world have spent years transforming prudential standards in order to repair the financial system. This is no time for a retreat. Jeopardising the benefits of a more stable financial system, which supports the real economy to grow and create jobs, would be misguided.

Naturally, where features of the new regime do not work properly, we should consider how to fix them—while remaining true to the goal of stability. Take, for example, the risk of a significant difference in capital requirements between the challenger and incumbent banks. Larger firms typically use internal models to calculate their capital requirements. This means that the weights used are sensitive to the specific risks they take. Smaller or younger groups typically use standardised weights. But, as the Treasury select committee has highlighted, there can be large disparities between the two calculations.

Research by the Bank of England has shown that the gap between internal models and the standardised approach for low loan-to-value mortgages has given smaller banks an incentive to increase lending for higher loan-to-value mortgages. That somewhat defeats the purpose.

Recent initiatives—such as the systemic risk buffer for large lenders—have already narrowed the effect of disparities between the two approaches.

The next stage at the global level is the subject of discussions in Basel. Meanwhile, the PRA is making an important and complementary step in the domestic framework.

Last week, the PRA published proposals to supplement its current risk-by-risk assessment, used for setting banks' requirements, with an overall assessment of the total level of capital needed for each firm. As a check, it already makes extensive use of business model analysis and peer reviews. But we can go further.

Under the plans, supervisors of a bank using the standardised approach would be informed by benchmarks calculated from the risk weights used by those employing internal models. And they will take into account factors such as the extent to which existing methodologies can lead to smaller banks maintaining capital in excess of a prudent coverage of the risks faced. Where this work shows the PRA can safely lower a bank's capital requirement, it will do so.

In short, the PRA will look at capital requirements in the round rather than assuming that a simple "sum of the parts" approach will necessarily deliver the right answer. This reduces any risk that smaller banks and building societies are disadvantaged by a prudent approach. It is an important step on the road to more effective competition in a safer banking system.

Words and Expressions

financial standard	财务标准
deputy governor	副总裁,副行长

safe and sound		安然无恙
secondary objective		次要目标
facilitate	vt.	促进,使便利
resilient	adj.	可迅速恢复的,有适应能力的,有弹性的,能复原的
capital framework		资本架构
authorise	vt.	授权,批准,委托
innovative	adj.	创新的,革新的,富有革新精神的,创新立异的
dedicated	adj.	专用的,专门用途的,献身的,专心致志的,一心一意的
incumbent	n.	在职者,现任者
	adj.	在职的,现任的,有责任的
prudential	adj.	谨慎的,明辨的
jeopardise	vt.	危及,损害
stable	adj.	稳定的
misguided	adj.	误入歧途的,被误导的,搞错的
feature	n.	特色,特征,特点
regime	n.	政治制度,政权,政体,管理,方法,[医]养生法,(病人等的)生活规则
weight	n.	砝码,权重
treasury	n.	国库,金库,(政府的)财政部
select committee		为某一特案组成的特别委员会
highlight	vt.	强调,突出
defeat	vt.	违背(初衷),挫败(行动或计划),使落空
initiative	n.	倡议,主动性,主动权,主动精神
	adj.	自发的,创始的,初步的
buffer	n.	缓冲器,起缓冲作用的人(或物)
narrow	vt.	使缩小,使变狭窄,限制
disparity	n.	悬殊,不同,不等,不一致
complementary	adj.	互补的,补充的,补足的
proposal	n.	建议,提议,求婚
supplement	vt.	增补,补充
	n.	增补,补充,补充物,增刊,副刊
check	n.	(对政治等权力的)规定,条令,约束,阻碍进程的事物,阻止恶化的事物
peer	n.	身份(或地位)相同的人,同龄人,同辈
peer review		同行评议

inform	vt.	知会,通知,通告
benchmark	n.	基准,标准检查程序
	vt.	用基准问题测试(计算机系统等)
risk weight		风险权重
employ	vt.	雇用,使用,利用
	n.	受雇,服务,工作
take into account		顾及,重视,考虑
methodology	n.	方法论,方法学,(从事某一活动的)一套方法
in excess of		多于,超出
coverage	n.	范围,规模
lower	v.	降低,减少,缩小
in the round		由所有角度(来看),全面地
deliver	vt.	交付,发表,递送,使分娩
disadvantaged	adj.	贫穷的,处于不利地位的,社会地位低下的
	n.	不利条件
	vt.	使处于不利地位(disadvantage 的过去式和过去分词)

Notes to the Text

1. Bank of England:英格兰银行,是英国的中央银行。1694 年由英国皇室特许苏格兰人威廉·彼得森(William Paterson)等创办。初期主要为政府筹措战费,并因此而取得货币发行权。1844 年根据新银行法(《皮尔条例》)改组,分设发行部和银行部,后逐渐放弃商业银行业务,成为中央银行,1946 年由工党政府收归国有。其主要职责是:发行货币;管理国债;同财政部和财政大臣协作,执行货币政策;对贴现行进行票据再贴现;代理财政金库;通过国际货币基金组织、世界银行、国际清算银行等机构办理同其他国家有关货币方面的事项;代理政府保管黄金外汇储备。

2. FSA(Financial Service Authority):英国金融服务管理局。该局于 1997 年 10 月由 1985 年成立的证券投资委员会(Securities and Investments Board,SIB)改组而成,作为独立的非政府组织,拟成为英国金融市场统一的监管机构,行使法定职责,直接向英国财政部负责。由于 2008 年金融危机的影响,2012 年 1 月 19 日,FSA 被拆分为两个机构:一个是金融行为监管局(Financial Conduct Authority,FCA),另一个是审慎监管局(Prudential Regulation Authority,PRA)。自此,FSA 不复存在。金融行为管理局则负责监督英国金融服务公司和金融市场的行为,以及作为未经 PRA 授权公司的审慎监管机构;审慎监管局主要负责审慎监管和银行、信贷、保险等主要的投资公司。任何一个在(或从)英国提供银行或者其他金融服务的英国注册组织都将被这两个机构监管。

3. The Parliament of United Kingdom：英国议会，又被称为"威斯敏斯特议会"，英国的最高立法机关，是英国政治的中心舞台。政府从议会中产生，并对其负责。国会为两院制，英国议会由上议院（贵族院，House of Lords）、下议院（平民院，House of Commons）和国王共同组成，行使国家的最高立法权。英国议会创建于 13 世纪，迄今已有 700 多年的历史，被称为"议会之母"。自有议会以来，通常在伦敦古老的建筑威斯敏斯特宫（议会大厦）举行会议。每年开会两次，第一会期从 3 月末开始，到 8 月初结束，第二会期从 10 月底开始，到 12 月圣诞节前结束。

4. real economy：实体经济。real economy 是与 fictitious economy（虚拟经济）相对应的概念，是指物质的、精神的产品和服务的生产、流通等经济活动。实体经济始终是人类社会赖以生存和发展的基础，而虚拟经济是指相对独立于实体经济的虚拟资本的经济活动。虚拟资本一般指以有价证券形式（如债券、股票）存在的未来预期收益的资本化。在实体经济系统中产生的风险，如产品积压、企业破产，都会传递到虚拟经济系统中，导致其失稳；虚拟经济中的风险，如股票指数大落、房地产价格猛跌、银行呆账剧增、货币大幅贬值等，也会对实体经济造成严重影响。

5. Treasury Select Committee：英国国会财政特别委员会。英国为君主立宪制政体，实行议会民主，国王或女王为国家元首。首相（Prime Minister）为政府首脑，从下议院多数党领袖中产生，并对议会负责。首相及 22 个重要部门的部长（Ministers）组成最高决策机构，即政府内阁（Cabinet）。下议院对应政府职能部门设立 20 个专责委员会（Commons Select Committees），对政府及其部门提出的财政、经济政策及预算、业务计划等重大议题进行审查、辩论及表决通过。财政部和税务海关总署两个部门对应一个下议院专责委员会——财政专责委员会（Treasury Select Committee）。

6. loan-to-value：贷款价值比（简称 LTV），放贷风险比率，计算方法为抵押或贷款总额除以物业的估值。

7. Basel [ˈbɑːzl]：巴塞尔，是瑞士西北部城市，在莱茵河畔。《新巴塞尔资本协定》简称《新巴塞尔协议》或《巴塞尔协议 Ⅱ》（英文简称 Basel Ⅱ），是由国际清算银行下的巴塞尔银行监理委员会（BCBS）所促成，内容针对 1988 年的《旧巴塞尔资本协定》（Basel Ⅰ）做了大幅修改，以期标准化国际上的风险控管制度，提升国际金融服务的风险控管能力。

8. risk assessment：风险评估，是指在风险事件发生之前或之后（但还没有结束），该事件针对给人们的生活、生命、财产等各个方面造成的影响和损失的可能性进行量化评估。风险评估就是量化测评某一事件或事物带来的影响或损失的可能程度。

从信息安全的角度来讲，风险评估是对信息资产（即某事件或事物所具有的信息集）所面临的威胁、存在的弱点、造成的影响及三者综合作用所带来风险的可能性的评估。作为风险管理的基础，风险评估是组织确定信息安全需求的一个重要途径，属于组织信息安全管理体系策划的过程。

9. mortgage [ˈmɔːgɪdʒ]：按揭，是英文的粤语音译，最初起源于西方国家，本意属于英美平衡法体系中的一种法律关系，后于 20 世纪 90 年代从香港引入内地房地产市场，先由深圳建设银行在当地试行，之后逐渐在内地流行起来，因为在房地产领域频频出现并正式运用于文本，其含义逐渐演化成"抵押贷款"，目前在国内已经被正式称为"个人购置商品房抵押贷款"。在会计学中，按揭贷款（Mortgage Payable）属于非流动负债。

Foreign Exchange: A Losing Battle

Why a cheaper currency can sometimes dampen economic growth
December 15, 2017, *The Economist*

In September 2010 Brazil's then-finance minister, Guido Mantega, gave warning that an "international currency war" had broken out. His beef was that in places where it was difficult to drum up domestic spending, the authorities had instead sought to weaken their currencies to make their exports cheaper and imports dearer. The dollar had recently fallen, for instance, because the Federal Reserve was expected to begin a second round of quantitative easing. The losers in this battle were those emerging markets, like Brazil, whose currencies had soared. Its currency, the real, was then trading at around 1.7 to the dollar.

These days a dollar buys 3.4 reais, but no one in Brazil or in other emerging markets with devalued currencies is declaring a belated victory. A cheap currency has not proved to be much of a boon. Indeed new research from Jonathan Kearns and Nikhil Patel, of the Bank for International Settlements (BIS), a forum for central banks, finds that at times a rising currency can be a stimulant and a falling currency a depressant. They looked at a sample of 44 economies, half of them emerging markets, to gauge the effect of changes in the exchange rate on exports and imports (the trade channel) and also on the price and availability of credit (the financial channel).

They found a negative relationship between changes in GDP and currency shifts via the trade channel. In other words, net trade adds to economic growth when the currency weakens and detracts from growth when it strengthens, as the textbooks would have it. But they also found an offsetting effect of currencies on financial conditions. For rich countries, the trade-channel effect is bigger than the financial-channel effect. But for 13 of the 22 emerging markets in the study, the financial effect dominates: a stronger exchange rate on balance speeds up the economy and a weaker one slows it down.

This attests to the growing influence of a "global financial cycle" that responds to shifts in investors' appetite for risk. Prices of risky assets, such as shares or emerging market bonds, tend to move in lockstep with the weight of global capital flows from rich to poor countries. These flows in turn respond to changes in the monetary policy of rich-country central banks, notably the Federal Reserve, which influences the scale of borrowing in dollars by governments and businesses outside America. Global financial conditions are thus responsive to attitudes to risk. When the Fed lowers its interest rate, it not only makes it cheaper to borrow in dollars but also drives up asset prices worldwide, boosting the value of collateral and making it easier to raise capital in all its forms. A few days before Mr Mantega declared a currency war, Brazil's government was celebrating a bumper $67bn sale of shares in Petrobras, its state-backed oil company, for instance.

The BIS researchers find the financial channel works mainly through investment, which relies more on foreign-currency borrowing than does consumer spending. Their results are sobering for emerging-market economies. They suggest that a cheap currency cannot be relied on to give a boost to a sagging economy. More worrying still, the exchange rate might not always act as a shock absorber; rather it may, through the financial channel, work to amplify booms and busts.

Words and Expressions

losing battle		败局,必败之仗
dampen	vt.	抑制,使潮湿,使……沮丧,隔音,防音
beef	n.	牛肉,菜牛(饲养以供肉食的牛),怨言,牢骚
	vi.	抱怨,大发牢骚
drum up		竭力争取(支持),兜揽(生意)
devalue	v.	使(货币)贬值,降低(某事物)的价值,贬低
belated	adj.	迟来的,延误的,姗姗来迟的
boon	n.	非常有用的东西,益处
stimulant	n.	刺激物,兴奋剂
depressant	n.	镇静剂
	adj.	有镇静作用的
gauge	n.	测量仪器(或仪表),计量器
	vt.	(用仪器)测量,估计,估算
trade channel		贸易渠道
availability	n.	可利用性,可得到的东西(或人)
net trade		净贸易,净交易

detract from		贬低,减损
offset	vt.	抵消,补偿
dominate	v.	支配,影响,占有优势
exchange rate		汇率,兑换率
on balance		全面考虑之后,总的说来
attest to		证实,证明
appetite	n.	强烈欲望,渴望,胃口,食欲
bond	n.	债券,纽带
lockstep	n.	步伐一致,同步发生
monetary policy		货币政策
notably	adv.	尤其
responsive	adj.	应答的,响应的,反应灵敏的
collateral	n.	抵押物,担保品
bumper	adj.	[only before noun] (approving) 异常大的,丰盛的
sobering	adj.	令人警醒的,使人冷静的
sag	vt.	消衰,委顿,萎靡
absorber	n.	吸收器,吸收剂,减振器
amplify	vt.	增强,详述,放大,扩大
bust	n.	破产,破碎,毁坏

Notes to the Text

1. The Federal Reserve System：美国联邦储备系统,简称为"美联储"(Federal Reserve),负责履行美国的中央银行的职责。这个系统是根据《联邦储备法》(Federal Reserve Act)于1913年12月23日成立的。美联储的核心管理机构是美国联邦储备委员会。联邦储备系统由位于华盛顿特区的联邦储备委员会和12家分布全国主要城市的地区性的联邦储备银行组成。杰罗姆·鲍威尔为现任美联储最高长官(美国联邦储备委员会主席)。作为美国的中央银行,美联储从美国国会获得权力,行使制定货币政策和对美国金融机构进行监管等职责。

2. quantitative easing：量化宽松的货币政策,又被称作"定量宽松的货币政策"。一般来说,中央银行在设立货币政策的时候会将目标放在一个特定的短期利率水准上,央行通过向银行间市场注入或者抽离资金来使该利率处于目标位置。此时中央银行希望调控的是信贷的成本。而定量宽松货币指的是货币政策制定者将政策关注点从控制银行系统的资金价格转向资金数量,货币政策的目标就是为了保证货币政策维持在宽松的环境下。对于这个政策而言,"量"意味着货币供应,而"宽松"则表示很多,当然定量宽松的货币政策也有自己的指标。采用"定量宽松"的货币政策往往意味着放弃传统的货币政策手段,因为对于央行而言,他们不可能既控制资金的价格又控制资金的数量。量化宽松货币政策俗称"印钞票",指一国货币当局通过大量印钞、购买国债或企业债券等方式,向市场注入超额资金,旨在降低市场利率,刺激经济增长。该政策通常是往常常规货币政策对经济刺激无效的情况下才被货币当局采用,即存在流动性陷阱的情况下实施的非常规的货币政策。

3. BIS (Bank for International Settlements):国际清算银行,是英、法、德、意、比、日等国的中央银行与代表美国银行界利益的摩根银行、纽约和芝加哥的花旗银行组成的银团。根据《海牙国际协定》成立于1930年,最初为处理第一次世界大战后德国战争赔款问题而设立,后演变为一家各国中央银行合作的国际金融机构,是世界上历史最悠久的国际金融组织。总部设在瑞士巴塞尔。刚建立时只有7个成员国,现成员国已发展至45个。

4. financial cycle:金融周期,主要是指由金融变量扩张与收缩导致的周期性波动。金融周期就是人们借贷的款项逐渐增加、资产增值、信贷条件放宽的过程。国际金融危机促使国际社会更加关注金融周期变化,各国央行也认识到只关注以物价稳定等为表征的经济周期来实施宏观调控显然已经不够,央行传统的单一调控框架存在着明显缺陷,难以有效应对系统性金融风险,在一定程度上还可能纵容资产泡沫、积聚金融风险。评判金融周期,最核心的两个指标是广义信贷和房地产价格,前者代表融资条件,后者反映投资者对风险的认知和态度。当经济周期和金融周期同步叠加时,经济扩张或收缩的幅度都会被放大;而当经济周期和金融周期不同步时,两者的作用方向可能不同甚至相反,会导致宏观调控政策的冲突和失效。金融周期结束时的情况未必是不好的,但在金融周期达到高峰时,往往会引发金融危机或偿债能力减低的问题。金融周期的时间颇长,从一个高峰到另一个高峰,平均历时15年。

5. Petrobras:巴西国家石油公司,成立于1953年10月3日,也被简称为"巴西石油公司",是一个以石油为主体、上下游一体化跨国经营的国家石油公司。当时第2004号法令宣布巴西的石油工业始于19世纪末期。1917年,国有企业石油国家垄断,巴西石油公司不仅参与石油政策的制定、执行,还统管巴西石油的勘探、开发、生产、运输及企业的经营管理,是巴西政府政企合一的国有企业。2018年7月19日,《财富》世界500强排行榜发布,巴西国家石油公司列第73位。

Not Passing the Buck: Global Capital Flows Have Slowed Down

Buttonwood

December 15, 2016, *The Economist*

For more than two decades after the early 1980s, it seemed as if the financial markets were moving in only one direction. More and more money was flowing across borders; capital markets were becoming increasingly integrated.

Since the 2008 financial crisis this particular aspect of globalisation has stalled, and even partly retreated. The reversal is illustrated by the triennial survey of foreign-exchange markets, conducted by the Bank for International Settlements (BIS). Daily turnover in April was $5.1trn, down from $5.4trn in April 2013.

That is still a huge number compared with the turn of the century, when daily turnover was around the $1trn mark. But it is a sign that markets are getting a little less frenetic; spot (or instant) currency trading has fallen by 19% in three years.

Other data from the BIS confirm the trend. Cross-border banking claims peaked in the first quarter of 2008 at $34.6trn. By the second quarter of 2010, they had dropped to $27.9trn, and they have never recovered their pre-crisis levels. In the second quarter of this year (the most recent data), claims were $28.3trn. Part of this may be a consequence of events in the euro zone, where the sovereign-debt crisis caused banks to cut back their lending to weaker economies. Add up all financial flows, including direct investment, and in 2015 cross-border volumes were only half 2007's level, according to McKinsey, a consultancy (see the following chart).

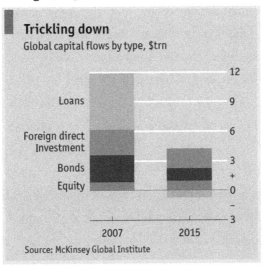

This is not necessarily bad news. After all, as Asian countries found out in the 1990s, too much "hot money" flowing into an economy can be destabilising. It can drive exchange rates out of line with economic fundamentals, making a country's exporters less competitive. A rising currency may also tempt domestic companies to borrow abroad. Then, when the hot money flows out and the exchange rate collapses, those borrowers will struggle to repay their debts. The result can be a financial crisis.

The implications of deglobalisation depend on why the slowdown is happening. There may be a link to economic fundamentals. World trade volumes were regularly growing at an annual rate of 5% ~10% in the run-up to the crisis; in recent years they have managed only 2% or so. In 2015 exports were a smaller proportion of global GDP than they were in 2008. If trade is growing less rapidly, so is the demand for credit to finance it.

However, as the BIS points out, trade accounts for only a small proportion of capital flows. The downturn is mainly because of events within the financial sector itself.

Before the crisis, cross-border banking activity was closely correlated with measures of risk appetites. When the economic outlook was good, banks were happy to lend abroad; in the face of shocks, they retreated back to their home base. Research by the Bank of England shows that the picture changed after the crisis; there was simply a more general retreat by the banking sector from foreign commitments.

Part of this may reflect a lack of demand for loans from companies and individuals that had overstretched during the boom years. But the biggest reason is probably the weakness of the banking sector. It has been deprived of some sources of funding (money-market mutual funds, for example) and has been forced by the regulators to rebuild its balance-sheet.

In the currency markets, the BIS says, there has been a shift in the type of people that are participating. Institutional investors such as pension funds and insurance companies are being more active. They may decide to buy, say, Japanese equities without wanting to be exposed to fluctuations in the yen, so they will hedge this exposure in the currency markets. In contrast, there has been a reduction in risk-taking activity by hedge funds and bank trading desks, which suffered a big shock in January 2015 when the Swiss National Bank suddenly abandoned its policy of capping the franc's exchange rate. The sharp jump in the value of the franc that followed caused turmoil for some brokers, forcing them to raise their fees and cut their client lists.

A market less in thrall to speculators might seem like an unalloyed boon. But the retreat of banks from currency trading (and from market-making in other instruments such as corporate bonds) may not be quite such good news. In a crisis, the banks may not be around to trade with investors seeking to offload their positions; the BIS notes signs of "volatility outbursts and flash events". Lots of investors and companies want to hedge their currency exposure. They need an institution to take the other side of the trade.

Words and Expressions

integrated	adj.	各部分密切联系的,综合的,完整统一的
stall	vt. & vi.	(使)熄火,(使)停止转动
reversal	n.	倒转,颠倒,反复,逆转,反转
illustrate	vt.	说明,表明,给……加插图,(用示例、图画等)说明
	vi.	举例说明
triennial	adj.	三年的,每三年一度的
	n.	三年生植物,三年一次的事物
turnover	n.	营业额,成交量,证券交易额
frenetic	adj.	狂热的,狂乱的,发狂的,非常激动的
	n.	疯子,狂人
spot currency		即期通货
banking claims		银行债权
consultancy	n.	咨询公司,顾问工作
equity	n.	(公司的)普通股
hot money		游资,(为追求高额利润而流动的)短期流动资金
destabilise	vt.	破坏稳定
out of line with		跟……不一致
tempt	vt.	吸引,引诱,怂恿,冒……的风险,使感兴趣
collapse	vi.	崩溃,倒塌,折叠,(尤指工作劳累后)坐下
	vt.	使倒塌,使坍塌,使瓦解
	n.	垮台,(身体的)衰弱
repay	vt.	偿还,报答,付还,酬报
	vi.	偿还,补偿
implication	n.	可能的影响(或作用、结果),含意,暗指
run-up	n.	(重要事情的)前期,准备阶段,助跑,助跑距离
credit	n.	学分,信誉,信用,贷款,荣誉
	vt.	相信,信任,归功于,记入贷方,赞颂
finance	n.	金融,财政,资金,财源
	vt.	为……供给资金,从事金融活动,赊货给……,掌握财政
downturn	n.	(价格或活动)开始下降,衰退,低迷时期

home base		本垒, 总部, 基地, 大本营
picture	n.	状况, 情形, 形势
commitment	n.	承诺, 许诺, 委任, 委托, 致力, 献身, 承担义务
overstretch	vt.	（使）勉强维持, 硬撑着, 超负荷运转
deprive of		剥夺某人的……
pension fund	n.	养老基金, 退休基金
fluctuation	n.	（价格、数量、水平等的）波动, 起伏
exposure	n.	面临, 暴露, 接触, 遭受（危险或不快）
risk-taking	adj.	冒风险的
hedge	vt. & vi.	回避, 避免
	n.	树篱, 保护手段, 防止损失（尤指金钱）的手段
	vt.	用树篱围起, 受……的束缚
bank trading desks		银行交易部门
abandon	vt.	放弃, 抛弃, 离弃, 丢弃, 使屈从, 停止进行, 终止
	n.	放任, 放纵
cap	vt.	限额收取（或支出）
franc	n.	法郎（瑞士等国的货币单位, 在法国、比利时和卢森堡于2002年为欧元所取代）
turmoil	n.	混乱, 焦虑
broker	n.	（股票、外币等）经纪人, 中间人, 代理人
	vt.	（国家或政府作为中间人）协调, 安排
client list		客户名单
in thrall to		被……束缚着, 拘泥于……
thrall	n.	奴役, 奴隶制, 奴隶, 奴隶般受支配的人
speculator	n.	投机倒把者, 投机商人, 思辨者, 思索者,〈美〉垄断收买（戏票）的人
unalloyed	adj.	纯粹的, 真正的, 非合金的, 不掺杂的
boon	n.	恩惠, 福利
	adj.	快乐的
offload	vt.	出手, 转手, 清理（不需要之物）, 卸（货）
position	n.	处境, 地位, 状况
note	vt.	指出, 特别提到
take the other side		充当另一方

Unit Four International Finance

Notes to the Text

1. pass the buck：把责任推给另一个人。它的起源和 poker game（纸牌游戏）有关。据说，在19世纪的纸牌戏中，buck 原意是"雄鹿"，但是这里指刀柄是鹿角做成的猎刀。在早年美国西部这种猎刀几乎人手一把。牌桌的规矩是轮流做庄发牌。打完一副牌就轮到坐在发牌人左边的那位发。为了不搞错，人们就在牌桌上传递一把猎刀帮助记忆。每人发完牌就把猎刀传给下一个发牌人。当轮到某个人发牌时，buck 就会被转交给这个人。在1865年，pass the buck 成为纸牌术语，意思是"把发牌权转交给某人"。后来 pass the buck 的意思就演变成"把责任推给另一个人"了。美国总统杜鲁门曾经有一句名言：The buck stops here，意思是"他会为政府部门的行为承担最终的责任"。buck 在这里的意思是"责任"。和 buck 相关的俚语还有：

buck for：为升迁或利益而努力，千方百计地谋求

buck up：（使）兴奋，鼓舞振作起来，打起精神

buck up against：反抗，不甘沉默

2. sovereign-debt ['sɒvrɪn det]：主权债务，是指一国以自己的主权为担保向外（向国际货币基金组织、世界银行或其他国家）借来的债务。历史上出现比较有影响的主权债务违约案例有：20世纪90年代阿根廷主权债务事件、2009年11月发生的迪拜主权债务违约事件。

3. economic fundamentals：基本经济要素，经济基本面。从一家公司的角度出发，经济基本面就是公司的经营业绩、盈利能力、财务状况、成长潜力等要素。从更宏观的角度出发，经济基本面包括国家宏观经济指标、经济政策走势、行业发展状况等经济基础要素。

4. de-globalization：去全球化，指的是全球主义的减弱。全球过去数十年间贸易一体化得到不断发展，互联网的出现更让世界密不可分，但自2008年金融海啸爆发以来，环球经济出现去全球化现象：出外打工谋生的人纷纷回流返国、外资大举撤出、贸易额大减、保护主义抬头等，令多个外向型经济体面临沉重打击。曾多次获选《时代周刊》百大最有影响力人物的经济学家萨克斯警告：20世纪的世界大战和大萧条后曾出现去全球化，今次亦有可能出现，各地民族主义抬头，各地政府只顾本地民众，全球化绝对有可能崩溃。全球化进程倒退迹象还出现在多方面。国际货币基金组织（IMF）前首席经济师约翰逊表示：过去20年来，带动全球经济增长的因素正开始倒退，随着劳工、资本流动性降低，未来将出现失落的十年，这就是去全球化。

5. risk appetite：风险偏好，是主动追求风险、喜欢收益的波动性胜于收益的稳定性的态度。风险偏好型投资者选择资产的原则是：当预期收益相同时，选择风险大的，因为这会给他们带来更大的效益。

6. mutual fund：共同基金，就是将众多投资者的余额集中在一起，等于众多投资者共同

聘请一个基金公司的专业投资经理,利用其专业的知识,分散投资于各种不同的投资类别上,使这一小额投资亦能在互惠基础下享受低风险及较高的回报机会。

7. Balance Sheet:资产负债表,是反映企业在某一特定时期(如年末、中期期末)财务状况的财务报表,属于重要的静态报表。它是以"资产=负债+所有者权益"这一会计等式作为理论依据,按照一定的分类标准和排序次序,将企业在某一特定时期的资产、负债和所有者权益项目进行排列编制而成的。

8. SNB(Swiss National Bank):瑞士国家银行,是瑞士的中央银行,它是根据1905年联邦宪法创建的联合股份银行。1907年在伯尔尼、巴塞尔、日内瓦、苏黎世、圣加伦开始营业。董事会大部人选由联邦政府指派,向联邦议院负责。

9. market maker:造市商,为证券交易所指定的买卖中间商,主要业务是为买方及卖方进行报价,并且为双方寻找好的价格撮合交易,本身则从买卖差价中获利。

European Insurers Feeling Squeezed

European insurers suffer from continued low interest rates
December 15, 2016, *The Economist*

Insurance is banking's boring cousin: it lacks the glamour, the sky-high bonuses and the ever-present whiff of danger. So European stress tests for insurers, whose results were due to be published on December 15 after *The Economist* went to press, have attracted far less attention than those for banks in July. Yet insurance also faces a grave threat, from prolonged low interest rates.

Insurers invest overwhelmingly in bonds, so low interest rates make their lives difficult. The last time the European Insurance and Occupational Pensions Authority (EIOPA) conducted an insurance stress test, in 2014, a quarter of participants scored poorly: they would not have met their capital requirements in the test's long low-interest-rate scenario. The proportion jumped to 44% in an alternative scenario involving an asset price shock. The new results are unlikely to be better. Each year of low interest rates worsens the problem. Higher-yielding bonds mature and

insurers end up with ever more newer ones with low, or even negative, interest rates.

Insurers are focused on the problem. One strategy is to outsource more to external asset managers, who are often cheaper because of their greater scale. Another is to buy new types of assets. According to Robert Goodman of Goldman Sachs, insurers want to allocate more to better-yielding, but more illiquid, asset classes like infrastructure, private debt and private equity. Access is hampered not only by a limited supply but also by regulatory capital requirements. So European insurers are looking at proxy investments, such as American municipal bonds (whose proceeds are often spent on infrastructure).

A shortage of capital is an especially acute problem for life insurers in northern Europe. Many, in better times, sold annuities with guaranteed annual returns of 3%~4%. Analysts expect German life insurers to be able to meet their promises for a while yet without going under. But profits will be hit badly. Stringent EU capital requirements, known as Solvency 2, introduced this year, have helped. But interpreting and policing the rules varies. Insurers are regulated only at the national level, even though insurance is as much a cross-border business as banking: the leading 30 insurers derive 31% of income from the rest of the EU, and only 41% at home (compared with 23% and 54% for the largest 30 banks).

Dirk Schoen maker of Bruegel, a think tank, proposes giving EIOPA greater supervisory powers over larger insurers as part of an "insurance union", analogous to the EU's banking union. But further regulatory centralisation may be a hard sell in today's EU.

The best hope for Europe's insurers would be an improved macroeconomic outlook. Long-term dollar and euro bond yields have perked up a bit in recent weeks. But the European Central Bank, by extending its quantitative-easing programme until the end of 2017, has pushed interest-rate rises far into the future. Europe's insurers still have a long hard slog ahead.

Words and Expressions

squeeze	vt. & vi.	挤,榨,捏,压迫,压榨
glamour	n.	魅力,魔力,诱惑力,迷人的美
	v.	迷惑,迷住
sky-high	adj. & adv.	极高(的)
bonus	n.	奖金,额外津贴,红利,额外股息,退职金,额外令人高兴的事情
ever-present	adj.	经常存在的

whiff	n.	轻微的迹象(或感觉),一点点,些许,一点儿气味,一股气味
grave	adj.	严重的,重大的,重要的
prolonged	adj.	延长的,持续很久的,拖延的
overwhelmingly	adv.	(数量)巨大地,压倒性地
scenario	n.	设想,方案,可能发生的情况,预测,(电影的)剧情梗概
alternative	adj.	替代的,另类的,备选的,其他的
	n.	可供选择的事物
high-yielding	adj.	高产的
mature	vi.	成熟,长成,(票据等)到期
end up with		<非正>以……结束
negative	adj.	消极的,否认的,[数]负的
outsource	vt.	(商业)交外办理,外包(工程)
allocate	vt.	分配,分派,把……拨给
illiquid	adj.	缺乏流动性的
hamper	vt.	妨碍,束缚,限制
	n.	(有盖的)大篮子
proxy	n.	代理权,代表权,代理人,受托人,代表
municipal bond		地方政府债券
proceed	n.	收入,获利
	vi.	进行,前进,(沿特定路线)行进,(尤指打断后)继续说
acute	adj.	尖的,锐的,敏锐的,敏感的,严重的,剧烈的,[医]急性的
life insurer		寿险公司
annuities	n.	养老金,年金保险,年金(annuity 的名词复数)
go under		破产,沉没,沉落,失败
hit	vt.	产生不良影响,打击,危害
stringent	adj.	严格的,迫切的,(财政状况)紧缩的,短缺的,银根紧的
solvency	n.	不负债,债务清偿能力
interpret	vt.	诠释,阐释,说明
policing	vt.	维护治安,(委员会等)监督管制,(警察、军队等)巡查(police 的现在分词)
regulate	vt.	调节,调整,校准,控制,管理
derive from		由……起源,取自
think tank		智囊团

supervisory	adj.	监督的,管理的
analogous	adj.	相似的,可比拟的
centralisation	n.	集中
hard sell		强行推销,硬性销售
perk up		(使)增加,(使)上涨,(使)增值,(使)振奋,(使)活跃,(使)快活,使更有趣
slog	n.	苦干,漫长而艰苦的跋涉
	vt. & vi.	猛击,步履艰难地行走,努力苦干

Notes to the Text

1. European Central Bank：欧洲中央银行,简称"欧洲央行",总部位于德国法兰克福,成立于1998年6月1日,负责欧盟欧元区的金融及货币政策。是根据1992年《马斯特里赫特条约》的规定于1998年7月1日正式成立的,是为了适应欧元发行流通而设立的金融机构,同时也是欧洲经济一体化的产物。首任欧洲中央银行行长为维姆·德伊森贝赫,荷兰人,曾任荷兰央行行长,曾在阿姆斯特丹大学教授宏观经济学。

Unit Five

International Investment

Defending a Good Company from Bad Investors

A Conversation with Former Allergan Ceo David Pyott

By Sarah Cliffe

May – June, 2017, *Harvard Business Review*

David Pyott had been the CEO of Allergan for nearly 17 years in April 2014, when Valeant Pharmaceuticals and Pershing Square Capital Management initiated the hostile takeover bid described in the accompanying article "The Error at the Heart of Corporate Leadership". He was the company's sole representative during the takeover discussions. When it became clear that the bid could not be fended off indefinitely, Pyott, with his board's blessing, negotiated a deal whereby Allergan would be acquired by Actavis (a company whose business model, like Allergan's was growth oriented).

HBR: Would you describe Allergan's trajectory in the years leading up to the takeover bid?

PYOTT: We'd experienced huge growth since 1998, when I joined as just the third CEO of Allergan and the first outsider in that role. We restructured when I came in and again 10 years later, during the recession. Those cuts gave us some firepower for investing back into the economic recovery. After the recession we were telling the market to expect double digit growth in sales revenue and around the mid-teens in earnings per share.

Your investor relations must have been excellent.

They were. I am extremely proud to say that we literally never missed our numbers, not once in 17 years. We also won lots of awards from investor relations magazines. You don't run a business with that in mind, but it's nice to be recognized.

In their article, Joseph Bower and Lynn Paine describe how difficult it is for any company to manage the pressure from investors who want higher short-term returns. You seem to have managed that well—until Valeant showed up. How?

Both buy-side and sell-side investors are like any other customer group. You should listen to what they say and respond when you can. But remember: Asking is free. If they say, "Hey, we want more", you have to be willing to come back with "This is what we can commit to. If there are better places to invest your funds, then do what you need to." Fortunately or unfortunately, I'm very stubborn.

Permit me a naive question: Since Allergan was going strong, why did it make sense to Valeant/Pershing Square to take you over and strip you down? I get that they'd make a lot of money, but wouldn't fostering continued growth make more in the long run?

Different business models. Valeant was a roll-up company; it wasn't interested in organic growth. Michael Pearson [Valeant's CEO] liked our assets—and he needed to keep feeding the beast. If he didn't keep on buying the next target, then the fact that he was stripping all the assets out of companies he'd already bought would have become painfully obvious.

He couldn't do it alone, given his already weak balance sheet, so he brought Ackman in—and Pershing Square acquired 9.7% of our stock without our knowledge. This was meant to act as a catalyst to create a "wolf pack". Once the hedge funds and arbitrageurs get too big a position, you lose control of your company.

I still thought we had a strong story to tell—and I hoped I could get long-term-oriented shareholders to buy new stock and water down the hedge funds' holdings. But almost nobody was willing to up their position. They all had different reasons—some perfectly good ones. It was a lesson to me.

That must have been disappointing.

Yes. It's poignant—some of those same people say to me now, "We miss the old Allergan. We're looking for high-growth, high-innovation stocks and not finding them." I just say, "I heartily agree with you."

Another thing that surprised and disappointed me was that I couldn't get people who supported what we were doing—who understood why we were not accepting the bid, which grossly undervalued the company—to talk to the press. Several people said they would, but then folks at the top of their companies said no. And the reporters who cover M&A don't know the companies well. The people who cover pharma are deeply knowledgeable—but once a company is in play, those guys are off the story day-to-day. So the coverage was more one-sided than we'd have hoped for.

Is the trend toward activist investors something that the market will eventually sort out?

Activist and hostile campaigns have been propelled by extraordinarily low interest rates and banks' willingness to accept very high leverage ratios. Recently investor focus has returned to good old-fashioned operational execution by management. But I do think that investment styles go in and out of fashion. I never would have guessed that when I went to business school.

Do you agree with Bower and Paine that boards and CEOs need to focus less on shareholder wealth and more on the well-being of the company?

Look at it from a societal point of view: A lot of the unrest we've seen over the past year is rooted in the idea that wealthy, powerful people are disproportionately benefiting from the changes happening in society. A lot of companies think that they need to make themselves look more friendly, not just to stockholders but to employees and to society. Having a broader purpose—something beyond simply making money—is how you do that and how you create strong corporate cultures.

I don't believe that strong performance and purpose are at odds, not at all. My own experience tells me that in order for a company to be a really high performer, it needs to have a purpose. Money matters to employees up to a point, but they want to believe they're working on something that improves people's lives. I've also found that employees respond really favorably when management commits to responsible social behavior. I used to joke with employees about saving water and energy and about recycling: "Look, I'm Scottish, OK? I don't like waste, and it saves the company money." That's a positive for employees.

Did that sense of purpose pay off when you were going through the takeover bid?

Absolutely. I left day-to-day operations to our president, Doug Ingram, that year. And we grew the top line 17%—more than $1 billion—the best operating year in our 62-year history. I remember an R&D team leader who came up to me in the parking lot and said, "Are you OK? Is there anything I can do?" I answered him, "Just do your job better than ever, and don't be distracted by the rubbish you read in the media." Employees all over the world outdid themselves, because they believed in the company.

What changes in government rules and regulations would improve outcomes for the full range of stakeholders?

My favorite fix is changing the tax rates. Thirty-five percent is woefully high relative to the rest of the world. If we got it down to 20%, we'd be amazed at how much investment and job creation happened in this country. The high rates mean that we're vulnerable to takeovers that have tax inversion as a motivator. We were paying 26%, and Valeant [headquartered in Canada] paid 3%. I think the capital gains taxes could be changed—in a revenue-neutral way—to incentivize holding on to stocks longer.

Shifting gears again: If a company wants to reorient itself toward long-term growth, what has to happen?

I think it's hard for a CEO to change his or her spots. Some can, but most can't. So in most cases you're going to need a new leader. And the board of directors really has to buy into it, because not only are you changing your strategy, you're changing your numbers. You must have a story to tell, for example: "For the next three years, we're not going to deliver 10% EPS growth. It's going to be 5% while we invest in the future. And that's not going to pay off until after three years, so you'll have to be patient." You have to be very, very clear about it. And then everyone—the board, the investors, the lab technicians, the salespeople—will watch you to see if you're serious. It will take a lot of fortitude and determination. It's not impossible, but it's extremely difficult.

Words and Expressions

hostile	adj.	怀有敌意的,(收购公司等的要约)不受(被购公司)欢迎的
sole representative		独家代理(人)
fend off		挡开,阻止……发生
indefinitely	adv.	无限期地,不定期地,不明确地,遥遥无期地
blessing	n.	上帝的恩宠,祝福,祝颂,赞同,许可
whereby	adv.	(formal)凭此,借以,由于
trajectory	n.	轨道,轨迹,(事业等的)发展轨迹,起落
lead up to		(一系列事件)导致,致使,引致
restructure	v.	重组,调整,重建
recession	n.	经济衰退,不景气,后退,撤退
firepower	n.	火力,弹药量
literally	adv.	逐字地,照字面地,确实地,真正地
miss	vt.	未达到
manage	vt.	经营,使用,完成(困难的事),明智地使用(金钱、时间、信息等)
	vt. & vi.	办理,设法对付
	vi.	能解决(问题),应付(困难局面等),凑合活下去,支撑
make sense		有意义,理解,讲得通,是明智的
foster	vt. & vi.	培养,促进,抚育,代养

acquire	vt.	收购(企业),获得(技能),养成(习惯)
be meant to		有意要,打算
catalyst	n.	催化剂,诱因,诱导者
wolf pack		一起捕猎的群狼
arbitrageur	n.	套利者
strong story		很好的故事
water down		加水稀释,掺水冲淡,使(提议、演讲、声明等)语气缓和,使打折扣,削弱
poignant	adj.	尖锐的,辛酸的,深刻的,(记忆)鲜活的
heartily	adv.	衷心地,强烈地,坚定地
bid	n.	出价,投标
	vt. & vi.	出价,投标
	vt.	恳求,命令,说(问候话),邀请,致敬
	vi.	投标,力求,企图得到或赢得某物,企图(for)
grossly	adv.	(形容令人不快的事物)极度地,极其,非常
undervalue	vt.	低估,对……认识不足,轻视
folks	n.	人们,父母,亲人,家属
cover	vt.	报道,电视报道
pharma	n.	制药行业,制药公司
knowledgeable	adj.	博学的,知识渊博的,有见识的,精明的
day-to-day	adj.	过一天算一天的,日常工作的,例行的
coverage	n.	新闻报道,(书、课程学习、电视等的)信息范围,信息质量提供的数量,覆盖范围(或方式)
activist	n.	积极分子,激进主义分子,积极行动者
	adj.	激进主义的,激进主义分子的
sort out		把……分类,整理,解决(问题),理清(细节),教训,规劝,惩处
campaign	n.	战役,运动(为社会、商业或政治目的而进行的一系列有计划的活动)
propel	vt.	推动,推进,驱使,驱动
willingness	n.	自愿,乐意
societal	adj.	社会的
unrest	n.	动荡,动乱,骚动
root	vt.	使生根,使固定,根源在于
disproportionately	adv.	不匀称,不相称

stockholder	n.	股东,股票持有者
strong corporate culture		强大深厚的企业文化
at odds		争执,不一致
high performer		表现杰出者
favorably	adv.	顺利地,好意地,亲切地
positive	n.	优势,优点,阳性结果(或反应),正极,(照片的)正片
sense of purpose		目的性,使命感
pay off		取得成功,使得益
operating year		运营年
outdo	vt.	胜过,优于
woefully	adv.	(人或事物)悲惨的,忧伤的,哀伤的,恶劣的,糟糕的,不合意的
relative to		关于……的,和……比较起来
be amazed at		对……感到惊讶
vulnerable	adj.	(身体上或感情上)脆弱的,易受……伤害的
motivator	n.	激起行为(或行动)的人(或物),促进因素,激发因素
incentivize	vt.	以物质刺激,鼓励
shift gear		(开车)换挡
reorient	vt.	(在迷失方向之后)重新定方向,转向
buy into it		彻底相信一套理念
lab technician		实验室技术人员
fortitude	n.	坚韧,刚毅

Notes to the Text

1. Allergan:美国艾尔建有限公司,建立于1950年,总部位于美国加州欧文市,是一家跨专业的健康医疗公司。公司研发并销售多种创新性药品、生物制剂、医疗器械等产品,帮助人们最大限度挖掘自身潜力——看得更清晰、行动更自由、更好地展现自我。公司在全球具有国际顶尖水准的研发机构和世界级的生产工厂。除了优秀的研发能力,艾尔建公司还具备卓越的全球营销能力,其产品已在100多个国家上市。

2. acquisition/takeover/buyout:收购。收购是一个商业公司管理学的术语,是指一个企业以购买全部或部分股票(或被称为"股份收购")的方式购买了另一企业的全部或部分所有权,或者以购买全部或部分资产(或被称为"资产收购")的方式购买另一企业的全部或部分所有权,是透过取得控制性股权而成为一个公司的大股东的过程,一般是指一个公司通过产权交易取得其他公司一定程度的控制权,以实现一定经济目标的经济行为。商业收购意指一个公司(收买方)买断另一个公司(收购目标)。该事件后果类似于合并,不过并没有形成一个新公司。股票收购可通过兼并(merger)或标购(tender offer)来实现。兼并特点是与目标企业管理者直接谈判,或以交换股票的方式进行购买;目标企业董事会的认可通常发生在兼并出价获得目标企业所有者认同之前。使用标购方式,购买股票的出价直接面向目标企业所有者。收购其他企业部分与全部资产,通常是直接与目标企业管理者谈判。收购的目标是获得对目标企业的控制权,目标企业的法人地位并不消失。

3. organic growth:有机增长,是指公司依托现有资源和业务,通过提高产品质量、销量与服务水平,拓展客户及扩大市场份额,推进创新与提高生产效率等途径而获得的销售收入及利润的自然增长。"有机增长"是与"非有机增长"(Nonorganic Growth)对应的概念,是剔除了并购、资产剥离、汇率影响后的增长,反映了核心业务增长的潜能和持久性。追求有机增长并不意味着全盘否定并购的积极意义。公司的有机增长过程中需要那些战略性的、与核心业务相关的小额并购,这些并购会为公司获得新技术、新产品、新理念或者新客户,尤其是涉及某些处于生命周期早期阶段的产品或者技术。

4. arbitrage [ˈɑːbɪtrɑːʒ]:套利,亦称"套现",通常指在某种实物资产或金融资产(在同一市场或不同市场)拥有两个价格的情况下,以较低的价格买进,以较高的价格卖出,从而获取无风险收益。套利是指从纠正市场价格或收益率的异常状况中获利的行动。异常状况通常是指同一产品在不同市场的价格出现显著差异,套利即低买高卖,导致价格回归均衡水平的行为。套利通常涉及在某一市场或金融工具上建立头寸,然后在另一市场或金融工具上建立与先前头寸相抵消的头寸。在价格回归均衡水平后,所有头寸即可结清以了结获利。套利者(arbitrageur)指从事套利的个人或机构。

5. position:头寸,也称"头衬",就是"款项"的意思,是金融界及商业界的流行用语,在金融、证券、股票、期货交易中经常用到。头寸就是资金,指的是银行当前所有可以运用的资金的总和。主要包括在央行的超额准备金、存放同业清算款项净额、银行存款以及现金等部分。头寸管理的目标就是在保证流动性的前提下,尽可能地降低头寸占用,避免资金闲置浪费。如果银行在当日的全部收付款中收入大于支出款项,就被称为"多头寸",如果付出款项大于收入款项,就被称为"缺头寸"。对预计这一类头寸的多与少的行为则被称为"轧头寸"。到处想方设法调进款项的行为被称为"调头寸"。如果暂时未用的款项大于需用量时则被称为"头寸松",如果资金需求量大于闲置量时就被称为"头寸紧"。

比如,在期货交易中建仓时,买入期货合约后所持有的头寸叫"多头头寸",简称"多头";卖出期货合约后所持有的头寸叫"空头头寸",简称"空头"。商品未平仓多头合约与未平仓空头合约之间的差额就叫作"净头寸"。只是在期货交易中有这种做法,在现货交易中还没有这种做法。

在外币交易中,建立头寸是"开盘"的意思。开盘也叫"敞口",就是买进一种货币,同时卖出另一种货币的行为。开盘之后,长了(多头)一种货币,短了(空头)另一种货币。选择适当的汇率水平以及时机建立头寸是盈利的前提。如果入市时机较好,获利的机会就大；相反，如果入市的时机不当，就容易发生亏损。净头寸就是指开盘后获取的一种货币与另一种货币之间的交易差额。

6. mergers and acquisitions（M&A）：企业并购，包括"兼并"和"收购"两层含义、两种方式。国际上习惯将兼并和收购合在一起使用，统称为 M&A，在我国被称为"并购"。商务印书馆出版的《英汉证券投资词典》解释为：合并；兼并。①任何形式两家以上公司之间的合并，常被称为"兼并"或"收购"。多用 merger and acquisition（M&A）。合并过程多通过公开证券市场实现。②收购方承担目标公司所有债权、负债的收购过程。

7. 财务报表最上面那个 Top 是收入，最下面那个 Bottom 是利润。top line growth = growth in revenues（公司整体收入增加）；而与此相对的是 bottom line growth = growth in net profit（公司净利增加）。

8. capital gains：（尤指出售固定资产所得的）资本收益，指人们卖出股票（或其他资产）时所获得的超过原来为它支付的那一部分。商务印书馆出版的《英汉证券投资词典》解释为：资本收益，英语为：capital gain；capital gains yield，亦作"资本利得"。投资工具如股票、互惠基金等买入与卖出差价，即转让价值（proceeds of disposition）与调整成本基价（adjusted cost basis）之间的正差额，指投资品种售出价格高于买入价格，即变现时得到的实际收益。

UK Workplace Pension Invests in UBS Climate Fund

Environmental change threatens retirement savings, says Nest

Chris Flood

February 5, 2017, *Financial Times*

Nest has invested £130m in a new climate-aware fund as part of a strategic push by the state-backed workplace pension provider to protect the retirement savings of 4.3m British workers from the threat of environmental change.

Pension schemes such as Nest have been stepping up their efforts to address the risks of global warming after governments around the world signed a historic agreement to tackle the climate change in Paris in December 2015.

Nest has shifted around one fifth of its current developed markets equity portfolio into a new UBS Life Climate Aware World Equity fund. It invests in companies that will help the global economy move away from producing and consuming environmentally polluting fossil fuels.

"We cannot afford to ignore climate change risks and we have committed to being part of the solution," said Mark Fawcett, chief investment officer at Nest which oversees the retirement savings of 291,000 employers.

He added that Nest wanted to send "a strong message" to companies that it expected them to make measurable progress towards environmental sustainability.

The UBS fund will invest more heavily in companies identified as making a positive contribution to combating the climate change, such as renewable energy providers. It will also have a reduced exposure to the companies that are heavy carbon emitters or that have large fossil fuel reserves.

Ian Ashment, head of systematic and index investments at UBS Asset Management said more investors wanted to achieve "a greater alignment" between their investment portfolios and their environmental policies.

The pool of assets managed by Nest, which stands at around £1.5bn, is expected to grow substantially, as most UK workers will have to be automatically enrolled into a workplace pension scheme by their employer. Monthly contributions from new and existing members will lead to significant growth in the new climate-aware fund.

Nest has decided that younger members, who are more likely to be affected by climate change, will be given a greater exposure to the new fund than older workers, who are closer to retirement and less likely to be affected by the transition to a lower-carbon economy.

Mr Fawcett said the transition to a greener global economy would take place over the next 20 to 30 years and many UK workers would be saving for their retirement with Nest for at least that long.

"The launch of Nest's climate aware fund is an excellent example of how institutional investors can incorporate climate-related issues into their portfolios in order to enhance returns," said Fiona Reynolds, managing director of the Principles for Responsible Investment, a UN-backed group of 1,500 investors.

Green Nest Egg

The UK workplace pension provider has invested to protect the retirement savings of 4.3m British workers from the threat of environmental change — Ian Dicks

"We need to remember that while climate change presents material risks to portfolios, it also presents new business opportunities in the form of developing alternative energy supplies, for example. Investment vehicles that recognize this fact will be welcomed by investors," she said.

 Words and Expressions

strategic	*adj.*	战略上的,战略的
pension schemes / pension plan		养老金计划
step up		增加(数量等),提高(速度、强度等)
address	*vt.*	设法解决,处理,对付
tackle	*vt.*	着手处理
equity portfolio		股票投资组合
afford to		容许,负担得起
oversee	*vt.*	监督,监视
sustainability	*n.*	可持续性
identify	*vt.*	确认,认出,鉴定
combat	*n.*	格斗,搏斗,战斗,〈美〉竞赛,比赛,论战
	vt.	与……战斗,与……斗争,防止,减轻
exposure	*n.*	暴露,接触
emitter	*n.*	发射者,排放者

index	n.	索引,<数>指数
alignment	n.	结盟,排成直线,调准,校正位置
substantially	adv.	非常地,巨大地,大体上,总的来说
automatically	adv.	自动地,机械地,无意识地,不经思索的
enroll	v.	招收,注册,登记,加入
significant	adj.	重要的,有重大意义的,值得注意的,别有含义的,意味深长的
likely	adj.	可能的,适合的,有希望的
	adv.	可能,或许,大概,多半
launch	n.	开始从事,发起,发动(尤指有组织的活动)
institutional	adj.	机构的,慈善机构的,根深蒂固的
incorporate into		并入,划归,使成为……的一部分,归并
material risks		实质性风险
alternative	adj.	替代的,另类的,备选的,其他的
	n.	可供选择的事物

Notes to the Text

1. UBS(Union Bank of Switzerland):瑞银集团,1998 年由瑞士联合银行及瑞士银行集团合并而成。瑞银集团是世界第二大的私人财富资产管理者,资本及盈利能力也是欧洲第二大银行。其中,瑞士银行共设有 96 个分行。

2. Bloomberg L. P. (Limited Partnership):彭博有限合伙企业,简称为"彭博"(Bloomberg),是全球商业、金融信息和财经资讯的领先提供商,由迈克尔·布隆伯格(Michael Bloomberg)于 1981 年创立,总部位于美国纽约市曼哈顿,业务遍及全球 180 多个国家与地区。

3. United Nations Framework Convention on Climate Change:《联合国气候变化框架公约》,是指联合国大会于 1992 年 6 月 4 日通过的一项公约。同年 6 月在巴西里约热内卢召开的由世界各国政府首脑参加的联合国环境与发展会议期间开放签署。1994 年 3 月 21 日,该公约生效。地球峰会上有 150 多个国家及欧洲经济共同体共同签署。公约由序言及 26 条正文组成,具有法律约束力,终极目标是将大气温室气体浓度维持在一个稳定的水平,在该水平上人类活动对气候系统的危险干扰不会发生。根据"共同但有区别的责任"原则,公约对发达国家和发展中国家规定的义务以及履行义务的程序有所区别,要求发达国家作为温室气体的排放大户,采取具体措施限制温室气体的排放,并向发展中国家提供资金以支付他们履行公约义务所需的费用。而发展中国家只承担提供温室气体源与温室气体汇的国家清单的义务,制订并执行含有关于温室气体源与汇方面措施的方案,不承担有法律约束力的限控义务。该公约建立了一个向发展中国家提供资金和技术,使其能够履行公约义务的机制。

《巴黎协定》是 2015 年 12 月 12 日在巴黎气候变化大会上通过、2016 年 4 月 22 日在纽约签署的气候变化协定,该协定为 2020 年后全球应对气候变化行动做出安排。《巴黎协定》主要目标是将 21 世纪全球平均气温上升幅度控制在 2 摄氏度以内,并将全球气温上升控制在前工业化时期水平之上 1.5 摄氏度以内。中国全国人大常委会于 2016 年 9 月 3 日批准中国加入《巴黎气候变化协定》,中国成为第 23 个完成批准协定的缔约方。2017 年 10 月 23 日,尼加拉瓜政府正式宣布签署《巴黎协定》,随着尼加拉瓜的签署,拒绝《巴黎协定》的国家只有叙利亚和美国。11 月 8 日,在德国波恩举行的新一轮联合国气候变化大会上,叙利亚代表宣布将尽快签署加入《巴黎协定》并履行承诺。2018 年 4 月 30 日,《联合国气候变化框架公约》(UNFCCC)框架下的新一轮气候谈判在德国波恩开幕。缔约方代表将就进一步制定实施气候变化《巴黎协定》的相关准则展开谈判。

4. fossil fuel:化石燃料,是指煤炭、石油、天然气等埋藏在地下和海洋下的不能再生的燃料资源。化石燃料中按埋藏的能量的数量顺序分有煤炭类、石油、油页岩、天然气、油砂及海下的可燃冰等。

5. renewable energy:可再生能源。按能源的基本形态分类,能源可分为一次能源和二次能源。一次能源是指自然界中以原有形式存在的、未经加工转换的能量资源,又被称为"天然能源",如煤炭、石油、天然气、水能等。一次能源可以进一步分为再生能源和非再生能源两大类型。再生能源包括太阳能、水能、风能、生物质能、波浪能、潮汐能、海洋温差能、地热能等。它们在自然界可以循环再生,是"取之不尽,用之不竭"的能源,不需要人力参与便会自动再生,是相对于会穷尽的非再生能源的一种能源。

6. pool of assets:资产池。资产证券化中的资产池其实就是一个规模相当大的具有一定特征的资产组合。证券化资产池的组建主要有三个步骤:第一,框定资产池的总体目标特征;第二,设定筛选标准,选择备选资产;第三,从备选资产中挑选组合,构成资产池。"资产池总体目标特征"是指资产池总体的预期期限、金额规模、资产类别、风险水平、行业构成、地区分布等特征,这主要是由发起人根据其资产配置的规划并结合市场的需求来决定。

7. LCE(low-carbon economy):低碳经济,是指在可持续发展理念指导下,通过技术创新、制度创新、产业转型、新能源开发等多种手段,尽可能地减少煤炭、石油等高碳能源消耗,减少温室气体排放,达到经济社会发展与生态环境保护双赢的一种经济发展形态。"低碳经济"最早的政府文件是 2003 年的英国能源白皮书《我们能源的未来:创建低碳经济》。作为第一次工业革命的先驱和资源并不丰富的岛国,英国充分意识到了能源安全和气候变化的威胁,它正从自给自足的能源供应走向主要依靠进口的时代,按 2003 年的消费模式,预计 2020 年英国 80%的能源都必须进口。并且,气候变化的影响已经迫在眉睫。2010 年 8 月,中国发改委确定在 5 省 8 市开展低碳产业建设试点工作。低碳经济的特征是以减少温室气体排放为目标,构筑低能耗、低污染为基础的经济发展体系,包括低碳能源系统、低碳技术和低碳产业体系。低碳能源系统是指通过发展清洁能源,包括风能、太阳能、核能、地热能、生物质能等,替代煤、石油等化石能源以减少二氧化碳排放。低碳技术包括清洁煤技术(IGCC)、二氧化碳捕捉及储存技术(CCS)等。低碳产业体系包括火电减排、新能源汽车、节能建筑、工业节能与减排、循环经济、资源回收、环保设备、节能材料等。

8. PRI(Principles for Responsible Investment):责任投资原则,是一种先进的投资理念,其核心要旨是帮助投资者理解环境(Environmental)、社会(Social)和公司治理(Governance)(三个要素简称ESG)对投资的重要影响,进而将ESG纳入投资决策之中。目前,PRI原则由联合国环境规划署金融行动机构和联合国全球合约机构提供支持。不过,PRI原则由投资者自行设计、自愿参与和遵守承诺,并非由官方机构强制性执行。从发展历程来看,秉持PRI原则对投资者的帮助十分明显。一方面,它可以提升投资者的投资业绩,特别是长期投资回报率,更好地履行基金经理的受托责任;另一方面,PRI原则具有显著的投资正外部性,更加有利于经济社会的绿色可持续发展。

9. investment vehicles:投资工具。对一般投资者而言,能够接触到的投资工具主要有以下几种:股票、债券、基金、期货。这些投资标的性质、投资策略、投资收益和风险各有不同,但按照投资标地是否有内生价值,可分为投资和投机两大类。什么是投资?投资标的本身会随着经济的发展不断地产生内生价值,让标的的价值不断增值,这种行为成为投资。什么是投机?投资标的本身不产生任何内生价值,其价值的波动完全取决于市场中的买卖行为及参与者的情绪,这种行为就是投机。投机行为就像一场对赌,有赢家就一定有输家,你的对立面永远站着其他投资者。因此,炒期货本身是一种投机行为,一般的投资者还是尽量远离它,除非你对市场有非常敏锐的嗅觉,能准确把握大部分投机者的心理变化,有严格的操作原则,那么你可以用少量资金去参与其中。

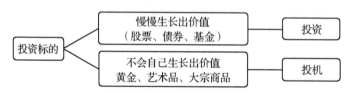

Fund Houses Turn Against Investment Consultants

February 27, 2017, *Financial Times*

UK regulator seeks more control over "opaque" and "uncompetitive" advisory industry, says Attracta Mooney

Asset managers have called for stricter oversight of the UK's hugely influential investment consulting industry after Britain's financial watchdog warned of conflicts of interest and a lack of transparency in the sector.

The Financial Conduct Authority expressed concerns about "opaque fees" and a lack of competition in the institutional advice sector in a damning interim report on the asset management industry last November.

The regulator said it was considering seeking more regulatory powers over investment consultants, who advise on where £1.6tn worth of people's savings should be invested. The FCA expressed concerns that a "very important part of the asset management value chain" is currently largely unregulated.

The FCA's stance has been backed by asset managers, trade bodies and some consultants, which claim greater regulation of the institutional advice sector is vital to improve services and investment returns for pension funds and other big investors.

The Investment Association, the trade body for fund houses in the UK, said in its response to the FCA report: "Investment consultants play a central role in the institutional asset management market and the quality of their advice is likely to be crucial in determining outcomes for institutional investors."

"Ensuring that this element of the investment value chain works well for institutional investors is therefore highly important."

The trade body added that it "strongly" supported proposals to bring institutional investment advice into the FCA's regulatory perimeter and backed proposals to refer the investment consulting industry for investigation by the Competition and Markets Authority, a government department responsible for strengthening business competition.

The FCA's spotlight on the investment consulting market comes as concerns mount about the influence of the sector.

In its 208-page report, the watchdog said consultants, on average, were unable to identify managers that offer better returns to investors and did not appear to have encouraged a rise in price competition between asset managers.

But investment consultants wield huge power in the UK due to rules that require pension funds to seek investment advice. With the exception of the largest schemes, most pension funds turn to investment consultants for this advice.

Consultants typically focus on helping pension schemes make decisions around asset allocation and risk, as well as suggesting suitable fund managers. In some cases, pension funds and other investors will entrust a consultant with the management of their assets, under a model known as fiduciary management.

Because consultants in the UK act as gatekeepers to more than a trillion pounds in assets, investment managers have traditionally been reluctant to condemn them publicly. In private, however, fund houses have been highly critical of the sector, especially its push into fiduciary management.

This move into fiduciary management has meant consultants are often in direct competition with the asset managers they are hired to assess independently.

The FCA said: "We heard a persistent concern from asset managers and institutional investors that once an investment consultant has developed its own product offerings, it will recommend its in-house propositions even if there are better investment products offered elsewhere."

£60bn	41%	4%	60%
The value of assets managed by investment consultants under a fiduciary arrangement	Percentage of revenues that came from fiduciary management for consultants that offer it	Percentage of assets under advice represented by fiduciary management	Estimated percentage of consultant market controlled by Willis Towers Watson, Aon Hewitt and Mercer

According to KPMG, the professional services company, three-quarters of all fiduciary mandates went to consultants last year.

One senior executive at a UK asset manager, speaking on condition of anonymity, says: "The problem [with consultants offering fiduciary management] is it creates a massive conflict of interest."

"[The consultants] have some clients who want to make their own investment decisions, but the consultant wants to push them down the route of fiduciary because it is hugely profitable."

According to the FCA, the value of assets managed by investment consultants under a fiduciary arrangement has tripled in the past five years to almost £60bn.

While dwarfed in size when compared with the £1.6tn in assets under advice, the regulator said that on a per-client basis, fiduciary management generates much higher revenues than traditional advisory business.

The FCA said that of consultants that offer fiduciary management services, 41 per cent of their combined advisory and fiduciary management revenues came from fiduciary management, despite representing just 4 per cent of assets under advice.

The regulator also warned that performance and fees of fiduciary managers appear to be among the most opaque parts of the asset management value chain.

John Walbaum, head of investment consultancy at Hymans Robertson, an investment consultancy that does not offer fiduciary management, says: "We would be in favour of more separation of the two roles [fiduciary and investment consulting]. We think these conflicts are unnecessary and they are too big."

The UK's largest consultants, Willis Towers Watson, Aon Hewitt and Mercer, said on Friday said they had put forward a series of proposals to the FCA that are aimed at improving competitiveness and transparency in the investment consultancy and fiduciary management industries.

Over the coming months, the UK's financial watchdog will have to decide whether to officially ask for regulatory powers over consultants.

Redington, one of the UK's five largest consultants, backs this approach. It says: "We believe it makes sense to bring those areas of advice that are most meaningful to pension fund outcomes under the FCA regulatory perimeter."

Patrick Disney, European managing director of the institutional group for SEI Investments, a fiduciary manager, argues that more efforts need to be made to ringfence consultancy work from fiduciary management. SEI stopped offering consultancy services in favour of focusing on fiduciary management because of concerns about conflicts between the two services.

He says: "More regulation is a logical next step, particularly if you have [companies] offering both [fiduciary and investment consulting] services."

The IA says: "We are particularly keen that, where consultants provide asset management products and services, they compete on a level playing field with asset managers, both in terms of regulatory oversight and client scrutiny of their performance."

The FCA will also have to decide whether to push the antitrust regulator to carry out a probe into the sector.

In its report, it raised concerns about the dominant "big three" investment consultants: Willis Towers Watson, Aon Hewitt and Mercer. It estimates that the trio collectively control 60 per cent of the market and take an estimated 71 per cent of revenues, down from 78 per cent in 2011.

Consultants have been quick to dismiss suggestions that the sector should be referred to the antitrust authority because of a lack of competition, arguing there has been an improvement over the past decade.

But others are less sure. The Transparency Task Force, a campaign group, believes a probe by the antitrust authority is a "good idea".

"It will help to shine a light on the workings of the investment consultancy sector and it therefore has the potential to identify and deal with issues that prohibit the efficient workings of the market, including conflicts of interest."

It also backed more regulatory oversight of consultants. "The fact that the institutional investment consulting sector has not been regulated to date may explain many of the sub-optimal market practices that have been taking place," the group argues.

Words and Expressions

fund house		基金公司
turn against		(使)与……反目,(使)反对,(使)反感
investment consultant		投资顾问
regulator	n.	(某行业等的)监管者,监管机构
opaque	adj.	(玻璃、液体等)不透明的,不透光的,浑浊的,(说话或写作)难懂的,模糊的,隐晦的,不清楚的
uncompetitive	adj.	无竞争力的,竞争力弱的
advisory	adj.	顾问的,劝告的,忠告的,提供咨询的
	n.	公告,报告
oversight	n.	负责,照管,疏忽,忽略,失察
financial watchdog		金融监督机构
transparency	n.	透明,透明度
damning	adj.	(证据或报告)确凿的,导致定罪的
interim report		期中(临时)报告
unregulated	adj.	未受管理(控制、约束)的,未校准(调整、调节)的
stance	n.	态度,立场,站姿
claim	vt.	宣称,声称,断言要求(拥有),索取,认领
vital	adj.	必不可少的,对……极重要的,生命的
perimeter	n.	周长,周围,边界
refer	vi.	提交,送交,委托
spotlight	n.	媒体和公众的注意

Unit Five International Investment

mount	vi.	逐步增加
identify	vt.	确认,认出,鉴定,找到,发现
consultant	n.	顾问,咨询者,会诊医生
wield	vt.	使用,行使,挥舞
exception	n.	例外,除外
suitable	adj.	合适的,适当的,适宜的,恰当的
entrust	vt.	委托,托付
fiduciary	adj.	信托的,受信托的,基于信用的
	n.	受托人,被信托者
gatekeeper	n.	看门人,把关系统
condemn	vt.	(通常因道义上的原因而)谴责
move in sth		涉足,出入,生活在(某群体)
persistent	adj.	(尤指不好或不受欢迎的状态或情况)持续存在的,继续发生的
product offering		产品提供,产品出售
in-house	adj.	机构内部的,在机构内部进行的
	adv.	在机构内部
proposition	n.	(尤指业务上的)提议,建议,见解,主张,观点
mandate	n.	(政府或组织等经选举而获得的)授权
	vt.	托管,批准
anonymity	n.	匿名
profitable	adj.	有利可图的,有益的,可赚钱的,合算的
triple	adj.	三倍的,三方的,三部分的
	vt. & vi.	(使)增至三倍
dwarf	vt.	使显得矮小,使相形见绌
	n.	侏儒,矮子
represent	vt.	等于,相当于,意味着
in favour of		支持……的活动
managing director		总裁,总经理,常务董事
level playing field		公平竞争环境
scrutiny	n.	详细的检查(或审查),仔细的观察
antitrust	adj.	反垄断的,反托拉斯的
probe	n.	盘问,追问,探究,(用细长工具)探查,查看
dominant	adj.	占优势的,统治的,支配的
trio	n.	三人小组,三件一套,三重奏乐团

dismiss	vt.	不予考虑,摒弃,对……不屑一提
campaign group		运动组织
potential	n.	潜力,潜能
prohibit	vt.	禁止,阻止,防止
to date		迄今,至今,直到今天,到目前为止
sub-optimal	adj.	次优的,不是最佳的
argue	vt.	主张,认为

Notes to the Text

1. FSA（Financial Service Authority）：在 2013 年 4 月 1 日之前,英国的金融服务管理都由英国金融服务管理局监管。随着 2007—2008 年金融危机的爆发,英国政府决定重新调整金融监管体系,最终 FSA 被废止,其架构革新并被两个新组织所取代,分别是金融行为监管局(FCA)与审慎监管局(PRA)。审慎监管局主要负责审慎监管和银行、信贷、保险等主要的投资公司;金融行为管理局则负责监督英国金融服务公司和金融市场的行为,以及作为未经 PRA 授权公司的审慎监管机构。任何一个在(或从)英国提供银行或者其他金融服务的英国注册组织都将被这两个机构监管。在新的监管体系下,零售外汇平台和差价合约、点差交易等零售外汇金融产品接受 FCA 监管。

2. value chain：价值链,是一个商业体系,用来详细描述企业运营或功能行为的顺序。为了获得更高的生产效率,人们可以同时使用两个或多个价值链。价值链中的每一个环节都为产品或服务增加价值,为实现同一个目标而努力,因此它们不是相互竞争而是相互合作的。只有完成了价值链中的最后一个环节,这个产品或服务才是完整的。

3. KPMG：毕马威,是世界上最大的一家专业服务机构。毕马威提供三类主营服务,分别是审计、税务和咨询。1911 年,William Barclay Peat & Co. 和 Marwick, Mitchell & Co. 合并成为一家网络遍布全球的会计及专业咨询机构—PMI（Peat Marwick International）。1979 年,Klynveld, Deutsche Treuhand-Gesellschaft 和跨国专业服务机构 McLintock Main Lafrentz 进行合并,组成 KMG（Klynveld Main Goerdeler）。1987 年,PMI 和 KMG 的成员机构进行合并。自此,它们在全球各地的所有成员机构均以毕马威的名义提供服务,或把毕马威之名纳入其机构名称内。

4. ringfence：围栏策略,是指投资者分离若干金额的资金,使之无须面对外部风险的策略,一般是离岸投资采用的策略。据英国央行新规,到 2019 年,英国大行在对其投行业务实施围栏策略时,银行间额外资本金储备至多达到 33 亿英镑。英国央行新规还允许实施围栏策略的银行将其零售部门的资金以分红形势划转给其他业务部门。该规定受到英国银行业的热烈欢迎。

5. antitrust law：反托拉斯法，即反垄断法，是国内外经济活动中用以控制垄断活动的立法、行政规章、司法判例及国际条约的总称。从广义上讲，垄断活动同限制性商业惯例（"限制"指限制竞争）、卡特尔行为及托拉斯活动含义相当；从狭义讲，国际间的限制性商业惯例指在经济活动中企业为牟取高额利润而进行的合并、接管（狭义的垄断活动），或勾结起来进行串通投标、操纵价格、划分市场等不正当的经营活动（狭义的限制性商业惯例）。

6. SEI Investments Co：SEI 投资公司，创立于 1968 年，总部位于美国宾夕法尼亚州，是一家资产管理公司，提供资产管理和资讯服务。

The Surprising Behaviors That Can Make a Difference

How venture capitalists really assess a pitch
May – June, 2017, *Harvard Business Review*

Before Lakshmi Balachandra entered academia, she spent a few years working for two venture capital firms, where she routinely witnessed a phenomenon that mystified her. The VCs would receive a business plan from an entrepreneur, read it, and get excited. They'd do some research on the industry, and their enthusiasm would grow. So they'd invite the company founder in for a formal pitch meeting—and by the end of it they'd have absolutely no interest in making an investment. Why did a proposal that looked so promising on paper become a nonstarter when the person behind the plan actually pitched it? "That's what led me to pursue a PhD," says Balachandra, now an assistant professor at Babson College. "I wanted to break down and study the interaction between the VC and the entrepreneur."

Even before she began her research, Balachandra had some hunches. Most entrepreneurs believe that the investment decision will hinge primarily on the substance of their pitch—the information and logic, usually laid out in a PowerPoint deck. But in fact most VCs review pitch decks beforehand; the in-person encounter is more about asking questions, gaining clarity, and sizing up personalities. To better understand those dynamics, Balachandra spent almost 10 years capturing what happens in pitch meetings and quantifying the results. Some patterns were obvious from the start. For instance, entrepreneurs who laugh during their pitches have more success, as do people who name-check friends they have in common with the VCs. But after drilling down, she drew four broad conclusions:

Passion is overrated.

Working with video recordings of 185 one-minute pitches during an MIT Entrepreneurship Competition (with real VCs as judges), Balachandra had coders turn off the sound and use only the visuals to assess how energetic and how positive or negative each founder appeared. (The coders controlled for presenters' gender and attractiveness along with the size of the market the start-ups were addressing.) Among both VCs and entrepreneurs, conventional wisdom holds that "passion" is a positive attribute, connoting high energy, persistence, and commitment. "There's this mythology that they want to see that you're dying to do this business and work hard," Balachandra says. But when the coders looked at their assessments in light of which start-ups were chosen as finalists in the competition, they found that the opposite was true: The judges preferred a calm demeanor. Follow-up studies showed that people equate calmness with leadership strength. So temper the enthusiasm and project stone-cold preparedness instead.

Trust beats competence.

In a second study, Balachandra worked with a California-based network of angel investors who gather monthly to hear 20-minute pitches from start-ups. Immediately after each pitch, the investors filled out detailed surveys about their reactions and indicated whether they wanted to send the company through to due diligence (the next step before investing). The results showed that interest in a start-up was driven less by judgments that the founder was competent than by perceptions about character and trustworthiness. Balachandra says that this makes sense: A CEO who lacks a skill-based competency, such as a financial or technical background, can overcome that through training or by hiring the right complementary talent, but character is less malleable. And because angel investors often work closely for several years with entrepreneurs on highly risky ventures, they seek evidence that their new partners will behave in honest, straightforward ways that don't heighten the risks. In fact, the research showed that entrepreneurs who projected trustworthiness increased their odds of being funded by 10%.

Coachability matters.

Particularly among angel investors, who get involved earlier than traditional VCs do, decisions aren't driven only by potential returns; they are driven by ego as well. Most angel investors are experienced entrepreneurs who want to be hands-on mentors, so they prefer investments where they can add value. For that to happen, a founder must be receptive to feedback and have the potential to be a good protégé. Balachandra reached this conclusion by conducting surveys and evaluating video sessions with the same California investors' network. Coders examined the videos for behaviors, such as nodding and smiling in response to questions, indicating that founders were open to ideas. When analysis and survey results indicated that they were, and when the investor was experienced in the relevant industry—giving him or her knowledge that could add value—the company was more likely to move on to due diligence.

Gender stereotypes play a role.

In Balachandra's first job in venture capital, she rarely encountered other women, whether among VCs or among entrepreneurs; in fact, she says, 94% of venture capitalists are male. (She then worked at an all-female firm that focused on funding start-ups headed by women.) In her research, she and her colleagues used videos from the MIT competition to test the perception that VCs are biased against female entrepreneurs. Coders noted whether the presenter was male or female and then measured whether he or she exhibited stereotypically masculine behaviors (such as forcefulness, dominance, aggressiveness, and assertiveness) or stereotypically female ones (warmth, sensitivity, expressiveness, and emotionality). The analysis revealed that although gender alone didn't inluence success, people with a high degree of stereotypically female behavior were less likely than others to succeed at pitching. "The study shows that VCs are biased against femininity," Balachandra says. "They don't want to see particular behaviors, so if you're overly emotional or expressive, you should consider practicing to avoid those things."

The most important takeaway for entrepreneurs is this: You should approach the pitching process less as a formal presentation and more as an improvisational conversation in which attitude and mindset matter more than business fundamentals. Listen hard to the questions you're asked, and be thoughtful in your responses. If you don't know something, offer to find out—or ask the investor what he or she thinks. Don't react defensively to critical questions. And instead of obsessing over the specifics of your pitch deck, Balachandra advises, "Think about being calm, cool, and open to feedback."

 Words and Expressions

academia	n.	学术界,学术环境
routinely	adv.	例行公事地,常规地,惯常地
witness	n.	目击者,见证人
	vt.	当场看到,目击(罪行或事故)
phenomenon	n.	现象,事件,奇迹,非凡的人
mystify	vt.	使神秘化,使迷惑,使困惑
entrepreneur	n.	创业者,(尤指涉及财务风险的)企业家
enthusiasm	n.	热情,热忱,热衷的事物
founder	n.	(组织、机构等的)创建者,创办者,发起人
pitch meeting		融资会议

absolutely	adv.	绝对地,完全地
proposal	n.	提议,建议,提案
promising	adj.	有希望的,有前途的,前景很好的
nonstarter	n.	无望成功的计划(或想法)
break down		划分(以便分析)
hunch	n.	预感,直觉
hinge on		取决于……,以……为转移
hinge	n.	铰链,折叶
	vi.	依……而转移
primarily	adv.	首先,首要地,主要地,根本上
substance	n.	物质,主旨,要点,实质,基本内容
lay out		阐述,讲解,说明,规划,布置,设计(场地或建筑)
in-person	adj.	亲自的,亲身的,本人的,现场的,实况的
encounter	n.	相遇,邂逅,遭遇,冲突
clarity	n.	清晰度,明确,透明,清楚
size up		打量,估量,估计,迅速对……做出判断(评价)
personality	n.	性格,个性,人格,名人,风云人物
dynamics	n.	相互作用,动力
capture	vt.	俘获,夺取,(用图画、文章、电影等准确地)表达,刻画,描述
quantify	vt.	确定……的数量,用数量来表示,量化
pattern	n.	模式,方式,图案,花样,样品
overrated	v.	对(质量、能力等)估价过高(overrate 的过去式和过去分词)
coder	n.	编码员
visual	adj.	视觉的,看得见的
	n.	画面,图像
attractiveness	n.	吸引力
conventional wisdom		传统观点(观念)
attribute	n.	属性,(人或物的)特征
connote	vt.	隐含,暗示,意味着
persistence	n.	持续,坚持不懈
commitment	n.	承诺,许诺,(对工作或某活动)献身,奉献,投入
mythology	n.	神话学,神话(总称),虚构的事实,错误的观点
dying to		渴望

in light of		按照,根据
finalist	n.	参加决赛者
demeanor	n.	<正式用语>行为,举止,态度
follow-up	n.	后续行动,后续事物
equate	vt.	等同,使相等,相当于,把……相提并论,与……等同
project	vt.	展现,表现,确立(好印象)
stone-cold	adj.	冰冷的,凉透的
preparedness	n.	有准备,已准备
beat	vt.	比……更好,赛过,胜过
competence	n.	能力,才干
send through		报告,通知(消息等)
due diligence		尽职调查,应有的注意
perception	n.	知觉,感知,看法,见解
trustworthiness	n.	信用,可信赖,确实性
competency	n.	资格,能力
complementary	adj.	互补的,补充的,补足的
malleable	adj.	(人、思想等)可塑的,易受影响(或改变)的
straightforward	adj.	直截了当的,坦率的
odds	n.	希望,可能性,概率,打赌的投注赔率
coachability	n.	(人的)可塑性,可培养潜力
potential	adj.	潜在的,有可能的
ego	n.	自我,自负,自尊心,自我意识
hands-on	adj.	亲自实践的,实际动手操作的
mentor	n.	有经验可信赖的顾问
receptive	adj.	(对新观点、建议等)愿意倾听的,乐于接受的
protégé	n.	被保护者,得宠者,受庇护者,宠儿
session	n.	开会,会议,(法庭的)开庭,会期,学期,(进行某活动连续的)一段时间
stereotype	n.	陈规旧习,旧规矩
biased	adj.	有偏见的,倾向性的,片面的
note	vt.	指出,特别提到
presenter	n.	(广播、电视)节目主持人,演讲人,发言人,(仪式上的)颁奖人
stereotypically	adv.	带有成见地(stereotype 的副词形式)

masculine	adj.	男子气概的,阳性的
forcefulness	n.	（人）强有力的,有说服力,雄辩才能
dominance	n.	优势,统治,支配
aggressiveness	n.	积极进取,好斗,挑衅
assertiveness	n.	观点明确,坚决主张
warmth	n.	热情,友情
sensitivity	n.	体贴,体恤,善解人意
expressiveness	n.	富于表情,富于表现力
emotionality	n.	富于感情,情绪
femininity	n.	女性气质,娇弱,温柔,妇女的总称
approach	vt. & vi.	接近,走近,靠近
improvisational	adj.	即兴的
improvise	vt. & vi.	临时拼凑,临时做,即兴创作（音乐、台词、演讲词等）
mindset	n.	观念模式,思维倾向
fundamental	n.	基本规律,根本法则,基本原理,基础
listen hard		倾听,留心听
thoughtful	adj.	沉思的,深思的,思考的,缜密思考过的,深思熟虑的
offer to		主动提出
defensively	adv.	防御地,守势地,心存戒备地
critical	adj.	极重要的,关键的,至关紧要的
obsess over		痴迷于,执着于

Notes to the Text

1. venture capital：风险投资,简称"风投",又译为"创业投资",主要是指向初创企业提供资金支持并取得该公司股份的一种融资方式。风险投资是私人股权投资的一种形式。风险投资公司是一个专业的投资公司,由一群具有科技及财务相关知识与经验的人组合而成的,经由直接投资获取投资公司股权的方式,提供资金给需要资金者（被投资公司）。风投公司的资金大多用于投资新创事业或未上市企业（虽然现今法规上已大幅放宽资金用途）,并不以经营被投资公司为目的,仅是提供资金及专业上的知识与经验,以协助被投资公司获取更大的利润为目的,所以是一追求长期利润的高风险、高报酬事业。

2. PhD：哲学博士学位,现泛指学术研究型博士学位,源自拉丁语 Philosophic Doctor。所谓"哲学博士",是指拥有人对其知识范畴的理论、内容、发展等都有相当的认识,能独立进行研究,并在该范畴内对学术界有所建树。因此,哲学博士基本上可以授予任何学科的博士毕业生。改革开放后,我国逐渐兴起的"专业学位"博士的称呼并没有照搬西方,一般不称作 PhD,而是每个专业各有其简称。

3. Angel Investor:天使投资者,在欧洲被称为 Business Angle,或者简称为 Angle,是具有丰厚收入并为初创企业提供启动资本的个人。具有一定净财富的人士,对具有巨大发展潜力的高风险的初创企业进行早期的直接投资。相应地,这些进行投资的富人就被称为投资天使、商业天使、天使投资者或天使投资家。

4. Angel Investment:天使投资,是权益资本投资的一种形式,属于一种自发而又分散的民间投资方式。天使投资者的投资通常会要求获得被投资企业的权益资本。天使投资一词源于纽约百老汇,1978年在美国首次使用,"天使"这个词是由百老汇的内部人员创造出来的,特指富人出资资助一些具有社会意义演出的公益行为。对于那些充满理想的演员来说,这些赞助者就像天使一样从天而降,使他们的美好理想变为现实。后来,天使投资被引申为一种对高风险、高收益的新兴企业的早期投资。那些用于投资的资本就叫天使资本。天使投资是风险投资的一种形式,根据天使投资人的投资数量以及对被投资企业可能提供的综合资源进行投资。

5. Due Diligence:尽职调查,是指企业在并购(简称 M&A)时,买方企业对目标企业进行的经营现状调查。其目的主要包括以下两个方面:搜集用于估算目标价值的信息;履行管理层应尽义务,收集信息并制作资料以期向股东说明此次并购决策的合理性。

Unit Six

Globalization

Saving Globalisation: The Reset Button

October 1, 2016, *The Economist*

How to make economic liberalism fairer and more effective

There may be few better advocates of the benefits to America of an open economy than Pin Ni, boss of Wanxiang America Corporation, part of a private firm based in Hangzhou that his father-in-law started as a bicycle-repair shop. Mr Ni launched the American subsidiary in 1994, suspending his studies at the University of Kentucky. He has been there ever since.

During the car-industry meltdown in 2007–2009 the company began buying moribund car-part suppliers and restoring them to health. It pushed its acquisitions to concentrate on their strongest suits, usually the relationship with the car manufacturers and engineering. It helped them to source components more cheaply and to gain a foothold in the Chinese market. Mr Ni is effusive about the prospects for American exporters. America has firms with technology and brands that are coveted around the world, he says.

Such optimism about globalisation is all too rare these days. Neither candidate in America's presidential race is an advocate of free trade. "If Trump is elected, it's a mandate for isolationism," says a seasoned observer at a think-tank in Washington, DC. "If Clinton is elected, the best we can hope for is we don't go back very far." Britain's trading relationships with the rest of the world are up in the air, following the vote in June's referendum to leave the EU. France is hostile to TTIP, a proposed trade agreement between the EU and America. Even in Germany, the self-declared world export champion, politicians are turning against the deal in the face of public opposition. Globalisation is increasingly blamed for job losses, rising wage inequality and sluggish GDP growth.

How should politicians respond? Closing borders to trade, capital and people would cause great harm and do very little to tackle inequities in the economy. In some respects it would increase them. People on low pay spend a far greater proportion of their income on imports than the well-off. A growing body of research links economic maladies to more oligopolistic economies. Blocking imports would only entrench the market power of rent-seeking firms, further harming the prospects for higher productivity and pay.

Easing the pain

As borders have been steadily opened up, policies needed to complement globalisation have not kept pace, particularly in America. They need to catch up. A good place to start is demand management. The stability of the labour market depends on macroeconomic policies, not trade. In Europe the most effective policy would be to use public money to fix the banks. With monetary policy overstretched and bond yields low or negative, it is a shame that countries with room to borrow more, notably Germany, are seemingly addicted to thrift. The case for free trade is undermined when many countries in Europe are free to rack up persistent trade surpluses, which are a drag on global demand.

In America and Britain, a strong case can be made for locking in low-cost long-term funding to finance a programme to fix potholed roads and smarten up public spaces. Private pension funds with expertise in infrastructure have a role to play in such schemes. Rich-country central banks, notably the Federal Reserve, can afford to be more relaxed about the threat of inflation. An economy at full pelt begins to draw people into the workforce who were thought to have opted out for good. "Ex-felons were doing pretty well in 2000," notes Larry Mishel, of the Economic Policy Institute, a think-tank in Washington, DC. The risks of slamming the brakes on too quickly outweigh those of excessive policy stimulus.

Demand management is (or ought to be) the bread and butter of economic policy. Curing the ills that feed public opposition to globalisation requires efforts to address two other problems. The first is the job churn caused by shifts in trade and technology. Too little effort and money has been expended on taking care of those who have been hurt by the opening up of markets. America in particular makes little attempt to assist people find new jobs to replace lost ones. Extra help need not blunt the incentives to look for work. For instance, more generous jobless benefits could be made conditional on attending a back-to-work programme. A valid criticism of government training schemes is that they cannot keep up with the fast-changing demands of the jobs market. A better option would be a system of wage insurance. That would nudge workers to acquire new skills by taking a less well-paid job when they lose a good one.

Yet there is little point in helping people change careers if a lack of dynamism in the economy means that too few good jobs are being created. So a second prong of reform should be to spur greater competition so that startups can thrive and incumbent firms are kept on their toes. More competition is a hard sell when many people are already anxious about their jobs and income; but without it there is less chance of the dynamism that boosts productivity (and earnings) and creates new job opportunities. Europe has long been notorious for restrictive practices such as occupational licences, but state-level licences in America have proliferated almost unnoticed. Some are necessary, but most are simply a way of keeping prices higher and restricting entry.

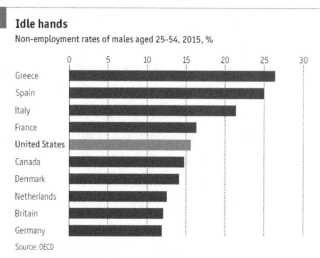

Competition policy needs to become more vigorous. In America the startup rate (the share of new firms in the total number) has fallen steadily since 1980. Most industries have become more concentrated. The profits of the leading companies have pulled well ahead of the rest. America's courts have tended to view windfall profits as the rightful reward for innovation. There is much to be said for redrawing the boundaries of intellectual property so that incumbents can be more readily challenged. The growing habit of big tech firms to swallow startups that might become rivals is worrying. Such deals often suit both sides—the buyer gets the innovation and the startup makes a lucrative exit—but the practice saps dynamism from the economy.

Trustbusters might be given more discretion when making judgments about how markets might evolve in future, though this is difficult to do well.

Unit Six Globalization

 Words and Expressions

reset button		复原按钮
suspend	v.	暂停
meltdown	n.	(公司、机构或系统的)崩溃,瘫痪,彻底失败
moribund	adj.	垂死的,奄奄一息的,(企业、机构等)即将倒闭的
be sb's strong suit		为某人所长
source	vt.	寻求(尤指供货)的来源
component	n.	零件
gain a foothold		站稳脚跟,取得立足点
effusive	adj.	溢于言表的,热情洋溢的
prospect	n.	前景,希望
covet	vt. & vi.	贪求,觊觎
optimism	n.	乐观,乐观主义
presidential race		总统竞选
mandate	n.	(政府的)任期
seasoned	adj.	富有经验的,老于此道的
observer	n.	观察员,评论员
up in the air		悬而未决
referendum	n.	全民公决,公民投票
hostile	adj.	怀有敌意的,强烈反对的
propose	vt.	提议,建议,求婚
self-declared	adj.	自行宣称的,公然自称的
champion	n.	捍卫者,声援者,拥护者
turn against		转为反对
inequity	n.	不公平,不公正
body	n.	大量,大批,大堆
malady	n.	疾病,病症,(制度或机构的)弊病,弊端
oligopoly	n.	寡头,垄断
oligopolistic	adj.	寡占的,由少数垄断的
entrench	vt.	使处于牢固地位,牢固确立
complement	vt.	补足,补充,补助
keep pace		与其他人并驾齐驱,跟得上步伐
macroeconomic	adj.	宏观经济的,总体经济的

fix	vt.	提供,准备
monetary	adj.	货币的,金钱的,金融的,财政的
overstretch	vt.	(使)勉强维持,超负荷运转
bond yield		债券收益率
negative	adj.	负的,小于零的
notably	adv.	尤其,特别
addicted	adj.	依赖的,习惯的
thrift	n.	节俭,节约
undermine	vt.	逐渐削弱,使逐步减少效力
rack up		获得,得到
persistent	adj.	持续的,持久的
drag	n.	拖沓
strong case		有力的证据
lock in		锁定(资金)
finance	vt.	为……供给资金
potholed		(路面)坑坑洼洼的,多坑洞的
smarten up		修饰,打扮,装修
private pension funds		私人养老基金
expertise	n.	专门知识,专门技能,专长
afford to		容许,能够,可以
pelt	vi.	快速奔跑,飞奔
at full pelt		全速,大力地
opt out		决定退出,决定不参加
for good		一劳永逸地,永远地
ex-felon	n.	获释重罪犯
slam the brakes on		急踩刹车
bread and butter		生计,主要收入来源
job churn		工作机会流失
blunt	vt.	使减弱,使降低效应
jobless benefit		失业补助
conditional	adj.	有条件的,有前提的
back-to-work programme		再就业计划
nudge	vt.	劝说,鼓动
dynamism	n.	(令人振奋的)发展变化,(经济)腾飞

prong	n.	(政策、计划等的)部分,方面
thrive	vi.	兴旺发达,繁荣
keep sb on their toes		让某人保持警觉
a hard sell		强行推销
notorious	adj.	众所周知的,臭名昭著的
proliferate	vi.	激增,扩散
idle hands		闲置人员
windfall profit		意外的利润,暴利
rightful	adj.	合法的,正当的
there is much to be said for		(某件事情)是很有道理的
redraw the boundary		重新划定界线
intellectual property		知识产权
readily	adv.	轻而易举地,容易地
swallow	vt.	吞并
lucrative	adj.	获利多的,赚钱的
exit	n.	退出市场
sap	vt.	消耗,削弱,逐渐破坏
discretion	n.	自行决定的自由,自行决定权

Notes to the Text

1. University of Kentucky:肯塔基大学,简称UK,创办于1865年,是美国一所著名的公立研究型大学,位于美国肯塔基州的莱克星顿市(Lexington)。

2. isolationism:孤立主义,是一种外交政策。它通常由防务和经济文化两方面政策组成。在防务上,孤立主义采取不干涉原则,即除自卫战争外不主动卷入任何外部军事冲突;在经济文化上,通过立法最大程度限制与国外的贸易和文化交流。美国孤立主义政策是华盛顿在其总统任满后发表的《告别词》中提出来的:"要将美国建成自由进步的伟大国家,最为重要的是应该排除对某些个别国家抱永久且根深蒂固的反感,而对另一些国家则又有感情上的依附;不要与任何外国建立永久的联盟;美国独处一方,远离他国,这种地理位置允许并促使美国能推行一条独特的外交路线,使好战国家不能从美国获得好处,也不敢轻易冒险向美国挑衅。"在此后的一百多年里,美国的领导人忠实地执行了这一政策。

3. TTIP(Transatlantic Trade and Investment Partnership):《跨大西洋贸易与投资伙伴协定》,俗称"经济北约",是指美国和欧盟双方通过削减关税、消除双方贸易壁垒等来发展经济、应对金融危机的贸易协定。该协定的谈判在2013年6月启动。谈判一旦达成协议,意味着欧美自贸区成形。这将一举成为世界上最发达和规模最大的自由贸易区,对欧美经济乃至全球贸易格局和规则的演变无疑都将产生重大影响。TTIP 从一开始就宣布是一个宏伟、全面和高标准的贸易和投资协定，要达成进一步开放市场、促进投资、消除关税和非贸易壁垒、统一监管标准等八大目标，涉及包括农业和工业产品市场准入、政府采购、投资、服务、能源和原材料、监管议题、知识产权、中小企业、国有企业等 20 项议题。

4. oligopoly：寡头，指为数不多的销售者。在寡头垄断市场上，只有少数几家厂商供给该行业全部或大部分产品，每个厂家的产量占市场总量的相当份额，对市场价格和产量有举足轻重的影响。

5. favorable balance of trade：贸易顺差。所谓"贸易顺差"，是指在特定年度一国出口贸易总额大于进口贸易总额，又被称为"出超"（trade surplus）。贸易顺差就是在一定的单位时间里（通常按年度计算），贸易的双方互相买卖各种货物，互相进口与出口，甲方的出口金额大过乙方的出口金额，或甲方的进口金额少于乙方的进口金额，其中的差额对甲方来说就叫作"贸易顺差"，反之，对乙方来说就叫作"贸易逆差"（trade deficit）。贸易顺差越多并不一定好，过高的贸易顺差是一件危险的事情，意味着经济的增长对外依存度过高。

Deregulation and Competition: A Lapse in Concentration

A dearth of competition among firms helps explain
wage inequality and a host of other ills
October 1, 2016, *The Economist*

In "The Fugitive", a 1960s television drama, David Janssen plays Richard Kimble, a doctor wrongly convicted of murdering his wife who escapes on the way to his execution. He claims, but cannot prove, that he encountered a one-armed man minutes before he discovered his wife's dead body. After his escape he drifts from town to town trying to find the ghostly figure and to elude the man obsessed with recapturing him.

The damage that globalisation has done to America's economy is as obvious to some as Dr Kimble's guilt was to his pursuers. Careful academic studies have linked competition by Chinese manufacturers to the growing propensity of prime-aged men to drop out of the labour force. A pillar of trade theory says that increased commerce with labour-rich countries will depress the pay of the low-skilled, and some reckonings of wage inequality in America pin part of the blame on trade and migration. GDP growth has been sluggish during the long hangover from the financial crisis. The globalisation of finance provided the kindling for America's subprime crisis and spread its effects around the world. Globalisation is on the run. But might there be another brig and who bears responsibility for its alleged crimes?

An intriguing line of research identifies an increase in the incidence of economic "rents" (profits over and above the levels needed to justify investment or input of work) as a possible villain. A study last year by Jason Furman, of the Council for Economic Advisers (CEA), and Peter Orszag, a former budget director for Barack Obama, found that the top 10% of firms by profit have pulled away sharply from the rest (see the following chart). Their return on capital invested rose from more than three times that of the median firm in the 1990s to eight times. This is way above any plausible cost of capital and likely to be pure rent. Those high returns are persistent. More than four-fifths of the firms that made a return of 25% or more in 2003 were still doing so ten years later.

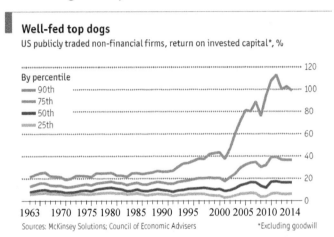

Well-fed top dogs
US publicly traded non-financial firms, return on invested capital*, %
By percentile: 90th, 75th, 50th, 25th
Sources: McKinsey Solutions; Council of Economic Advisers *Excluding goodwill

Other research suggests that this increasingly skewed distribution of profits goes a long way to explaining the rise in wage inequality. A paper in 2014 by Erling Bath, Alex Bryson, James Davis and Richard Freeman found that most of the growing dispersion in individual pay since the 1970s is associated with variations in pay between companies, not within them. In other words, the most profitable companies pay handsomely and people who work for them earn more than the rest.

This finding was confirmed in a more recent study by Nicholas Bloom and David Price, both of Stanford University, with others, which found that virtually all of the rise in income inequality is explained by a growing dispersion in average wages paid by firms. This finding, the authors conclude, holds across all industries, regions and firm sizes. One of the most striking implications is that inequality within firms has not changed much: the relationship between managers' and shop-floor workers' pay in each firm is still roughly the same. But the gap between what the average and the best firms pay their workers at all levels has widened. Alan Krueger, of Princeton University, illustrated this point nicely at a presentation he gave while working at the CEA in 2013. Using data from the decade after 2003, he showed that where managers are well paid, so are janitors (see the following chart).

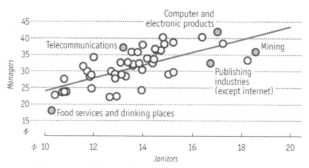

A rising tide floats all boats
US, average hourly wages by industry, 2003–2012, $, 2012 prices

Sources: US Census Bureau; US Bureau of Labour Statistics; Council of Economic Advisers

More power, more profit

This wider range of profits is likely to be related to increases in market power. Some of this is due to the rise of Internet giants, which dominate their respective markets thanks to network effects. But many of America's industries have also become more concentrated by a slow creep of acquisitions. A study by *The Economist* earlier this year divided the economy into 900-odd sectors covered by the five-yearly economic census and found that two-thirds of them were more concentrated in 2012 than they had been in 1997. The weighted average share of the total held by the leading four firms in each sector rose from 26% to 32%.

America used to be famous for its workers' willingness to follow the jobs, but they have become far less mobile. A paper by Raven Molloy and Christopher Smith of the Federal Reserve and Abigail Wozniak of the University of Notre Dame finds that over the past three decades migration rates between states have fallen by at least a third for most age groups. For those aged between 20 and 24, the most mobile group, the annual rate of internal migration fell from 5.7% in 1981–1989 to 3.3% in 2002–2012.

Many of the reasons put forward for this are not wholly convincing. It cannot be the rise of the two-income family, because the trend to less mobility holds for workers of all ages. Nor is it the housing boom and bust: the decline in mobility started long before that, in the early 1990s, and has continued since. It is certainly not trade unions (membership of which has declined), labour-market regulation or unemployment benefits, claims for which have dropped sharply.

A few researchers have made an intriguing link between the decline in labour mobility and the wider profit dispersion. The argument has several steps. The average age of established businesses has risen steadily because fewer new firms are formed. Startups have a high labour turnover, but in mature firms fewer people join and leave in any given year. The lower the churn rate of jobs, the fewer the opportunities for job-changers to find new work.

So it is possible that less dynamism in American business, characterised by industry concentration and lower job turnover, has reduced the incentive for job seekers to go and look for work in another state.

Another reason may be rent-seeking within the labour force itself. Another paper from the CEA finds that the share of America's workforce covered by state-licensing laws has risen to 25%, from less than 5% in the 1950s. Much of this red tape is unnecessary. On the most recent estimates, over 1,000 occupations are regulated in at least one state but only 60 are regulated in all states. The scope of the rules vary from state to state. A licensed security guard requires three years of training in Michigan but only around two weeks in most other states, for instance. Licensed workers can command higher pay than the unlicensed kind because entry to the occupation is restricted, so consumers have to pay more.

Success stories

For much of the past 40 years economic liberals have argued for the dismantling of barriers to the free flow of commerce, such as state monopolies, trade unions and restrictive practices. Such policies have produced some clear successes. In Britain the privatisation of monopoly utilities, such as British Telecom, and the opening up of other sectors to competition was a spur to productivity and innovation, leading to better and cheaper services for customers. In America the deregulation of airlines brought lower fares and an increase in the number of trips. Labour markets in America and Britain became more flexible, and unemployment has generally been lower than in continental Europe.

Deregulation is almost always a difficult task. Those whose interests are hurt by such reforms protest noisily. The political costs quickly become apparent, whereas the gains may not become clear before the next polling day. It is even harder to make changes when so many people feel that the cost of liberalising markets in the past was unfairly distributed. Critics of such liberalisation point to a decline in labour income as a share of GDP as evidence that wage earners have the odds stacked against them. They argue that blue-collar workers provide the flexibility, having to accept lower pay and less job security, whereas white-collar workers and bosses are protected. The increased openness to trade and the growing mobility of capital have made it harder for workers to push for pay rises, so they cling to the jobs they have. In an age of insecurity, it is hard to persuade anyone that they should give up such protections for the greater good.

Market power is supposed to be policed by competition agencies, but they have lost some of their vim, particularly in America, where competition cases are fought out in the courts. A landmark Supreme Court judgment in 2004 said monopoly profits were the just reward for innovation. That has made it harder for trustbusters to root out rent-seeking or block mergers. Most big firms got where they are by being good at what they do, not because of coddling by regulators. But if firms can hold onto their market share for years, they create distortions in the rest of the economy. Incumbent firms are powerful lobbyists.

Big tech firms also have a penchant for so-called "shootout" acquisitions, whereby a startup is bought to eliminate a budding rival. For many tech startups and their financiers, a buyout by one of the big platform companies is a badge of success. But if small firms cannot become independently big, the market power of incumbents is not sufficiently challenged.

Competition policy faces difficult questions in an age of superstar firms that dominate global markets. But the trickiest political problem for reformers is how to inject some dynamism into the economy without getting people even more worried about their livelihoods. Raising import tariffs or closing borders to people and capital is not the answer. Instead, policymakers should encourage more competition while putting in place adequate protections for those who lose out from it.

Words and Expressions

deregulation	n.	解除控制
lapse	n.	小错,过失
	vi.	时间流逝,合同终止
dearth	n.	缺乏,不足
a host of		许多,一大群
convict of		宣判(某人)犯有(某罪)
execution	n.	处决
ghostly	adj.	鬼似的,幽灵般的,鬼魂萦绕的
elude	vt.	逃避,躲避
be obsessed with		痴迷,着迷于,痴迷于,执着于
recapture	vt.	重温,重新捕获
pursuer	n.	追求者,追赶者,追捕者
propensity	n.	倾向,习性,癖好
pillar	n.	富有某种素质的人,某种素质的化身
pin sth on sb		使……承担……过失
hangover	n.	遗留的感觉,沿袭下来的风俗(或思想等)
kindling	n.	引火柴,引火物
on the run		失败,逃跑
brig	n.	(尤指军舰上的)禁闭室

Unit Six Globalization

alleged	adj.	声称的,所谓的,被断言的
intriguing	adj.	非常有趣的,引人入胜的,神秘的
incidence	n.	发生率,影响范围
villain	n.	(小说、戏剧等中的)主要反面人物,反派主角,坏人
CEA		(美国总统的)经济顾问委员会
budget director		预算主管
pull away		远离,疏远
median	adj.	中间值的,中间的
way	adv.	远远地,大大地
persistent	adj.	持续的,持久的
top dog		(尤指竞争中的)夺魁者,优胜者
percentile	n.	百分位(数)
skewed	adj.	偏的,斜的,歪的
distribution	n.	分配,分布
go a long way		对……大有帮助
dispersion	n.	离散,偏离(平均值)
variation	n.	变化,变更,变异
handsomely	adv.	(金额)相当大地,可观地
virtually	adv.	几乎,差不多,事实上,实际上
hold	vi.	正确,有效
striking	adj.	引人注目的,显著的
implication	n.	可能的影响(或作用、结果)
shop-floor	n.	生产车间
roughly	adv.	粗略地,大致上
illustrate	vt.	说明,解释
nicely	adv.	成功地,进展顺利地
presentation	n.	提交,演出,陈述,报告,展示会,介绍会,发布会
janitor	n.	看门人
range	n.	(变动或浮动的)范围,界限,区间
creep	n.	非常缓慢地行进,不知不觉产生,渐渐出现
odd	adv.	(紧接在数字后面)大约,略多
census	n.	人口普查,统计
weighted	adj.	加权的
two-income family		双收入家庭
bust	n.	破产,倒闭

unemployment benefit		失业救济,失业补贴(或津贴)
claim	n.	(尤指向公司、政府等)索款,索赔
turnover	n.	人事变更率,人员调整率
incentive	n.	激励,刺激,鼓励
licensing	v.	批准,许可,颁发执照
occupation	n.	职业,工作
security guard		保安人员,安全警卫
liberal	n.	自由主义者
dismantle	vt.	废除,取消,拆卸,拆开
privatisation	n.	私有化,非国有化(将国有企业转为民营企业)
monopoly	n.	垄断,专卖
spur	n.	马刺,激励因素
noisily	adv.	吵闹地,喧喧嚷嚷地
polling day		选举日
critic	n.	批评家,批评者
push for		急切、强烈地要求,为……奋力争取
cling to		坚持,保留
police	vt.	(委员会等)监督,管制
vim	n.	精力,生气
fight out		解决矛盾
trustbuster	n.	要求解散托拉斯的人,联邦反托拉斯检察官
root out		肃清,彻底根除
block	vt.	阻止,阻塞,限制
coddle	vt.	姑息,纵容,娇惯
hold onto		紧紧抓住,保持
distortion	n.	扭曲,歪曲,变形,失真
incumbent	adj.	在职的,现任的
lobbyist	n.	(对政府或委员会进行游说的)说客
penchant	n.	(强烈的)倾向,爱好,嗜好
shoot	vi.	萌芽
budding	adj.	初露头角的,正发芽的
rival	n.	对手,竞争者
buyout	n.	控制股权收购
tricky	adj.	难办的,难对付的,棘手的
livelihood	n.	生活,生计,谋生之道

Unit Six Globalization

Notes to the Text

1. economic rent:经济租金,是指从要素的所有收入中减去那部分不会影响要素总供给的要素收入的一部分,它类似于生产者剩余,等于要素收入和其机会成本之间的差额。

2. Barack Obama:贝拉克·侯赛因·奥巴马,美国民主党籍政治家,出生于1961年,第44任美国总统,为美国历史上第一位非裔美国总统。2017年1月20日正式卸任美国总统。

3. Princeton University:普林斯顿大学,简称"普林斯顿"(Princeton),成立于1746年,是世界著名私立研究型大学,位于美国新泽西州的普林斯顿市,是美国大学协会的14个始创院校之一,也是著名的常春藤八盟校的成员。

4. market power:市场势力,也被称为"市场权力",是指卖方(seller)或买方(buyer)不适当地影响商品价格的能力。对于卖方来说,市场势力也就是卖方的垄断倾向。它是指一个人(或一小群人)不适当地影响市场价格的能力。

5. *The Economist*:《经济学人》,是一份由伦敦《经济学人》报纸有限公司出版的杂志,于1843年9月由詹姆士·威尔逊创办。在杂志创刊之初,"经济主义"(economism)意思是"经济保守主义",但是今天该杂志无论是经济上还是政治上的立场都是倾向自由主义的,反对政府在经济和政治方面过度的介入。

6. weighted average:加权平均值,即将各数值乘以相应的权数,然后加总求和得到总体值,再除以总的单位数。

7. University of Notre Dame:圣母大学,又音译为"诺特丹大学",始建于19世纪中期,经历了一个多世纪的辉煌,享誉全美,是一所私立天主教大学、研究型大学,位于美国印第安纳州的南本德。

8. attrition rate/churn rate:顾客流失率,又被称为"客户流失率",是指顾客的流失数量与全部消费产品或服务顾客的数量的比例。它是顾客流失的定量表述,是判断顾客流失的主要指标,直接反映了企业经营与管理的现状。

9. rent seeking:寻租,又被称为"竞租",是指在没有从事生产的情况下,为垄断社会资源或维持垄断地位,从而得到垄断利润(亦即"经济租")所从事的一种非生产性寻利活动。政府运用行政权力对企业和个人的经济活动进行干预和管制,妨碍了市场竞争的作用,从而创造了少数有特权者取得超额收入的机会。根据美国经济学家J. 布坎南和A. 克鲁格的论述,这种超额收入被称为"租金"(rent),谋求这种特权以获得租金的活动,被称作"寻租活动",俗称"寻租"。寻租就是"寻求经济租金"的简称,是为了获得和维持垄断地位从而得到垄断利润(亦即"垄断租金")所从事的一种非生产性寻利活动。其整个寻租活动的全部经济损失要远远超过传统垄断理论中的"纯损"三角形。

10. State of Michigan:密歇根州,是美国的一个州,位于五大湖地区。这个州作为汽车工业的诞生地而闻名。密歇根州以制造业和农业为主,是全美和世界上最主要的汽车产地,也是美重要农业州之一。

11. BT（British Telecom）：英国电信集团,原为英国国营电信公用事业,由英国邮政总局管理,1981年10月1日脱离英国皇家邮政,变成独立的国营事业。在英国保守党撒切尔夫人执政下,1984年向市场出售50%公股,成为民营公司。该公司始终是全英最大电信设施硬件的营运者。英国电信在全球170个国家设有营业点或办事处。

Unit Seven

Enterprise Development Strategy

The Data: Where Long-Termism Pays Off

Dominic Barton, James Manyika and Sarah Keohane Williamson

May – June, 2017, *Harvard Business Review*

Dominic Barton *is the global managing partner of McKinsey & Company and a trustee of the Brookings Institution.* **James Manyika** *is a director of the McKinsey Global Institute.* **Sarah Keohane Williamson** *is the CEO of FCLT Global.*

Does short-termism destroy value? The question is increasingly debated by leaders in business, government, and academia. But little hard evidence has been presented on either side of the issue, in part because the phenomenon involves many complex factors and is hard to measure.

Seeking to quantify the effects of short-termism at the company level and to assess its cumulative impact on the nation's economy, we tracked data on 615 nonfinancial U.S. companies from 2001 to 2014 (representing 60% to 65% of total U.S. market cap). We used several standard metrics as proxies for long-term behavior, including the ratio of capital expenditures to depreciation (a measure of investment), accruals as a share of revenue (an indicator of earnings quality), and margin growth. To ensure valid results and avoid bias in our sample, we compared companies only to industry peers with similar opportunity sets and market conditions. Adjusting for company size and industry, we identified 167 companies (about 27% of the total set) that had a long-term orientation.

Then we examined how all 615 companies performed. The results were clear: As these graphs show, the long-term-focused companies surpassed their short-term-focused peers on several important financial measures and created significantly more jobs. They also delivered above-average returns to shareholders and had a 50% greater likelihood of being in the top quartile or decile at the end of the period we measured. (One caveat: We've uncovered a correlation between managing for the long-term and better financial performance; we haven't shown that such management caused that superior performance.)

What if all U. S. companies had taken a similarly long-term approach? Extrapolating from the differences above, we estimate that public equity markets could have added more than $1 trillion in asset value, increasing total U. S. market cap by about 4%. And companies could have created five million more jobs in the United States—unlocking as much as $1 trillion in additional GDP.

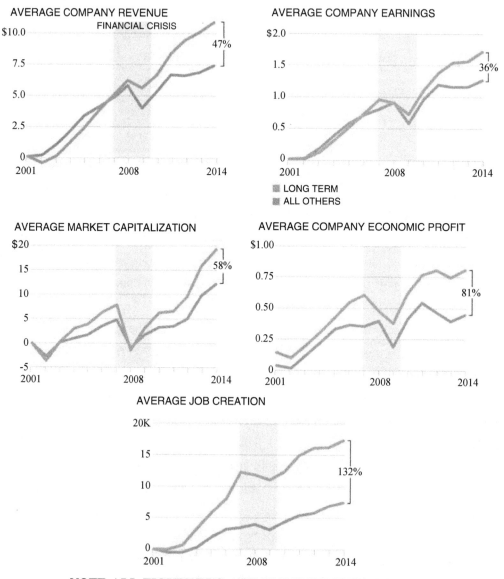

NOTE ALL FIGURES US $BILLIONS INDEXED TO 2001

Unit Seven Enterprise Development Strategy

 Words and Expressions

pay off		使得益,有报偿
trustee	n.	受托人
short-termism	n.	短期效益主义(只注重眼前利益)
academia	n.	学术界,学术环境
hard evidence		确凿的证据
cumulative	adj.	累积的,渐增的
market cap		市场总值,上市公司的股票市值总合
metric	n.	度量标准
proxy	n.	(测算用的)代替物,指标
depreciation	n.	(资产等)折旧,货币贬值
indicator	n.	指示信号,标志
margin	n.	利润,盈余
industry peer		业界同行
adjust for		考虑到
likelihood	n.	可能,可能性
quartile	n.	四分位数
decile	n.	十分位数
caveat	n.	附加说明,事先声明,警告
extrapolate	v.	(由已知资料对未知事实或价值)推算,推断
unlock	vt.	释放(潜能)

 Notes to the Text

1. Brookings Institution:布鲁金斯学会,美国著名智库之一,是华盛顿学术界的主流思想库之一,其规模之大、历史之久远、研究之深入,被称为美国"最有影响力的思想库"并不为过。布鲁金斯学会总部在美国首都华盛顿,是一家研究公共政策的非营利组织。

2. CAPEX (Capital Expenditure):资本性支出,一般是指资金或固定资产、无形资产、递延资产的投入。这类资产在使用过程中会持续多个计费期间,需要在使用过程中将其资本化,并分期将成本转为费用,如固定资产的折旧、无形资产、递延资产的摊销等。对电信运营商来说,网络设备、计算机、仪器等一次性支出的都属于 CAPEX。

3. opportunity set:机会集合,是指在预算约束和时间约束下经济个人所能够做出的选择的集合,即那些在实际中可行的全部选择所构成的集合。对于经济个体的决策而言,只有在处于机会集合内的那些选择行为才是切实可行的,而处于机会集合外的选择都是不可行的。就个人或者厂商而言,对任何选择进行经济分析的第一步是找出什么是可能的,即所谓"机会集合",也是一组实际存在的不同选择办法。在做选择和决定的时候,只有机会集合内的选择才有意义。

Why High Potentials Struggle and How They Can Grow through It

Jennifer Petrieglieri & Gianpiero Petriegliei

May – June, 2017, *Harvard Business Review*

Jennifer Petrieglieri is an assistant professor of organizational behavior at INSEAD. Gianpiero Petrieglieri is an associate professor of organizational behavior at INSEAD. Both teach in the INSEAD MBA program and direct the Management Acceleration Program for emerging leaders along with experiential leadership-development workshops for global corporations.

In Brief

The Problem

When people are groomed as future leaders, they often feel trapped by others' expectations and fixate on proving themselves worthy. Sometimes they end up blandly conforming to their organization's established leadership ideal and losing their edge. Sometimes they leave altogether, depriving themselves of an opportunity and the organization of their talent.

The Remedy

High potentials struggle with this "talent curse" again and again as they take on new roles and challenges. But they can grow from the experience by accepting the help they need to thrive, bringing all facets of themselves to the job (not just those that say "leadership material"), and treating the present like a final destination.

There were many late nights during Thomas's time at a private equity firm, but two of them really stand out. On the first, he was at a bar. Earlier in the day, his boss had let him know that he was the top performer in his cohort. Over drinks that evening, he struck up a conversation with a partner at a rival firm. "You're the guy who closed two deals in six months, aren't you?" the man asked. It was a moment Thomas had dreamed of and worked for since leaving his small town for college, the first in his family, years before.

On the second, he was at his desk, working on a high-profile IPO. He was the only associate on the deal—the kind of assignment reserved for top talent on the firm's fast track to partnership. Dawn was breaking, and he had no memory of the past six hours, even though his e-mail and phone logs chronicled a busy all-nighter. A neurologist later ran some tests and warned him of the dangers of sleep deprivation. "I would go to bed at five, wake up at seven with palpitations, and go to work," Thomas recalled. "I never stopped to think that it was wrong. It's how it works, I told myself. Everyone does it."

Thomas slowed down briefly after the doctor's warning but soon came back full throttle. His talent and drive were intact, though somehow he'd lost his sense of purpose. He created an opportunity for the firm to do a $1.3 billion deal, and then surprised his bosses by suddenly quitting. His performance was strong and his prospects bright as ever, but as he put it when we spoke, he had fallen victim to a vicious cycle: "I did not want to step off the fast track, so I could not slow down." Thomas felt trapped by his firm's expectations, but his desire to prove deserving of his bosses' endorsement kept him from challenging the culture or asking for support. He felt both overwhelmed and underutilized, and concluded that this firm was not the right place to realize his leadership ambitions.

In our two decades of studying and working with "future leaders" like Thomas, we've met many people who struggle with what appears to be their good fortune. In most cases, these managers and professionals have been accurately identified as star performers and fast learners. But often, placement on a fast track doesn't speed up their growth as leaders in the organization, as it's meant to do. Instead, it either pushes them out the door or slows them down—thwarting their development, decreasing their engagement, and hurting their performance.

In an age when companies wage wars for talent, it is hard to acknowledge that for some people, being recognized as talented turns out to be a curse. But it does. Aspiring leaders work hard to live up to others' expectations, and so the qualities that made them special to begin with—those that helped them excel and feel engaged—tend to get buried. They behave more like everyone else, which saps their energy and ambition. They may start simply going through the motions at work—or, like Thomas, look for an escape hatch.

This curse strikes the talented even in companies that invest heavily in their development—places where executives are sincerely dedicated to helping people thrive. We began to notice it long ago, when one of us (Jennifer) worked in various multinationals and the other (Gianpiero) practiced as a psychotherapist in a global MBA program. Since then, we've studied hundreds of managers and professionals from various sectors and parts of the world—many of whom we have followed over time—and met thousands more in our teaching, consulting, and coaching engagements. Through that work with high potentials, we've examined talent development from their perspective and identified common psychological dynamics, signs of trouble, and ways of breaking the curse.

THE PSYCHOLOGY BEHIND THE CURSE

Often, the curse begins when an organization gives an employee a platform to hone his or her skills in hopes of earning some reward, such as partnership, a senior leadership position, or just a broader range of career options. Although that person is lattered and grateful at first, a resentful angst eventually sets in—a feeling that's difficult to explain or justify. It's not garden-variety uncertainty, which you'd expect of anyone facing new challenges; the roots reach much deeper, into the self.

Two psychological mechanisms, idealization and identification, turn out to be a destructive combination for high potentials. Others idealize their talent as a defense against the company's uncertain future, and then the high potentials identify with that image, shouldering the uncertainty themselves. That's what happened to Thomas. After his early successes brokering deals, his bosses and colleagues began to see him as a rainmaker the firm could rely on in the volatile PE world. The combination of idealization and identification is evident in many workplaces where people praise the promise of the talented, and the talented feel the burden of their promise. If the future isn't as bright as everyone hoped, it will be them who have failed.

As their talent increasingly defines them, high potentials sense that their own future is at stake too. They fixate on what they should do to ensure their place in the organization. Though these expectations might be amplified in their minds, they aren't simply self-imposed. They're spelled out in lists of company values and competencies, which up-and-coming leaders are meant to model, and reinforced through performance feedback and informal interactions.

Lars, a rising star at a manufacturing company, explained it like this at a leadership workshop: "One day I'm told that those like me must transform the way we do business; the next day, I must make sure that the executives whose business I must transform appreciate me."

We often hear this sort of thing. In companies whose executives want strong cultures and rapid change, talented managers feel pressured both to be revolutionaries and to win the establishment's approval. The inherent tension between those pursuits wears people down. Their sensitivity to cultural and political cues—part of the reason they've been lagged as future leaders—makes them especially vulnerable once they're on that track.

Every opportunity becomes an obligation; every challenge, a test. The high potential strives to be a perfect manager, now suppressing the very talents—the passions and idiosyncrasies—that made her stand out in the first place. And so the curse twists talent management against its intent. Rather than empowering those who deserve to lead, it increases their insecurity and pushes them to conform, like a protection racket of sorts—a company's costly demands in exchange for safety from the threats that working there presents. "Future leader" becomes a synonym for "exceptional follower".

THREE SIGNS OF TROUBLE

You must have high standards for yourself and be ready for extra scrutiny—no aspiring leader can ignore others' expectations. But you can shine only so long under the spotlight of opportunity and the magnifying glass of expectations before burning out—unless you put some protections in place. That requires learning to spot and deal with three signs of trouble.

1. A shift from simply using your talent to proving it

After being placed in a high-potential pool, you may find that your excitement about the recognition soon fades, whereas the new expectations create ongoing pressure. That's what typically happens. Caught between the acknowledgment of their past achievements and the possibility of future opportunities, aspiring leaders often view the present as a time to prove that they deserve both. In an effort to ensure that they fulfill their promise, they become more calculating about where and how they apply themselves.

Companies with a formal high-potential track aren't the only places where this happens. In some organizations, senior executives just take an interest in certain employees, and things snowball from there. Take Laura, who left halfway through a PhD program in artificial intelligence to try her hand in the business world. Laura joined a consultancy and then moved on to a role in the strategy function of a consumer goods company. About a year into that new job, her boss's boss recognized her skills in data analytics. So he brokered an introduction that led Laura into a role managing digital marketing for one of the company's floundering products.

"It was as if everything came together in that moment," Laura told us. Her understanding of data analytics and her experience in business strategy made her a great woman for the job. All she had to do now was delivery. Succeeding in her new role, the hiring executive assured her, would "open every door in this industry". The pressure was on.

Laura then fell into a spiral of overwork, anxious to show others—and herself—that she could handle the challenge. Although sales grew, she felt that no one noticed her dedication and results. Perhaps, she thought, her work wasn't impressive enough. "I feared that people were nice to me," she said, "but didn't have the guts to tell me that maybe I had plateaued, that my time was up." This was hardly what others thought. Accustomed to her competent and composed demeanor, her bosses and colleagues assumed that she needed little help. And they were more than happy to let her carry on, praising her independence and initiative without realizing the struggle beneath both.

In her seminal research, Stanford psychologist Carol Dweck has drawn a distinction between a performance orientation and a learning orientation. When children believe that their intelligence is a fixed quantity, she found, they tend to become easily discouraged by tough school assignments and give up quickly on the problems they cannot easily solve. Children who sense that their intelligence is malleable, conversely, stay on those problems longer, seeing them as a way to keep improving. Those with a performance orientation are embarrassed by failure, whereas those with a learning orientation are spurred on by it—they work harder. The same is true for adults at work, Dweck found.

The amplified expectations that high potentials internalize are a classic circumstance that, Dweck's research predicts, will elicit a performance orientation. Though Laura and many others we have studied didn't give up on hard challenges or stop striving to develop their skills, their learning itself became a performance of sorts—a way of affirming their talent. As a result, extra experiments and side projects—which could further expand their skills but also reveal their laws—began to feel like risks they could not afford.

This is how special people become ordinary. After being placed on the partnership track at a global firm, one consultant recalled, "I knew I could succeed, so I focused on where I knew my talents shone. It was great in the short term, but over time I began to lose my edge."

The pressure is even stronger for minorities, who may also feel obligated to serve as role models and advocates for those whose talent often goes unseen. Consider how a female junior partner in a male-dominated elite law firm changed her mindset after finding out she was in the running to become an equity partner. "I have no doubt that I deserve a place at the table," she told us, "but I feel totally paralyzed. I am being very conservative because I feel that if I fail at anything, I will let everyone down." She knew she was a role model for other women, which raised the stakes even more. Rather than expand her expertise, she stuck to areas where she knew she would perform well and to clients with whom she had established relationships. When she was not able to bring in the number of new clients expected from an equity partner, her career progress slowed.

2. A preoccupation with image despite a yearning for authenticity

An investment banker who ended up leaving his firm told us, "I was always in the spotlight, always performing, always trying to be the leader they expected me to be." Though he had worked very hard to get to that visible position, once on the fast track, he felt strangely invisible. It was as if the firm had hijacked his identity along with his ambition. As he put it, "No one saw the real me."

The preoccupation with image is a natural consequence of the pressure to prove one's talent—and it's a common problem, our INSEAD colleague Herminia Ibarra has found in her research on leadership transitions. At most firms, the promise of future leadership is bestowed on those who conform to the desired organizational culture—the values and vision established by those at the top. So while many companies invite employees to "bring themselves" to work, people on a high-potential track often bring only those aspects that say "leadership material"—and this makes them feel inauthentic.

This isn't a problem just for those uncomfortable with "faking it" until they acquire new leadership skills—which, as Ibarra argues, can actually help people discover new facets of themselves. It can also happen to people who take on roles that seem like a natural it. Laura, the data scientist, could easily put forward the problem-solving, data-driven self that her company valued. But there was more to her than that. No matter how fitting the role, when people continually display just one aspect of themselves, it flattens and limits them. That happened to Laura. By being true to just part of her identity—on demand—she lost her sense of ownership and spontaneity.

Like many others caught in this position, Laura considered leaving and fantasized about getting a job where she would be "free to be myself". In one study we conducted with CEIBS professor Jack Wood, in which we followed a cohort of MBAs for a year, nearly half the participants said that they sought a similar escape. They hoped business school would provide a retreat—a space where they could discover and recover who they really were.

In her classic research, psychologist Alice Miller examined what she provocatively labeled "the drama of the gifted child". She described how inquisitive and intelligent children often learn to hide their feelings and needs to meet their doting parents' expectations. They do this so well that over time they no longer know what they feel and need. The sense of emptiness and alienation that Miller chronicled resembles what we have encountered among high-potential managers: Paradoxically, being recognized as talented robs them of their talents. Their talents still exist but are no longer their own; they belong to a distant and demanding organizational "parent".

3. Postponement of meaningful work

When people feel trapped by their organization's expectations and anticipate great rewards for enduring that captivity with dignity, the present loses meaning for them. They begin to locate their dreams for recovering and expressing themselves in the future—when they will finally, they hope, be free to say what they mean, relate to others openly, fulfill their true calling, and lead as they have wanted to all along.

Some just wait for the numbness to dissipate. Others harbor flourishing images of what they will do once they've quit the rat race—goals they share with only a few trusted friends for fear that those dreams, too, might be hijacked. This amounts to what Jungian analyst H. G. Baynes labeled, long ago, the "neurosis of the provisional life": While developing leaders view their current work as instrumental to future opportunities, they imagine that their future work will be much more meaningful. Who they will be becomes more important than who they are. The present loses value, so they stop giving their best.

By the time the engaged self escapes to the future, the talent curse has taken hold. While the high potential might appear immersed in her work, she is sealed off from it. And if she continues to view her present work as empty, not even leaving the organization will help. In the study we mentioned earlier, people who had begun an MBA program in search of a retreat found themselves caught in the same spiral of striving to meet expectations that they resented, and dreaming of other escapes. "Every day I woke up and wanted to leave," one participant recalled. "I wanted to go and tell no one."

Another explained how he began to second-guess his past choices. "When I finished my undergraduate degree," he recalled, "I got arguably the most enviable job in my class, and of course I took it. It was the prestigious thing to do. I never really sat back and thought, Do I really want to do this?" He was hoping to transition out—somehow. He didn't know where he'd go, but he imagined that almost any option must be better than where he was.

When Laura told us her story, she talked about maybe returning to finish her PhD—immediately after wondering if she could be a COO one day. It was as if the thought of another step in her career progression demanded a counterthought of escape, a way out for the self from a job she excelled at and an organization that valued her work.

BREAKING THE TALENT CURSE

Though the curse can hamper the personal growth, engagement and career progress of the most gifted high potentials, it can be broken. We recommend three steps:

1. Own your talent—don't be possessed by it

Once your talent becomes your identity, every challenge to it (there will be plenty if you are stretching to learn) feels like a challenge to the self. As Laura put it when one peer questioned her ability, "It struck me to my core." Slavishly bowing to everyone's expectations, including your own, is no solution; you'll just become a follower of what you believe others want. Nor is ignoring those expectations; at best, you will be seen as a rebel. Instead, remain mindful of what you need and what others want—without allowing either to consume you.

Striking that balance often involves learning how to accept help, even when you don't think you need it, rather than going it alone. This is something that Michael Sanson, an executive coach at INSEAD, emphasizes with his clients. "A key shift occurs," he says, "when a high potential realizes that his or her role is not to deliver more than others, but to deliver more with others." People sometimes resist feedback and coaching, he explains, because they view both as vehicles for more expectations. When they begin to see the input not as judgment but as a source of support, they become great listeners and fast learners—which helps them perform better and grow as leaders.

2. Bring your whole self, not just your best self, to work

It's tempting to show only the shiny, polished facets of ourselves—especially when we value them and others appreciate them. But our greatest talents often spring from wounds and quirks, from the rougher, less conformist sides of ourselves. Much resolve lows from restlessness, creativity from angst, and resilience from having faced challenges we'd rather not share. Managers who are empathetic (and thus great with people) sometimes get overwhelmed by emotions. Don't fight these darker sources of your talent. Learn to channel them.

The last time we spoke to Thomas, the former private equity associate, he was transitioning into the field of talent management. He brought his business acumen to it, but also a deep personal understanding of how organizations can boost or hinder employees' growth, and vice versa. His firsthand struggle to develop and thrive at his old firm gave him insight that allowed him to help others develop and thrive. He was no longer just gifted. He was purposeful and revitalized.

3. Value the present

This is the most important step in breaking the curse. Ask yourself: What if this is it? What if my current work is not a stepping-stone, but a destination? You must invest in the work you're doing now—make it matter—in order to grow from the experience. Look at the expectations, the pressures, and the doubts you face as challenges that all leaders face. They aren't tests for leadership; they are features of leading. They won't go away once you prove yourself worthy—they'll only intensify. So now is the time to muster the resources you'll need to manage them over the long run. And accept that even with plenty of resources, leading will always require courage. As Mette Stuhr, a former head of talent management at a multinational corporation who has taught and coached scores of high potentials all over the world, puts it: "If you wait for it to be safe to speak up, you never will."

A RITE OF PASSAGE

For all the pain it causes and the risks it entails, the talent curse is a rite of passage. Breaking the curse is an important part of learning how to lead. And it's an ongoing process—high potentials must do this again and again as they grow into new roles.

Let's return to Laura's example: During a team retreat, she finally took the plunge and confessed that she was thinking about leaving. In a well-rehearsed argument, she explained how the structure of her department was creating friction between her and two peers. Much to her surprise, what she thought might become a farewell speech was very well received. Voicing her concerns paid of. The structure changed. She stayed.

Soon after that, Laura was offered a bigger role leading a team of five managers, with 52 people below them. She felt energized at first, because she could have an impact on the whole company. But then new doubts started gnawing at her—and again, she asked for no support. Six months into the new role, she had not yet negotiated her package. "I got a great job," she said. "What would they think if I worried about the contract, the salary, and things like that?" Upholding her image as a passionate go-getter prevented her from making arrangements to succeed. "I have not yet proved myself," she said. "How can I ask for more? I should be grateful."

Once more, an opportunity turned into a burden, and Laura became sad and frustrated. Neither her boss nor her organization had intended any of this. They had been happy to give a stretch assignment to an ambitious and responsible young manager. They did not maliciously withdraw support, but they didn't encourage her to seek it, either. They never invited her to take it a little easier or told her that she shouldn't expect to get everything right. And so they reinforced her modus operandi.

That brings us to our final point: Organizations should do their part to break the curse too. They should stop referring to talented young managers as "future leaders", since it encourages bland conformity, risk-averse thinking, and stilted behavior. They should stop offering responsibility in the present with the promise of authority later on. And they should allow people room to deviate from the image of leadership that others have drawn. That will ease the pressure for managers to prove their talent, freeing them to simply use it—to engage with their work and grow into better leaders.

The best way to develop leaders, in the end, is to help them lead. The best way to learn to lead is to accept that help in the end here and now.

Words and Expressions

assistant professor	助理教授（级别高于讲师而低于副教授）
INSEAD	欧洲工商管理学院
associate professor	副教授

Unit Seven Enterprise Development Strategy

MBA (Master of Business Administration)		工商管理学硕士
cohort	n.	(尤指作为研究对象的相同年龄、社会阶层等的)一批人,一群人(术语),同伙,支持者(含贬义)
close the deal		完成交易,达成协议
chronicle	vt.	将(一系列事件)载入编年史,按时序记载
	n.	编年史,年代记
neurologist	n.	神经病学家,神经科医生
sleep deprivation		睡眠剥夺
palpitation	n.	心悸
full throttle		加足马力,全速
intact	adj.	(不可用于名词前)完好无损的
vicious cycle		恶性循环
endorsement	n.	(公开的)赞同,支持,认可,宣传,代言,(支票、汇票等)背书
thwart	v.	阻挠,阻碍
sap	vt.	(逐渐)削弱,消耗(尤指力量或决心)
	n.	(植物的)液,(非正式)傻瓜,容易上当的人
escape hatch		逃生出口,安全舱口
psychotherapist	n.	精神治疗医师
hone	vt.	磨炼,训练,提高(技艺),磨(刀、剑等)
angst	n.	焦虑不安,烦恼
rainmaker	n.	(通过商定交易吸引客户或资金为公司获利的)商界能人,求雨法师,(运用科学方法的)人工造雨者
idiosyncrasy	n.	(个人特有的)习性,癖好,(某物的)异质,特点
scrutiny	n.	仔细的审视,彻底的检查
snowball	vi.	(计划、问题、生意等)滚雪球似的迅速增大
	n.	雪球
artificial intelligence		人工智能
broker	v.	(国家或政府作为中间人)协调,安排
	n.	(为别人买卖股票或外汇的)经纪人,(为别人安排交易的)经纪人,掮客
plateau	vi.	达到稳定时期(阶段),达到并保持稳定增长
	n.	高原,平稳时期,(尤指某物增长后的)稳定期
malleable	adj.	有展延性的,可锻(压、拉)的,易受影响的,易改变的,可塑的

paralyze	vt.	使不能正常运作,使陷入瘫痪,使瘫痪,使麻痹
expertise	n.	专门技能(知识)
preoccupation	n.	全神贯注,使人全神贯注的事物
yearning	n.	渴望,向往
hijack	vt.	劫持(飞机、车辆或船),控制,操纵
	n.	劫持事件
conform to		符合,遵照
facet	n.	(性格、情况等的)方面
spontaneity	n.	自发性,自然
CEIBS (China Europe International Business School)		上海中欧管理学院
provocative	adj.	(行为、话语等)使人生气的,挑衅的,煽动的,引起争论的,(衣服、动作、图片等)挑逗性的
inquisitive	adj.	过分好奇的,爱打听的,好追根究底的,好问的
dissipate	vt.	(使)(某事物)消散,消失,浪费(时间),挥霍(金钱),耗费(精力)
the rat race		(大城市里的)永无休止的激烈竞争,你死我活的竞争
neurosis	n.	神经(官能)症,过分的恐惧(或焦虑)
COO (Chief Operating Officer)		首席运营官
quirk	n.	怪异性格(或行为),怪癖,(尤指偶发的)怪事,奇事
resilience	n.	恢复力,复原力,适应力,弹性
acumen	n.	敏锐,聪明,机智
vice versa		反之亦然
stepping-stone	n.	(过小溪用的)踏脚石,成功的途径,进身之阶,敲门砖
take the plunge		冒险一试
gnaw	vt.	咬,啃,使烦恼,折磨
stretch assignment		延展性任务(指派员工做一些可以让他们自我挑战,并且超越以前工作的任务来延展能力)
maliciously	adv.	怀有恶意地,恶毒地
modus operandi		(from Latin, formal)(abbr. MO)做法
risk-averse thinking		规避风险的想法
stilted	adj.	(文体、言谈)呆板的,生硬的,不自然的

Unit Seven Enterprise Development Strategy

Notes to the Text

1. INSEAD:欧洲工商管理学院,是一所营利性商学院,在欧洲(法国枫丹白露)、亚洲(新加坡)和中东(阿布扎比)设有分校。欧洲工商管理学院一直是世界上最好的商学院之一,在2016年和2017年的所有全日制MBA课程中排名第一,在2018年排名第二。欧洲工商管理学院提供全日制工商管理硕士(MBA)课程、高级管理人员工商管理硕士(EMBA)课程、金融硕士课程、管理博士课程和各种高管教育课程。

2. IPO:首次公开募股,是一种公开发行的方式,其中一家公司的股票出售给机构投资者,通常也出售给散户(个人)投资者;IPO由一家或多家投资银行承销,投资银行还安排在一家或多家证券交易所上市。通过这一过程,俗称"浮动"或"上市",一家私营公司转变为一家上市公司。首次公开募股可用于:为有关公司筹集新的股本;将公司创始人或私人股本投资者等私人股东的投资货币化;通过成为公开交易的企业,使现有持有的股份或未来的资本易于交易。

Don't Try to Protect The Past

A Conversation with IBM CEO Ginni Rometty by Adi Ignatius
(January 2012 Ginni Rometty becomes CEO)
July – August, 2017, *Harvard Business Review*

When Virginia Ginni Rometty became the CEO of IBM, in early 2012, she dutifully adopted her predecessor's strategy. Sam Palmisano, who held the position for a decade, had vowed in 2010 that IBM would roughly double its per-share earnings within five years. Two-plus years into her tenure, Rometty concluded that trying to meet that goal would end up crippling IBM's efforts to reinvent itself. She abandoned the plan in October 2014, thereby taking full ownership of the company's future strategy and financial health. It's been an interesting ride ever since. Rometty, 59, is on a protracted mission to make IBM a cloud-based "solutions" business. She has invested billions in advanced technologies while selling off legacy divisions that don't fit the new model.

IBM is still hugely profitable, with net income in 2016 of $13.0 billion on revenue of $79.9 billion. But it's also still a work in progress. Amid the transformation, the company has suffered 20 consecutive quarters of falling revenue. Rometty says the decline is due primarily to her selling off legacy businesses and to unavoidable currency hits. Moreover, she says, moving to new, higher-margin businesses requires some short-term pain. "My job is to build an IBM that's durable," she says.

So far her board has been supportive. Despite the shrinking revenue, it recently raised Rometty's pay package to $33 million, making her the eighth-highest-paid CEO in the United States. The question is whether investors will remain as patient. In May, IBM's biggest shareholder, Warren Buffett, said he had dumped about 30% of his holdings, noting that the company faces "some pretty tough competitors". Rometty, who also serves as IBM's chairman and president, seems undaunted. She says IBM's ability to change is "in its DNA". She should know. She has spent 36 years at the company and earned her stripes developing IBM's business-services division and leading the successful purchase and integration of PwC Consulting.

Now she is betting the farm largely on Watson, IBM's artificial intelligence platform. Watson debuted in 2011, when it took on two former champions of the TV quiz show *Jeopardy*! Watson won, demonstrating just how far machine learning had come. IBM commercialized Watson two years later, and its big brain now does everything from advising doctors on cancer treatment to predicting the weather.

Rometty met with HBR in her office at IBM's leafy headquarters in Armonk, New York.

HBR: You've been running IBM for more than five years now, overseeing big changes. Do you view this process as a turnaround?

ROMETTY: I wouldn't use that term. This is a transformation. We're a 106-year-old technology company, and we're the only tech company that has moved from one era to the next. When you're in tech, you have to transform.

How much transformation can your employees and investors handle? When will you be able to declare that you've made it to the other side?

That's a good question. Let me answer in a couple of ways. First, you need to be clear about what you are transforming to. For us, it's all about data, and we have a very clear view of what our enterprise clients will need. When people talk about data, they often mean things that are searchable via public search engines. But that's only 20% of the data in the world. What we're trying to unlock is the 80% that's behind everyone's firewalls, because that's where the value is. Everybody has tons of data; they just can't make use of it. Our belief is that you'll make better decisions if you can unlock that data and that there's a $2 trillion market around better decision making. That's the market we are going after.

How do you know you're on the right strategic path? And are you making changes as you go?

Oh, goodness, have I made changes! It's important to have deeply held beliefs about the vision. But then you have to look at the results. I'm confident about where we are at this point. Our new businesses around cloud, data, and security add up to almost $34 billion in revenue. They're growing at 13% to 14% a year and make up 42% of the company. Watson, our artificial intelligence platform, will touch one billion people by the end of this year. I consider these numbers proof that we're on the right track.

Yet you've had 20 consecutive quarters of revenue decline.

Yes, but that includes divestitures and the strong U.S. dollar. Currency is responsible for $14 billion of that decline. And I divested $8 billion to $9 billion worth of revenue sources. So that is the bulk of it.

However you account for it, is this extended revenue slide part of the plan? Or is it a disappointment?

What's positive is that the plan is proceeding as we believe it should, with the growth of large new businesses that are adjacent to our core franchises. IBM will grow again. But we need to grow in the right ways. We're moving into areas that have value and shedding ones that don't. We could have higher growth rates, but we made a bold decision to divest commoditizing businesses before they commoditize further. The new areas are higher margin, but we have to invest in them and then scale them up.

Warren Buffett just sold a big chunk of his IBM holdings. Does he not get it?

I never talk about our shareholders; they can speak for themselves. But our clients vote through their use of our offerings, and they are showing that we're on the right track. H&R Block, for example, took Watson for the tax season to assist its professionals in handling millions of customers. The company gained market share and had an unbelievable Net Promoter Score.

ONGOING TRANSFORMATION

IBM's former CEO Lou Gerstner came from the outside and pretty much wrote the playbook on how to transform a company. Is it harder to accomplish something like that when you've already been at the company for a few decades?

I don't think it's any harder. I really believe the company has in its DNA the ability to change. We've done it over and over again. And Lou would agree that this is a more extensive transformation because of the convergence of multiple trends that are accelerating the pace of change. It doesn't matter if you're an insider so long as you don't try to protect the past. Then you have the freedom to reinvent yourself for the long term.

What's the hardest thing about trying to take this transformation through to the other side?

You have to have passion. And you have to have clarity. But I think the most difficult thing is perseverance. This is a large, highly profitable company that continues to do mission-critical work serving clients around the world—and at the same time reinventing itself. As the familiar metaphor has it, that's like changing the wheels while you're driving. And we're doing it all in the public eye. Above all, we need to stay focused on our clients and keep moving forward. I think the team has done a super job at this.

Do you feel pressure to get this done quickly?

Sure we do. Every leader wants things to go faster. You have to set the bar high and keep moving faster. But my job is to build an IBM that's durable for a whole era. We take seriously our ongoing responsibility to the clients that run our systems today, to make their work more productive. Supporting those clients takes my revenue down, but I'm proud of it: We run the world's systems. Without IBM, banks couldn't operate. Railroads couldn't move. Airlines couldn't fly.

Don't you worry that advances in cloud-based computing and data analytics could commoditize some of your new areas of growth?

I don't. Our analytics business is worth more than $19 billion. So there's no problem there. The cloud is accretive to our services business, which makes up 60% of IBM. And the cloud works in a standardized way, which means the margins can be higher. Most important, we believe that the basis of competitive advantage in the future will be data. As I've said before, data is the next natural resource. Think of oil. Where it sits is not necessarily where the wealth is. The wealth goes to whoever can refine it, process it, and turn it into something else.

How is transformation affecting your processes and your people?

For starters, we've adopted "design thinking" in our offices around the world. The goal is to make our B2B products as consumerish as possible in terms of ease, feel, simplicity. Then, to increase our speed, we've adopted agile work flows in every part of the company. And we've changed the tools we use, forming partnerships with Box, Apple, Slack, and others. We now have probably one of the most modern work environments in the world. And we're doing this with a workforce of 380,000 people.

What's the plan for your core businesses?

Our new businesses have been built of our core franchises and couldn't have grown to the size they are without them. That said, the core businesses are not necessarily in growth markets. So we need to continually reinvent them. One example is our Global Business Services. We've been transitioning to digital, but it takes time, because it's a people business. Although areas like that aren't big growth markets, they are big cash producers, and they do mission-critical work for our clients.

BUILDING THE RIGHT TEAM

In a fast-paced environment like this, how do you construct the right management team?

I've brought in five direct reports from the outside, because you need people who really understand how the new systems work. About 15% of IBM's managers up and down the company came from the outside. That adds up to a lot of people when you consider our size. We've spent $2 billion in the past three years on training in new methods and approaches and on the new areas we've gone into, such as Watson Health, where we now have hundreds of doctors and nurses. With Watson we are also exploring creativity and music, and we've been hiring musicians. A new spectrum of career types are part of IBM now.

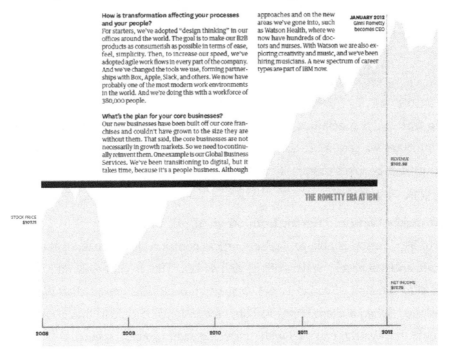

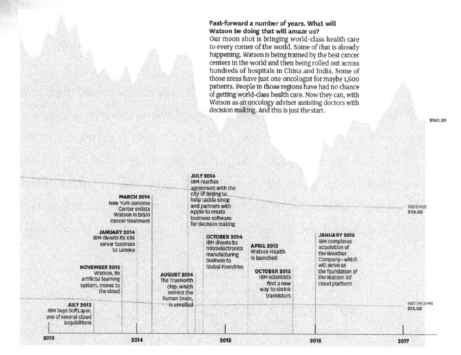

Aside from such specialties, what are the attributes you look for in new hires?

The attributes we care most about are intelligence and adaptability. Our own Watson is helping us predict people's propensity to learn.

WATSON'S ROLE

What makes Watson different from other AI platforms?

First of all, Watson is able to deal in vertical domains. It understands the languages of medicine, financial services, underwriting, and so on. That is extremely difficult to achieve, and it's a differentiation. Second is our business model: We ensure that Watson protects clients' insights. When a client brings its data, the insights go only to that client. Third is the range of data that Watson can deal with, including sight, sound, speech.

What does all this look like in practice?

Think about a conversation. Generally, people miss about 5% of the words. Watson is at 5.5%. That makes it number one in the field. It can also sense motion; the Watson Internet of Things group has developed for customers applications such as cognitive ball bearings, which use sensors to record work-process data. And Watson can "see". In analyzing melanoma, for example, Watson achieves 95% accuracy. Try to do this task with other systems, and at best they'll score 50/50.

Fast-forward a number of years. What will Watson be doing that will amaze us?

Our moon shot is bringing world-class health care to every corner of the world. Some of that is already happening. Watson is being trained by the best cancer centers in the world and then being rolled out across hundreds of hospitals in China and India. Some of those areas have just one oncologist for maybe 1,600 patients. People in those regions have had no chance of getting world-class health care. Now they can, with Watson as an oncology adviser assisting doctors with decision making. And this is just the start.

Do you worry that Watson and other AI programs will wipe out entire categories of jobs?

There will be an impact, of course. But in many cases AI will automate only parts of jobs, meaning people can do the rest of their jobs better. Over the years, I've watched professionals—chemists, researchers, doctors, financial analysts—say, "Uh-oh, I'm going to be replaced." And eventually they end up saying, "I can't do my job without this technology." That's what always happens when there's a dislocation in technology: We learn what it is that man innately does better.

To what extent is IBM trying to write the rules of human-AI interaction?

We're leaders in the field, and we will have influence over these technologies. In January we published our "Principles for the Cognitive Era". There are three tenets. The first is *purpose*: We believe that "cognitive" will augment humans and extend what they do, not replace them. The second is *transparency*: We need to be able to tell people not just how and when our technologies are being used, but also how they were trained and by whom. If you're sick and Watson is assisting your doctor, you want to know that it was trained by the 20 best cancer centers in the world. The third is about *skills*: We need to help prepare a whole new cadre to live in this world. We're working with 50,000 kids in 100 high schools to help build these skills.

ENGAGING ON THE ISSUES

You've decided to engage with the Trump administration, even though some of your employees oppose that. What have you learned from trying to navigate the new political era?

I wrote a letter to employees noting that IBM CEOs have interacted with every president since Woodrow Wilson. My view is that you have to be engaged on the issues that matter so that you can have influence. You need a seat at the table to advocate for what's really important to your company—and to the world. But we stand up for policies and positions, not for politics. In fact, we're one of the few companies in our industry that don't make political contributions.

Let's talk about gender. Some female executives like talking about gender issues, and some don't, preferring to be judged solely on their records. Where do you come down?

In the past I would have said I wasn't interested in the topic. I would rather have people just look at me for what I'm capable of doing. But some years ago I realized that wasn't a sufficient answer. I was in Australia making a presentation, and a man came up to me at the end and said, "I really wish my daughter could have been here." I realized that whether I like it or not, I have to be a role model. Women and girls need role models. There aren't enough out there.

Have you faced gender-related challenges in your career?

My biggest obstacles were self-imposed, which I think is true for many women. I often tell the story of how, years ago, my boss offered me a big promotion. I told him I wasn't sure I was ready—that I needed two more years to prepare and become more confident. Later I spoke to my husband, who asked, "Do you think a man would have responded that way?" And I said, "No, he wouldn't have." The next day I accepted the job.

So what's your advice to women who are facing such a challenge?

You have to learn to be comfortable with being uncomfortable, or you won't grow. I often ask people, "When do you feel you grew the most during your career?" They typically mention a time when they took a risk. Growth and comfort never coexist. If you're not nervous about something, it means you're not learning.

Is that why there are so few female CEOs? Women are holding themselves back? Or do you think something else is going on?

There are many reasons. One thing we've worked on at IBM is keeping women in the workforce. Many women deal with realities such as having children, taking care of elderly parents, or coming in and out of the workforce, and we focus on flexible programs that help keep women in the leadership pipeline. We also have to deal with the issue of bias. For every open position, you have to demand a diverse slate of candidates. And I'm talking not only about racial and gender diversity but also about diversity of thought. You need to be sure that your people are comfortable speaking up. As we say at IBM, "Treasure wild ducks."

Words and Expressions

dutifully	adv.	忠实地,忠贞地
predecessor	n.	前任,前辈,原有事物,前身,祖先
per-share	n.	每股
tenure	n.	占有(职位、不动产等),占有期,终身职位
cripple	vt.	使跛,受伤致残,严重削弱,使陷于瘫痪
	n.	跛子,瘸子,瘫子
abandon	vt.	放弃,抛弃,离弃,丢弃,使屈从,停止进行,终止

Unit Seven Enterprise Development Strategy

	n.	放任,放纵
protracted	adj.	拖延的,延长的
revenue	n.	收益,财政收入,税收收入
currency hit		汇率影响
margin	n.	利润,盈余,边缘,范围,极限,(版心外)的空白
durable	adj.	持久的,耐用的,耐久的,长期的
dump	vt.	倾倒,倾销,丢下,卸下,摆脱,扔弃
	vi.	突然跌倒或落下,卸货,转嫁(责任等)
	n.	垃圾场,仓库,无秩序的累积
undaunted	adj.	顽强的,不惧怕的,无畏的
debut	n.	初次露面,初次表演,首次出场,处女秀
	vi.	初次表演,初次登台
	adj.	首张的,首场的,首次的
jeopardy	n.	危险,危险境地
commercialize	vt.	使商业化,利用……牟利
leafy	adj.	多叶的,叶茂的,多树木的
oversee	vt.	监督,监视,俯瞰
turnaround	n.	转身,转向,车辆调头处,(思想、立场的)转变,(飞机等)卸货、加油、服务、重新装货所需时间
transformation	n.	(彻底的)改革,变化,改观,转变
bulk	n.	主体,大部分,(大)体积,大(量)
account for		说明(原因、理由等),导致,引起,(在数量、比例上)占,对……负责
adjacent	adj.	相邻的,邻近的,毗邻的,(时间上)紧接着的
core franchise		核心业务
shed	vt.	去除,摆脱,剥离
	n.	简易房,棚(用于贮藏物品),(工业上用于生产或存放设备的)厂房,工棚,库房,剪羊毛棚,挤奶棚
scale up		按比例增加/提高
chunk	n.	厚厚的一块,(某物)相当大的数量或部分
public offering		公开销售证券
playbook	n.	剧本,剧本集,战术手册
convergence	n.	会聚,融合,集合
clarity	n.	清晰度,明确,透明,清楚,明晰的思维(或理解)能力
perseverance	n.	毅力,韧性,不屈不挠的精神

mission-critical	adj.	关键的,至关重要的
set the bar high		树立一个很高的标杆或者门槛
analytics	n.	分析学,解析学,分析论
accretive	adj.	增生的
agile	adj.	灵活的,灵巧的,轻快的,机敏的
work flow		业务流程,加工流程
spectrum	n.	光谱,波谱,范围,系列
attribute	n.	属性,(人或物的)特征,价值,定语
	vt.	认为……是,把……归于,把……品质归于,认为某事/物属于
new hire		新员工,新雇员
adaptability	n.	适应性,合用性
propensity	n.	倾向,习性,癖好,偏爱
differentiation	n.	区别,分化,分异
insight	n.	领悟,顿悟,洞察力,洞悉,直觉,眼光
melanoma	n.	(恶性)黑色素瘤
moon shot		(乘太空船的)登月旅行
roll out	vt. & vi.	启动,开展
oncologist	n.	肿瘤学家
dislocation	n.	错位,混乱,紊乱
innately	adv.	内在地,固有地
tenet	n.	原则,信条,教义
augment	vt.	增强,加强,增加,增添,(使)扩张,扩大
	n.	增加,补充物
transparency	n.	透明度,透明,透明性,透明的东西
cadre	n.	骨干,干部,核心
navigate	vt.	驾驶,航行于,找到正确方法(对付困难复杂的情况),使通过
	vi.	航行,驾驶
gender	n.	性别
come down		决定并宣布(支持或反对)
self-imposed	adj.	自愿承担的,自己强加的
pipeline	n.	渠道,传递途径管道,输油管道
a slate of		一系列

Unit Seven　Enterprise Development Strategy

Notes to the Text

1. revenue：一般指主营业务收入，一般出现在利润表中（income statement）。

2. profit：利润，经常出现在报表项目中，比如 PBIT = profit before interest & tax，"营业利润"是 operating profit。

3. turnover：(1) 收入，营业额；(2) 周转，如 inventory turnover rate（存货周转率）；(3) staff turnover rate（人员变动率）。

4. gain：利得，指单笔交易收入扣除成本及费用之后的数字，如 gain of disposal of fixed assets（处置固定资产的利得）。

5. income：收入。这个词很少单独使用，一般与其他词合在一起形成专有名词，income statement（利润表），taxable income（应税收入）。

6. proceeds：一般指单笔交易的收入所得、用在处置的收入。比如，你要表达处置金融资产的收入额，一般用 proceeds from disposal of financial assets，而不用 revenue 或者 income。

7. earn one's stripes：凭借工作的努力而得到晋升。stripe 本来是指军装或警服上表示等级的条纹标志。

8. bet the farm：(在赌博、投资或风险事业上)孤注一掷，破釜沉舟。

9. firewall：防火墙（自动防止未经授权者通过网络侵入计算机的系统或程序）。

10. IBM Watson：沃森，能够在 10 分钟内阅读并剖析 2000 万份医学文献、论文和病理报告，相比之下，一名研究人员一年只能够阅读 200—300 份医学文献。作为与行业结合最深的 AI 平台，在中国市场 IBM Watson 早已深入医疗行业，帮助千万中国患者改善医疗服务。

11. H & R Block：美国最大的连锁税务服务供应商，在美国经营税务门店 10000 多家。

12. net promoter score（NPS）：净推荐值，是一种满意度调查方法，旨在衡量客户推荐某项产品或服务的可能性。这种方法将客户划分为三类：推荐者、被动接受者、叛离者。

通过向客户提一个简单的问题：你将[这家公司]推荐给朋友或同事的可能性有多大？客户在 0—10 分之间进行打分。然后你就能通过客户的眼光来度量公司和品牌的表现，并将客户划分为以下三类：

推荐者（9—10 分）：是忠实的热心客户，他们会不断购买，并引荐他人，促进你的业绩增长。

被动接受者（7—8 分）：是满意的客户，但他们对你的品牌缺乏热情，并且易受竞争者的诱惑而背叛。

叛离者（0—6 分）：是不满的客户，他们会损害你的品牌形象，并通过负面口碑传播来阻碍你的业绩增长。

要计算你的净推荐者得分NPS,只需简单地把推荐者占总体客户的百分比减去叛离者的百分比。

13. Box.net:一家文件存储与协作公司。该公司表示其用户数量已超过500万,其中包括思科系统(Cisco Systems)、戴尔(Dell)、梦工厂动画(DreamWorks Animation SKG)等企业。

14. vertical domain:垂直领域。垂直即纵向深层次,行业垂直领域即相对综合性下的特定领域,只专注于某一领域。

Unit Eight

Merger and Acquisition

Aldo Ernesto Belloni Lured from Retirement to Tackle $65bn Chemical Tie-Up Challenge

New Linde chief faces threat to Praxair merger from union unrest and antitrust concerns

Patrick McGee—Munich

February 27, 2017, *Financial Times*

The stakes are high for Aldo Ernesto Belloni. Lured out of retirement in December to complete the mega deal between German chemical group Linde and Praxair of the US, the new chief executive of the Munich-based company may on occasions yearn for the quieter life of a pensioner.

The merger has already collapsed once and claimed the jobs of Linde's former chief executive and finance director. Now, as Mr Belloni races to seal the terms of the deal before the German group's annual meeting on May 10, antitrust concerns and unrest from trade unions pose a threat to the tie-up.

"Not being able to communicate [the signing of the merger] on that day would be very embarrassing for all of us and it would disappoint the people," he admits in an interview at Linde's headquarters.

If the two companies can join forces, the rewards could be high as the merger would create a global leader worth $65bn that could capitalise on "megatrends" in society and industry, from an ageing population to the challenges of renewable energy, he says.

But first, he must deal with the competition issues and the unions.

Analysts at Bernstein have estimated the enlarged Linde would hold 40 per cent of the global market in industrial gases. In some countries, it would be so big that regulators are likely to intervene.

Meanwhile, Jürgen Wechsler, head of the metal workers' union IG Metall in Bavaria, came out against the merger, airing worries about job losses and querying whether the deal was a merger of equals, given Praxair's larger size. "Linde doesn't need Praxair," he said.

If Mr Belloni, a 67-year-old Italian who emerged from retirement to take charge on December 8 after a 35-year career with Linde, is ruffled, he does not show it. He is confident the group can pre-empt antitrust worries by disposing of certain assets where their presence is too large. Analysts say this would be in the US, Brazil, Spain and Italy.

Praxair, which is more specialised and attains higher margins, will maintain its dominant role in North America and Brazil, while Linde will keep its stronghold in Europe and Asia. But Mr Belloni says "sacrificial lambs" will be offered in a plan that preserves competition.

He acknowledges that labour unrest has been a source of annoyance, given the board's approval of the deal in December. But he thinks the problem is a lack of information. Linde employs 65,000 people in more than 100 countries, with just 11 per cent of them in Germany. "The merger won't happen at the cost and detriment of the German work force and locations," he says.

"There is this sense of losing a German jewel—that's the fear. In the recent past there have been acquisitions of German technology, and we do not want to be associated with that. It's a totally different thing. We are partners in a merger of equals."

The merger is important in an industry that is not well understood but which plays an "all-pervading" role across society, industry and in medicine, Mr Belloni adds. "If you eat and handle food, you're touching us," he says. "We do a lot of things where you don't see us because we are not at the customer touch point, but we are in the second row of an infinite array of industries."

Mr Belloni rattles off examples where Linde plays a part—drilling for oil and providing healthcare, but also conserving sperm and oxidising shrimp. "Your frozen pizzas have to be 'shock frozen' with liquid nitrogen," he says.

"The materials in your car have been produced by chemical and steel companies that require our products. Even rockets are propelled by hydrogen that we provide."

With Praxair, the enlarged company could save 1bn a year in reduced costs and synergies.

That would help propel Linde to capitalise in areas such as respiratory chemicals, where Mr Belloni sees the potential for demand to "increase exponentially" as society ages.

Given the long-term demise of combustion engine cars, Linde has also built 160 hydrogen fuel stations to prove fuel cell technology could be "a major business model" to compete with battery driven cars.

The collapse of merger talks in September surprised Praxair and threatened the dealmaking reputation of Linde chairman Wolfgang Reitzle. Heads rolled as a result, with the departure of the top executive and finance chief, prompting Mr Belloni's return.

Coming out of retirement is clearly a gamble for him, but hopes are high that Mr Belloni can complete the merger without hitches before handing over the reins to Praxair CEO Steve Angel.

"I'm the ferryman," he says. "I'm transporting the company into a new era."

Only then will he be able to contemplate a quieter life of retirement.

 Words and Expressions

tackle	vt.	处理,解决
union unrest		工会罢工
be lured out of		退休后受到诱惑重出江湖
mega deal		巨型交易
yearn for		渴望
pensioner	n.	领养老金者,领取抚恤金者
collapse	vi.	倒塌,瓦解,暴跌
claim	vt.	夺去,使丧失
seal	vt.	确定,明确定下来,使成定局
communicate	vt.	(与某人)交流(信息、消息、意见等),传达
capitalise on		从中获利
megatrend	n.	大趋势
intervene	vi.	干涉,调停
air	vt.	公开发表
query	vt.	怀疑,表示疑虑,询问
emerge from		自……出现
ruffled	adj.	心情烦躁不安的,心烦意乱的
pre-empt	vt.	预先制止,防止,避免
dispose of		丢掉,清除,处理
margin	n.	利润
stronghold	n.	有广泛支持的地方,势力强大的地方
sacrificial lamb		替罪羊,代人受过者,牺牲品
annoyance	n.	使人烦恼的事,令人生气的事物
detriment	n.	伤害,损害,造成伤害(或损害)的事物

be associated with		和……联系在一起,与……有关,与……有关系
all-pervading	adj.	普及的,普遍的
infinite	adj.	极大的,无法衡量的,无限的
array	n.	大堆,大群,大量
rattle off		不假思索地说出,脱口而出
sperm	n.	精子,精液
nitrogen	n.	氮,氮气
hydrogen	n.	氢,氢气
capitalize	v.	给(企业)提供资金
respiratory	adj.	呼吸的
exponentially	adv.	迅速增长地,成指数倍增地
age	vt. & vi.	变老,使变老,使成熟
demise	vi.	终止,消亡,死亡
combustion engine		内燃机
hitch	n.	(短暂的)小故障,小障碍
hand over the reins to		把控制权交到某人手中
ferryman	n.	渡船船工,渡船主
contemplate	vt.	考虑,思量,考虑接受(发生某事的可能性)

Notes to the Text

1. Linde:林德集团,是全球领先的气体和工程集团,是工业气体、工艺与特种气体的全球领先供应商,是盈利最多的工程公司之一。林德产品和服务几乎遍及每个行业,分公司遍及全球 100 个国家。1879 年,著名的德国科学家、低温技术的先驱者卡尔·冯·林德博士创建了林德低温设备公司,这就是林德集团的前身。1902 年,卡尔博士建立了世界上第一套空气分离装置,开创了世界工业气体的先河。林德气体的空分装置广泛应用在国内诸多大型石化、煤化工项目上,诸如镇海炼化、神华宁煤以及大连恒力炼化项目中。

2. Praxair:普莱克斯,是一家全球领先的工业气体专业公司,同时也是北美和南美洲最大的工业气体供应商,向来自各行业的用户提供大气气体、工艺气体、特种气体、高性能表面涂料和相关的服务与技术。普莱克斯这个名字从 1992 年起开始使用,它源于希腊文字 Praxis,意为"实际应用",而 Air 是指公司产品的主要原料空气。公司最初创建于 1907 年,也是首家将深冷分离氧气商业化的公司。

3. antitrust laws:反托斯法,即反垄断法,是国内外经济活动中用以控制垄断活动的立法、行政规章、司法判例以及国际条约的总称。从广义上讲,垄断活动同限制性商业惯例("限制"指限制竞争)、卡特尔行为以及托拉斯活动含义相当;从狭义上讲,国际间的限制性商业惯例指在经济活动中企业为牟取高额利润而进行的合并、接管(狭义的垄断活动),或勾结起来进行串通投标、操纵价格、划分市场等不正当的经营活动(狭义的限制性商业惯例)。

4. Munich ['mjuːnɪk]:慕尼黑,是德国巴伐利亚州的首府。慕尼黑分为老城与新城两部分,总面积约 310 平方公里,是德国南部第一大城、全德国第三大城市(仅次于柏林和汉堡)。慕尼黑位于德国南部阿尔卑斯山北麓的伊萨尔河畔,是德国主要的经济、文化、科技和交通中心之一。慕尼黑同时又保留着原巴伐利亚王国都城的古朴风情,被人们称作"百万人的村庄",是生物工程学、软件及服务业的中心。慕尼黑是德国第二大金融中心(仅次于法兰克福),慕尼黑是欧洲重要的出版中心之一,拥有南德意志报出版社等众多出版社。

5. Bavaria [bə'veərɪə]:巴伐利亚。巴伐利亚自由州(德语:Freistaat Bayern;英语:Free State of Bavaria)也常被称为"拜恩""拜仁",位于德意志联邦共和国东南部,是德国面积最大的联邦州(占全国面积 1/5)、人口第二大州(次于北莱茵-威斯特法伦),首府位于慕尼黑。巴伐利亚来自其拉丁文名称 Bavaria 的音译。巴伐利亚最著名的品牌有 BMW(宝马汽车),特产有啤酒,景点有新天鹅堡(迪士尼城堡原型),还有欧洲最古老的钟楼。

6. fuel cell:燃料电池,是一种把燃料所具有的化学能直接转换成电能的化学装置,又被称为"电化学发电器"。它是继水力发电、热能发电和原子能发电之后的第四种发电技术。燃料电池效率高,利用燃料和氧气作为原料;同时没有机械传动部件,故没有噪声污染,排放出的有害气体极少。由此可见,从节约能源和保护生态环境的角度来看,燃料电池是最有发展前途的发电技术。

EU Vetos Deutsche Boerse-London Stock Exchange Merger Deal

Foo Yun Chee

March 29, 2017, *Reuters*

BRUSSELS (Reuters)—An attempted merger between the German and British stock exchanges was struck down by European regulators on Wednesday, formally ending a deal that unraveled in the wake of Britain's vote to leave the European Union.

"We could not approve this merger on the terms ... proposed," said European Competition Commissioner Margrethe Vestager, blocking the 29 billion-euro ($31 billion) deal to combine Deutsche Boerse and the London Stock Exchange.

A merger would have created Europe's biggest stock exchange. But the European Commission objected, saying the deal, which was the pair's fifth attempt to combine, would have resulted in a monopoly in the processing of bond trades.

Selling MTS, the LSE's Italian fixed income trading platform, would have removed the

Commission's concerns but LSE declined to do so.

"How exactly these markets work and the products traded can seem like rocket science," said Vestager. "But actually our competition concerns with this merger are very simple."

"In some markets Deutsche Börse and London Stock Exchange both provide the same services. And in some of these markets they are essentially the only players and the merger would therefore have led to a de facto monopoly."

The EU rejection comes on the day the British government started proceedings for leaving the European Union, a move which industry sources have said undermined the merger plans.

The Brexit decision had prompted German politicians to demand that the headquarters of the exchange group move from London to Frankfurt, creating a conflict that caused the deal to unravel.

Further complicating the picture, German police and prosecutors had opened an investigation into possible insider trading by Deutsche Boerse Chief Executive Carsten Kengeter, the man who was set to lead the combined group.

"It is always the same," said one Deutsche Boerse manager, commenting on the long saga of the two exchanges trying to join together. "Attempt to merge. Fall on your face. Save up money. Next merger attempt. Fall on your face," he said.

While Wednesday's announcement marks the official end of the deal, there was already no hope left that it would go ahead after the LSE took the unusual step last month of saying it would not accede to EU demands that MTS had to be sold if the deal was to be approved.

Shares in the LSE were up 2 percent at 3,085 pence by 1130 GMT on Wednesday, after it announced a share buyback, while shares in Deutsche Boerse were up 1.7 percent at 83.23 euros.

POWER STRUGGLE

The proposed merger threw a spotlight on clearing, whereby stock, bond and derivatives trades are completed, even if one side of the deal goes bust.

The LSE's clearing arm, LCH, is one of the world's biggest, and the exchange had agreed to sell its LCH's Paris arm to French bourse Euronext if the merger went ahead. That sale will now not happen, the LSE said.

This presents a problem for Euronext, which had opposed the tie up of London and Frankfurt, because it uses LCH in Paris to clear its own share trades under a deal that expires next year.

Euronext Chief Executive Stephane Boujnah said on Wednesday that it was still willing to buy the business.

"But in the absence of obtaining an agreement, Euronext is fully committed to securing the best long-term solution for its post-trade activities," Boujnah said.

LCH in London dominates the clearing of euro-denominated derivatives, an activity some EU policymakers want shifted to the euro zone to come under the supervision of the European Central Bank because Britain is leaving the EU.

The bourse merger could have helped by shifting euro clearing to Deutsche Boerse's Eurex arm in Frankfurt. The collapse of the deal may now prompt the European Union to take action to engineer such a shift.

Words and Expressions

veto	vt.	行使否决权,拒绝认可
attempted	adj.	未遂的
strike down		废止,取缔,终结(非法的法律或规定)
unravel	vi.	(系统、计划、关系等)解体,崩溃,瓦解
monopoly	n.	垄断,专营服务
decline	vt.	婉拒,谢绝
rocket science		高深的事,难做的事,考验智力的事
de facto		实际上存在的(不一定合法)
proceeding	n.	诉讼,诉讼程序
industry sources		行业人士
complicate	vt.	使情况复杂化
prosecutor	n.	公诉人,检察官
saga	n.	传说,传闻
accede to		答应,同意
GMT		格林尼治标准时间
threw a spotlight on		专注于,聚焦于
go bust		破产,倒闭
bourse	n.	(尤指巴黎的)证券交易所
expire	vi.	(因到期而)失效,终止,到期
be committed to		致力于,承担
denominate	vt.	以(某种货币)为单位
clearinghouse	n.	(技术情报,票据)交换所
derivative	n.	派生物,衍生物
engineer	vt.	尽力谋划,精心安排

Notes to the Text

1. EU(European Union):欧洲联盟,简称"欧盟",总部设在比利时首都布鲁塞尔(Brussel),是由欧洲共同体发展而来的,创始成员国有6个,分别为德国、法国、意大利、荷兰、比利时和卢森堡。该联盟现拥有28个会员国,正式官方语言有24种。欧盟的条约经过多次修订,运作方式依照《里斯本条约》。经济上欧盟为世界第一大经济体,军事上绝大多数欧盟成员国为北大西洋公约组织成员。

2. LSE(London Stock Exchange):伦敦证券交易所,是世界四大证券交易所之一。作为世界上最国际化的金融中心,伦敦不仅是欧洲债券及外汇交易领域的全球领先者,还受理超过三分之二的国际股票承销业务。伦敦的规模与位置,意味着它为世界各地的公司及投资者提供了一个通往欧洲的理想门户。在保持伦敦的领先地位方面,伦敦证券交易所扮演着中心角色,它运作世界上最强的股票市场,其外国股票的交易超过其他任何证交所。

3. insider trading:内幕交易,是指内幕人员根据内幕消息买卖证券或者帮助他人,违反了证券市场"公开、公平、公正"的原则,严重影响证券市场功能的发挥。同时,内幕交易使证券价格和指数的形成过程失去了时效性和客观性,它使证券价格和指数成为少数人利用内幕消息炒作的结果,而不是投资大众对公司业绩综合评价的结果,最终会使证券市场丧失优化资源配置及作为国民经济晴雨表的作用。内幕交易行为必然会损害证券市场的秩序,因此《证券法》明文规定禁止这种行为。

4. Euronext:泛欧证交所,是阿姆斯特丹交易所(AEX)、巴黎交易所和布鲁塞尔交易所(BXS)合并而成的一家泛欧洲联合体,其管理结构为"一家公司,三个中心",是世界上第一家全方位融合并实行单一货币清算的跨国衍生品市场。自2002年起,Euronext进一步扩大,其先是兼并了伦敦国际金融期货与期权交易所(LIFFE),后又与葡萄牙证交所(BVLP)合并,成为欧洲领先的证券与期货产品兼备、集交易与清算于一身的跨国证券交易机构。2007年4月4日,纽约证券交易所和巴黎的泛欧证券交易所成功合并,在纽交所和欧交所同时挂牌上市,交易代码为NYX,成为全球第一个跨大西洋股票交易市场。

5. EUREX:欧洲期货交易所,为一全面电子化交易所,其电子交易平台可以提供广泛的国际基准产品的访问。该平台是由Deutsche Borse AG和瑞士交易所创建的。Eurex位于欧洲,于1998年秋由德国期货交易所(DTB)和瑞士交易所(Soffex)合并而成。Eurex是世界上最大的期货和期权交易所。

6. futures:期货,与现货完全不同,现货是实实在在可以交易的货(商品),期货主要不是货,而是以某种大众产品如棉花、大豆、石油等及金融资产如股票、债券等为标的标准化可交易合约。因此,这个标的物可以是某种商品(例如黄金、原油、农产品),也可以是金融工具。交收期货的日子可以是一星期之后、一个月之后、三个月之后甚至一年之后。买卖期货的合同或协议叫作"期货合约"。买卖期货的场所叫作"期货市场"。投资者可以对期货进行投资或投机。

7. OTC（over-the-counter market）：场外交易市场，是指在证券交易所外进行证券买卖的市场。它主要由柜台交易市场、第三市场、第四市场组成。

美国的 OTC 市场包括四个层次：NASDAQ 全国资本市场、NASDAQ 小型资本市场、OTCBB 和 Pink Sheets。NASDAQ 建立于 1971 年，是"全国证券商协会自动报价系统"的简称。目前在 NASDAQ 挂牌的股票大致可分为工业股、其他金融股、电脑股、银行股、通讯股、生化股、保险股、运输股八大类。这八大类中有 80% 的公司与高科技产业有相关，这就使 NASDAQ 指数代表了高科技的领先指标。让 NASDAQ 与众不同原因还有：首先 NASDAQ 发达的计算机和通信网络系统形成了一个庞大的电子交易网络。通过这个网络，所有投资者都可以通过这个系统被紧密地联系在一起。NASDAQ 另外一个令人瞩目之处在于它的柜台交易板，因为这个交易板块由多位做市商操作，使市场为买卖随时做好准备，即便在市场上无人提出买卖时也是如此。而在向纽约和多伦多股票交易所这样的拍卖市场中，做市商只能作为买卖中间人。NASDAQ 没有一个集中交易大厅，除了有一个大型行情显示屏外，交易数据都是通过电脑系统同步传送到全世界上万台的电脑终端上，电脑撮合的速度，加上网络联系的不断发展，使投资者能够从四面八方迅速注入资金，也使 NASDAQ 的吸引力远远超过了像纽约股票交易所靠人工跑单的传统交易所。

8. Synergy Effects：协同效应，指并购后竞争力增强，导致净现金流量超过两家公司预期现金流量之和，又或合并后公司业绩比两个公司独立存在时的预期业绩高。

9. clearing businesses：清算业务。证券交易所的清算业务是指将买卖股票的数量和金额分别予以抵消，然后通过证券交易所交割净差额股票或价款的一种程序。清算的意义在于同时减少通过证券交易所实际交割的股票与价款，节省大量的人力、物力和财力。证券交易所如果没有清算，那么每位证券商都必须向对方逐笔交割股票与价款，手续相当烦琐，占用大量的人力、物力、财力和时间。

Unilever's Best Option May Be to Do Nothing

After a bid attempt, the inclination to overreact needs to be resisted

February 27, 2017, *Financial Times*

Don't just do something—sit there. This old joke, which might do double duty as a Zen *koan*, is not to be dismissed. It is of particular use for the boards of public companies, who are under constant pressure to take action, even when inertia would be wiser.

The pressure is never greater than when a company has rejected a premium bid from a rival. So Paul Polman, Unilever's chief executive, and Marijn Dekkers, its chairman, will be feeling the heat. They have seen off a $50—a share cash-and-stock offer from Kraft Heinz, an 18 per cent premium to the share price before the bid became public, saying the bid undervalued their company. An iron law of convention dictates that Unilever must now perform a review aimed at discovering and realising the value that the suitor overlooked. It has done so. "The events of the last week have highlighted the need to capture more quickly the value we see in Unilever," the company said.

A company in this position has a short list of options. It can announce a bold cost-cutting plan; pay a bigger dividend; do a share buy-back; split itself up; buy another company, or some combination of these.

One or more of these choices may be fitting. This may indeed be true in Unilever's case. But there are four good reasons for Unilever, given its particular circumstances, to be suspicious of all of them.

That the bid from Kraft Heinz was seen off with such ease suggests that it was a misjudged effort by the Kraft Heinz team. It is absurd to contemplate a new strategy because someone else made a mistake. There is the old saw that any company receiving a bid is "in play". But this is no game. A suitor with as much financial fire power as any in the industry has just been turned away. Imitators will think twice.

Second, Unilever's long-term record is respectable. This does not imply that management is doing a good job but it does suggest that its problems are not of the structural sort that may require a big transaction to solve. Over 20 years, Unilever's shares have returned nine per cent a year on average, better than most benchmarks. Its performance does trail Nestlé—but Nestlé is, arguably, the best-run consumer company in the world. Over ten years, the performance has been closer to average and revenue growth has been modest, three per cent a year. Margins are lower than some competitors. So there is clear room for improvement. Unilever's special strength, however, is its deep presence in the emerging world, where it earns more than half its revenue. It has been an uneven decade for the developing world. As a long-term bet, though, these make as much sense as ever.

Next, doing big things—as companies under pressure do—is expensive, even if those costs are often hidden. Fat fees for bankers and lawyers are just the start. Restructuring costs that follow a big acquisition or spin-off are often left out of the "adjusted" profits reported when the deal is done. This is unfortunate, because the costs are real, and go on for years.

Finally, Mr Polman and Mr Dekkers must realise that because the "normal" behaviour expected from leaders in their position is bold action, they will be dangerously biased in that direction. They know that if they do nothing, and Unilever's fortunes do not improve, they will face more criticism, and possibly feel more regret, than if they had "at least tried something". But this is irrationality itself. Choosing to do nothing is, ultimately, an action like any other, to be assessed in just the same way. If more business leaders recognised this, we would live in a richer, if less exciting, world.

 Words and Expressions

double duty		双重功能,双重用途
dismiss	vt.	不予考虑,摒弃,对……不屑一提
inertia	n.	惰性,迟钝
bid	n.	出价,(尤指拍卖中)喊价
see off		送别,送行,赶走某人或者某物
suitor	n.	求婚者,有意收购另一公司的公司
highlight	vt.	突出,强调
bold	adj.	明显的
be suspicious (of/about sb/sth)		对……感觉可疑
ease	n.	容易,轻易,不费劲
absurd	adj.	荒谬的,荒唐的,怪诞不经的
turn away		拒绝……进入
think twice		重新考虑一下,思忖再三
respectable	adj.	体面的,得体的,值得尊敬的
benchmark	n.	基准
trail	vt.	(被)拖,拉
arguably	adv.	(常用于形容词比较级或最高级前)可论证地,按理说
emerging world		新兴国家
uneven	adj.	不均衡的,不公平的,不规则的
make sense		有道理,讲得通
fat fees		暴利,丰厚的费用
spin off		剥离公司,独立经营
be left out of		被忽略掉
"adjusted" profits		调整后的利润
biased	adj.	有偏见的,倾向性的,片面的
irrationality	n.	不合逻辑,不合理,荒谬

Notes to the Text

1. Unilever：联合利华公司，联合利华集团，是由荷兰 Margarine Unie 人造奶油公司和英国 Lever Brothers 香皂公司于 1929 年合并而成。总部设于荷兰鹿特丹和英国伦敦，分别负责食品及洗涤用品事业的经营。经过 90 多年的发展，联合利华公司已经成为世界上最大的日用消费品公司之一。联合利华全球个人护理用品的主要品牌有 dove（多芬）、lux（力士）、ponds（旁氏）、clear（清扬）、Axe（中国大陆地区 LYNX）、Rexona（舒耐）、Sunsilk（夏士莲，中国大陆地区英文为 hazeline），通用商标 Vanseline（凡士林）也是联合利华旗下品牌。

2. Kraft Foods：卡夫食品有限公司（简称"卡夫"），是全球第二大的食品公司，是菲利普·莫里斯公司旗下的子公司之一。卡夫公司的四大核心产品系列为咖啡、糖果、乳制品及饮料。卡夫北美及卡夫国际两个单位分别管理美国及加拿大市场与欧洲及发展中国家市场。美国卡夫食品公司和美国亨氏公司在 2015 年 3 月 25 日宣布合并成为全球第五大食品和饮料公司——卡夫亨氏公司。

创办人占士·卡夫（James L. Kraft）于 1903 年在美国芝加哥开展干酪批发事业，经历第一次世界大战后生意渐上轨道，自 1924 年起上市，其间不时收购其他公司，并扩展至非食品业务。1988 年 Altria 集团的前身菲利浦莫里斯收购卡夫食品，1989 年菲利浦莫里斯将旗下的通用食品（General Foods）与卡夫（Kraft Foods）合拼为 Kraft General Foods。2000 年菲利浦莫里斯收购纳贝斯克后再拼入卡夫食品。2007 年 1 月卡夫食品脱离 Altria 集团独立。2007 年 7 月收购竞争对手达能（Danone）的饼干业务。

2014 年 12 月 18 日，卡夫食品宣布该公司首席执行官托尼·弗农（Tony Vernon）将会退休，并宣布任命董事长约翰·卡希尔（John Cahill）为首席执行官。卡希尔此前曾担任百事瓶装集团（Pepsi Bottling Group Inc.）的首席执行官，他在 2012 年 1 月加盟卡夫食品。

3. Kraft Heinz：亨氏公司是在 1869 年由 H. J. Heinz 在美国宾夕法尼亚州夏普斯堡创立的，经过一百多年卓有成效的发展，由当时的小农场成为世界最大的营养食品生产商之一。亨氏的产品有 5700 多种，除了人们熟知的婴幼儿食品，如婴儿米粉、面条、佐餐泥、果汁、果汁泥零、婴幼儿配方奶粉，还有番茄酱、调味品、沙司、冷冻食品等。该公司的分支机构遍及全球 200 多个国家和地区。

4. A kōan [ˈkəuɑːn]：公案。"公案"并非来自禅宗，它原指官府的案牍，包括法律命令及其相应的案例。可以定法，可以判断是非。禅宗运用它专指前辈祖师的言行范例。通俗地说，公案就是对禅宗祖师言行范例所做的总结和归纳。"公案"是禅门中常用的术语，凡禅宗祖师"拈弄"或"评唱"的因缘或"上堂""小参"所做垂示的话头，后人都称之为"公案"。师徒之间的机锋、现存祖师的语录或偈颂也都属公案范畴。

5. dividend：红利，股息。股息就是股票的利息，是指股份公司从提取了公积金、公益金的税后利润中按照股息率派发给股东的收益。红利虽然也是公司分配给股东的回报,但它与股息的区别在于:股息的利率是固定的(特别是对优先股而言),而红利数额通常是不确定的,它随着公司每年可分配盈余的多少而上下浮动。因此,有人把普通股的收益称为红利,而股息则专指优先股的收益。红利则是在上市公司分派股息之后按持股比例向股东分配的剩余利润。获取股息和红利是股民投资于上市公司的基本目的,也是股民的基本经济权利。股息与红利合起来被称为"股利"。

Unit Nine

Innovation

City University of London professor Paolo Aversa and his colleagues documented every innovation on more than 300 Formula 1 race cars over 30 years and then cross-referenced that data with information on F1 race results. They discovered that in certain situations, more innovation led to poorer performance. Their conclusion:

Sometimes, Less Innovation Is Better

Professor Aversa, Defend Your Research
Interview by Scott Berinato
May - June, 2017, Harvard Business Review

AVERSA: It started with the observation that in some races, no-frills cars, meaning those that didn't innovate beyond F1's minimum requirements, were doing well. My research partners—Alessandro Marino of LUISS University, Luiz Mesquita of Arizona State, and Jaideep Anand of Ohio State—and I then took it to a higher level and ran statistical models on 30 years' worth of races. And it was clear that innovation didn't always lead to better results. When we mapped the relationship between the two, we got an inverted U, showing that increases in innovation initially helped performance but after a point began to hurt it. But the real breakthrough was seeing that in certain circumstances, less innovative cars performed better. And average drivers were winning with average cars.

HBR: Why would less innovative cars perform better?

We think it has to do with the environment around the innovation. If you have a complex product, like an F1 car, and are in a turbulent market, your instinct might be to innovate—to invest in getting ahead of all the change. But your chances of failing with an innovation in a dynamic, uncertain environment are very high. Often, it seems, it's better to wait until things are more stable and let others who are busy innovating during times of turmoil fail.

That's what happens in F1?

Yes. Here's an example. In 2009, F1 announced that teams could compete using hybrid technology. This was exciting but generated great uncertainty. No one had raced a hybrid at the F1 level before. But most teams dove into reengineering their cars to take advantage of hybrid technology. There was deep investment in innovation.

One team didn't innovate—one owned by Ross Brawn, a legend in the business. Before he'd purchased the team, it had been failing, so it was short on cash. Instead of investing in the new technology, Brawn's team just built a really solid, basic race car. With Jenson Button, a driver who had finished the 18th the year before, it blew away everyone racing the super innovative hybrid cars and won the championship.

Maybe it was luck—or a good year for the driver?

The math we ran afterward suggests it wasn't. Also, once the hybrid technology started to stabilize—once it wasn't so uncertain—Brawn invested in it, and guess what? His team, rebranded as Mercedes, won again. He waited until the technology was better understood.

But how do you know you're in a turbulent environment?

A time of turbulence is mainly defined by three factors. One: the magnitude of change. How much is the industry changing compared with other times? Two: the frequency of change. How often are changes coming at you? And three: predictability. Can you see changes coming? The most important of these is predictability. You can absorb almost any change you can see coming. But if predictability is low, and either frequency is high or magnitude is large, you should scale back innovation until things get more stable. Certainly if all three are working against you, you should innovate less.

F1 seems so specialized. Does this really apply to other businesses?

We already use this framework in other fields. Think of any complex product: a cell phone, a drug. We've seen that anytime exogenous forces or shocks to the system happen in their markets—for instance, a new set of regulations or a major political shift—innovators tend to lose. Sudden changes create instability that seems to beg for innovation, but it's probably better to sit tight and focus on execution and efficiency.

We can apply these three factors to lots of industries. In fashion, magnitude is generally moderate—styles, materials and so forth keep coming back in cycles. Frequency is steady, seasonal. But predictability—knowing what the next big thing will be—is wildly low. Think about music formats: The frequency of change is increasing, but it's still not that often—vinyl was around for decades, CDs were around for years. But magnitude is massive when changes take you from something like a CD to a streaming service. And predictability is really low now.

> **HOW TURBULENT IS YOUR ENVIRONMENT?**
>
> Innovating in an industry in turmoil can be perilous. To evaluate how uncertain things are in your industry, ask these questions:
>
> **MAGNITUDE OF CHANGE**
> - Are any of the forces that shape competition undergoing a radical shift?
> - Is the industry experiencing major changes in its structure, technological standards, or competitors?
> - Are regulations stable?
> - Are there major fluctuations in demand or prices?
>
> **FREQUENCY OF CHANGE**
> - Does the industry change before you've fully implemented an innovation?
> - How many changes has the industry experienced in recent periods?
> - Are competitors continually releasing innovations?
> - Are they releasing innovations much faster than you are?
>
> **PREDICTABILITY OF CHANGE**
> - Can you foresee how industry forces will change?
> - Can you predict when the next changes will happen?
> - Was there a pattern in competitors' recent moves?
> - Can you influence the nature and timing of future industry events?

We've applied these principles to everything from beer to finance and, of course, F1 racing.

Are executives surprised to hear you say, "Maybe you shouldn't be innovating so much"?

We wouldn't put it that way. F1 teams really have one product, the race car, but most companies have a portfolio of products. So we look at their different markets and think about where they should be scaling back innovation because of uncertainty. I would never say stop innovating altogether. I would say maybe push the envelope in this stable market but scale back and focus on efficiency in that market.

Why did you study F1?

I'm the son of an engineer. I've always loved Formula 1. I've driven race cars myself and helped design a car and build a team. Since I was a kid, I've watched the races with my father. It's this amazing sport where it always seemed like the most cutting-edge cars would win. But I noticed that sometimes the lackluster cars with mediocre drivers and low budgets won. And we'd argue about why that was. My father thought it was luck, but I thought it was something else. I said to him, "Someday I'll prove you wrong."

So basically you're settling a bet with your dad.

It wasn't easy, either. We had to amass blueprints to document data on six elements of the cars subject to innovation, like chassis, tires, and aerodynamics. We also had to find out if cars were updated each season. Then we graded each element's innovativeness on a scale of 0 to 3, where 3 was radical innovation and 0 was little to none. And we vetted that with engineers.

You were really committed to proving your dad wrong.

I showed him the paper. He liked it. He gave me credit for winning that argument. It only took me 20 years.

Where else do you want to take this research?

We're looking at other effects of turbulence. Specifically, we want to understand how it affects the likelihood that managers will create partnerships and alliances. There are lots of ways to look at what happens in times of instability. The chase goes on.

Words and Expressions

cross-reference	v.	（书等）加注使相互参照
no-frills	adj.	只包括基本元素的，无装饰的
frill	n.	（衣服、窗帘等的）饰边，褶边，荷叶边，不实用的装饰，虚饰
a week's, month's, etc. worth of sth		能用（一个星期、一个月等）的东西
inverted	adj.	颠倒的，倒置的
innovative	adj.	引进新思想的，采用新方法的
turbulent	adj.	动荡的，动乱的

turbulence	n.	骚乱,动乱
instinct	n.	本能,天性,直觉
turmoil	n.	动乱,骚动
uncertainty	n.	不确定性,令人无把握的局面
dove into		投入某事当中
reengineer		改造,再设计
be short on cash		现金短缺
predictability	n.	可预报性,可预测性
absorb change		承受变化
magnitude	n.	程度,重要性,数量级
scale back		缩小,缩减
exogenous	adj.	外源性的
beg for		恳求,乞求
sit tight		待在原处不动,不轻举妄动
wildly	adv.	极其,非常
format	n.	(文件)格式
vinyl	n.	黑胶唱片,乙烯基,乙烯基塑料,(尤指旧时)压制唱片的塑料,乙烯基唱片
be around		在某一领域(行业)中突出,有经验
perilous	adj.	危险的,艰险的
fluctuation	n.	波动,涨落,起伏
release	vt.	公开,发行,发布
pattern	n.	模式,方式

Notes to the Text

    1. City University of London:伦敦大学城市学院,拥有 120 多年的教学和研究历史。学校创建于 1894 年,于 1966 年获得皇家特许状,并于 2016 年正式加入伦敦大学(University of London),更名为"伦敦大学城市学院"。学校 2/3 以上的课程都得到相应专业机构的认可。

    2. FIA Formula 1 World Championship:世界一级方程式锦标赛,简称 F1,是由国际汽车运动联合会(FIA)举办的最高等级的年度系列场地赛车比赛,是当今世界最高水平的赛车比赛,与奥运会、世界杯足球赛并称为"世界三大体育盛事"。F1 比赛可以说是高科技、团队精神、车手智慧与勇气的集合体。F1 是赛车中的顶级赛事,全年的统筹安排、每站比赛的赛事组织、车队工作、电视转播等各个方面都井井有条,F1 世界已被整改得经非常健全。但同任何其他事物一样,F1 也有它的起源、发展过程,而且在前进道路上也有不少曲折。

3. LUISS University:国际社会科学自由大学或意大利路易斯大学(意大利语 Libera Università Internazionale degli Studi Sociali "Guido Carli" LUISS ROMA),位于意大利首都罗马市的市中心,拥有三个校区,是一所成立于 1966 年的私立大学,在意大利享有盛誉。该校属于意大利工业联合会(Confindustria)下属私立顶级商学院,在意大利排名前三,在意大利乃至欧洲拥有庞大而实力雄厚的校友资源。在校生许多来自欧洲贵族及意大利企业家、银行家集团,因该校实行精英化教育,每年招生很少,更鲜于参加国际排名而不被外界知晓。

4. Arizona State University:亚利桑那州立大学,简称 ASU,坐落在亚利桑那州的州府和最大城市菲尼克斯(又译"凤凰城"),是美国一所著名的公立研究型大学。该校于 1885 年成立。1945 年,学校开始由亚利桑那州评议委员会监管,并更名为亚利桑那州立学院,1958 年更为现名。亚利桑那州立大学是美国学生人数最多的大学,现有在校本科生、研究生及职业学生 8 万多名,分散在州府凤凰城大都会区的 5 个校区与哈瓦苏湖城的 1 个校区。学校共拥有 22 个学院,每个校区都提供学士学位、硕士学位及博士学位。2015 至 2019 年,该校连续三年被 U. S. News & World Report 评为美国最具创新力大学。

5. Ohio State University:俄亥俄州立大学,简称 OSU,创建于 1870 年,坐落于美国俄亥俄州首府哥伦布市(Columbus),是世界著名研究型大学、国际顶尖的研究型大学联盟 Universitas 21 成员之一、北美洲顶级的学术联盟美国大学协会(AAU)最早加入(1916 年)的成员之一及十大联盟成员。该校是北美五大湖地区最顶尖的公立大学之一,被誉为"公立常春藤"(Public Ivy)。大学主校区占地面积 65 平方千米,是全美面积最大的校园之一。开设的专业几乎涵盖所有学术领域,尤其以社会学、政治学、经济学、物理学、天文学、新闻传播学等学科于世界名列前茅。其商学院是 AACSB 在 1916 年的最初 16 所创始成员之一。其医学院为全美排名前 30 的医学院。US News 将其排在全美公立大学第 16 名。

6. hybrid technology:混合动力技术。混合动力是一种区别于传统车辆的新能源车辆技术,通常意义上是指油电混合动力,即车辆在保留传统内燃机的基础上,配合使用电动机提供辅助动力,系统可按照整车实际运行工况要求而进行灵活调控,使得发动机始终保持在综合性能最佳的工作区域,可有效降低其油耗与排放。油电混合动力技术开展较早,是目前混合动力系统中应用最广泛的一种,已有多款小型汽车产品投放市场,按照连接方式可以将其划分为串联式、并联式和混联式 3 种。

7. Ross James Brawn:罗斯·布朗,出生于英格兰的曼彻斯特,英国企业家。他曾经是法拉利车队技术主管,日常工作是直接监控赛车的开发和调校,但是他最显眼的工作还是为车队和车手制订比赛策略,特别是临场策略。2008 年 12 月 5 日,由于受到金融风暴的影响,本田公司 CEO 福井威夫对外宣布,不再向本田车队注资。本田车队退出 F1。2009 年新赛季即将开展前的 3 月 5 日车队经理罗斯·布朗挺身而出以 8000 万欧元成功接盘车队,组建了布朗 GP 车队。布朗百分百持有车队所有权,因此以自己姓氏为名命名了车队,即布朗 GP(Brawn GP)。这个声明中同时宣布,车队将使用梅赛德斯-奔驰引擎参赛。他于 2017 年被任命为 F1 总经理。

8. Jenson Button:简森·巴顿,1980 年 1 月 19 日出生于英国索美塞得弗罗姆,英国人,F1 赛车手,2000 年成为威廉姆斯车队的正式比赛车手,参加 2000 年的 F1 比赛。2006 年匈牙利大奖赛上首次获分站赛冠军。2009 年,在经历了 9 年 F1 生涯之后,巴顿终于拿下了车手总冠军。2009 年 10 月 19 日,布朗 GP 车队英国车手巴顿在 F1 巴西站比赛中夺取第五名,积分达到 89 分,在全年比赛还剩 1 站的情况下,领先第二名 15 分,从而提前一站夺取了车手年度总冠军,他也成为 F1 史上第 10 位来自英国的世界冠军。2011 年 6 月,其在加拿大正赛经历六次进站后最终夺得分站赛冠军。2016 年 9 月 4 日,简森·巴顿宣布不再参加 F1 比赛,但他坚称自己将留队,不会退役。

9. Mercedes-Benz:梅赛德斯-奔驰是世界闻名的豪华汽车品牌,总部位于德国斯图加特。1886 年 1 月,卡尔·本茨发明了世界上第一辆三轮汽车,获得专利,被誉为"汽车的发明者"。与此同时,奔驰的另一位创始人戈特利布·戴姆勒发明了世界上第一辆四轮汽车。从此,世界发生了改变。1926 年 6 月,戴姆勒公司与奔驰公司合并成立了戴姆勒-奔驰汽车公司,以梅赛德斯-奔驰命名的汽车是高质量、高性能的汽车产品的代表。除了高档豪华汽车外,奔驰公司还是世界上著名的大客车和重型载重汽车的生产厂家,梅赛德斯-奔驰为戴姆勒集团(Daimler AG)旗下公司。

10. streaming service:流媒体服务。流媒体指以流方式在网络中传送音频、视频和多媒体文件的媒体形式。相对于下载后观看的网络播放形式而言,流媒体的典型特征是把连续的音频和视频信息压缩后放到网络服务器上,用户边下载边观看,而不必等待整个文件下载完毕。由于流媒体技术的优越性,该技术广泛应用于视频点播、视频会议、远程教育、远程医疗和在线直播系统中。作为新一代互联网应用的标志,流媒体技术在近几年得到了飞速的发展。

What's Your Best Innovation Bet?

By mapping a technology's past, you can predict
what future customers will want by melissa schilling
July - August, 2017, *Harvard Business Review*

Melissa Schilling is a professor of management and organizations at New York University Stern School of Business. She is the author of *Strategic Management of Technological Innovation* (McGraw-Hill Education, 2017), now in its fifth edition.

IN BRIEF
The Challenge
Successful technology innovation requires firms to make good predictions about product and service capabilities that consumers will value in the future. Getting this wrong can be costly.
The Solution
By studying how a technology has evolved along key dimensions, and understanding the degree to which consumers' needs have been satisfied on those dimensions, it's possible to determine where best to invest in further technology development.
The Proof
Applying this approach, teams across industries have conceived of promising new products that are now in development or launched, including a financial data mobile app and a noninvasive glucose-monitoring technology.

When companies develop new technologies, they can never be certain how the market will respond. That said, the future of a given technology is not as unforeseeable as it might seem. When I work with tech companies on crafting or refining their innovation strategy, I start with an exercise that helps them anticipate where the next big breakthroughs will—or should—be. Central to the exercise is an examination of the key dimensions on which a technology has evolved—say, processing speed in computing—and the degree to which users' needs have been satisfied. This can give companies insight into where to focus their effort and money while helping them anticipate both the moves of competitors and threats from outsiders.

One of my favorite examples comes from the consumer electronics and recording industries, which competed on the basis of audio fidelity for decades. By the mid-1990s, both industries were eager to introduce a next-generation audio format. In 1996 Toshiba,

Hitachi, Time Warner and others formed a consortium to back a new technology, called DVD Audio, that offered superior fidelity and surround sound. They hoped to do an end run around Sony and Philips, which owned the compact disc standard and extracted a licensing fee for every CD and player sold.

Sony and Philips, however, were not going to go down without a fight. They counterattacked with a new format they had jointly developed, Super Audio CD. Those in the music industry gave a collective groan; manufacturers, distributors and consumers all stood to lose big if they bet on the wrong format. Nonetheless, Sony launched the first Super Audio players in late 1999; DVD-Audio players hit the market in mid-2000. A costly format war seemed inevitable.

You may be scratching your head at this point, wondering why you've never heard about this format war. What happened? MP3 happened. While the consumer electronics giants were pursuing new heights in audio fidelity, an algorithm that slightly depressed fidelity in exchange for reduced audio file size was taking off. Soon after the file-sharing platform Napster launched in 1999, consumers were downloading free music files by the millions, and Napster-like services were sprouting up like weeds.

You might be inclined to think that Sony, Philips and the DVD-Audio consortium were just unlucky. After all, who could have predicted the disruptive arrival of MP3? How could the consumer electronics giants have known that a format on a trajectory of ever-increasing fidelity would be overtaken by a technology with less fidelity? Actually, with the methodology outlined below, they could have foreseen that the next breakthrough would probably not be about better fidelity.

Understanding what's driving technological developments isn't just for high-tech firms. Technology—the way inputs are transformed into outputs, or the way products and services are delivered to customers—evolves in every market. I have used the three step exercise described here with managers from a wide range of organizations, including companies developing blood-sugar monitors, grocery store chains, hospitals, a paint-thinner manufacturer, and financial services firms. It often yields an "Aha!" moment that helps managers refine or even redirect their innovation strategy.

STEP ONE: IDENTIFY KEY DIMENSIONS

It's common to talk about a "technology trajectory", as if innovation advances along a single path. But technologies typically progress along several dimensions at once. For example, computers became faster and smaller in tandem; speed was one dimension, size another. Developments in any dimension come with specific costs and benefits and have measurable and changing utility for customers. Identifying the key dimensions of a technology's progression is the first step in predicting its future.

To determine these dimensions, trace the technology's evolution to date, starting as far back as possible. Consider what need the technology originally fulfilled, and then for each major change in its form and function, think about what fundamental elements were affected.

To illustrate, let's return to music-recording technology. Tracing its history reveals six dimensions that have been central to its development: desynchronization, cost, fidelity, music selection, portability, and customizability. Before the invention of the phonograph, people could hear music or a speech only when and where it was performed. When Thomas Edison and Alexander Graham Bell began working on their phonographs in the late 1800s, their primary objective was to desynchronize the time and place of a performance so that it could be heard anytime, anywhere. Edison's device—a rotating cylinder covered in foil—was a remarkable achievement, but it was cumbersome, and making copies was difficult. Bell's wax-covered cardboard cylinders, followed by Emile Berliner's lat, disc-shaped records and, later, the development of magnetic tape, made it significantly easier to mass-produce recordings, lowering their cost while increasing the fidelity and selection of music available.

For decades, however, players were bulky and not particularly portable. It was not until the 1960s that eight-track tape cartridges dramatically increased the portability of recorded music, as players became common in automobiles. Cassette tapes rose to dominance in the 1970s, further enhancing portability but also offering, for the first time, customizability—the ability to create personalized playlists. Then, in 1982, Sony and Philips introduced the compact disc standard, which offered greater fidelity than cassette tapes and rapidly became the dominant format.

When I guide executive teams through Step One of the exercise, I emphasize the need to zero in on the high-level dimensions along which a technology has evolved—those that are broad enough to encompass other, narrower dimensions. This helps teams see the big picture and avoid getting sidetracked by its details. In audio technology, for example, recordability is a specific form of customizability; identifying customizability, rather than the narrower recordability, as a high-level dimension invites exploration of other ways people might want to customize their music experience. For example, they might value a technology that automatically generates a playlist of songs with common characteristics—and indeed, services like Pandora and Spotify emerged to do just that.

It's important to identify dimensions at the optimal "altitude"—neither so low nor narrow that they miss the big picture, nor so high nor broad that they won't offer adequately detailed insight about a specific technology. In the case of automobiles, for example, climate control may be a technology dimension, but it's so narrow that it's not the most useful one to study; examining the higher-level "comfort" dimension under which it falls will be more illuminating. By the same token, the sweeping "performance" dimension in automobiles is probably too broad a choice, because it includes speed, safety, fuel efficiency, and other dimensions where meaningful advances could be made. Even a product as simple as a mattress involves technology with multiple performance dimensions—such as comfort and durability—that are useful to consider separately.

Selecting dimensions to examine isn't a strict science; it depends substantially on knowledge of your industry—and common sense. I usually ask teams to agree on three to six key dimensions for their technology. The exhibit "A Sampling of High-Level Technology Dimensions" lists those identified by workshop participants for their respective industries. Notably, some dimensions, such as ease of use and durability, come up frequently. Others are more specific to a particular technology, such as magnification in microscopes. And with rare exceptions, cost is an important dimension across all technologies.

A final step in this part of the exercise can add further insight about the identified dimensions and in some cases suggest future dimensions worth exploring. I ask team members to disregard cost and other constraints and imagine what customers would want if they could have anything. This sounds like it might unleash a flood of creative but impractical ideas. In fact, it can be highly revealing. Folklore has it that Henry Ford once said, "If I had asked people what they wanted, they would have said faster horses." If any carmaker at the time had really probed people about exactly what their dream conveyance would provide, they probably would have said "instantaneous transportation". Both consumer responses highlight that speed is a high-level dimension valued in transportation, but the latter helps us think more broadly about how it can be achieved. There are only limited ways to make horses go faster—but there are many ways to speed up transportation.

Most of the time this exercise indicates that people want further improvements in the key dimensions already identified. Sometimes, however, the exercise suggests dimensions that have not been considered. Would consumers want an audio device that could sense and respond to their affect? If so, perhaps "anticipation of needs" is another key dimension.

A SAMPLING OF HIGH-LEVEL TECHNOLOGY DIMENSIONS

Industry professionals can generally agree on three to six dimensions that significantly drive development of their technology.

TECHNOLOGY	DIMENSIONS
AUDIO	Desynchronization, fidelity, music selection, portability, customizability, cost
LIGHTING	Durability, brightness, comfort, design selection, cost
MICROSCOPES	Magnification, ease of use, versatility, cost
PAINKILLERS	Strength, reliability, safety, convenience, cost
TRANSPORT	Speed, comfort, safety, reliability, ease of use, fuel efficiency, cost

MORE MUSIC, MORE VALUE—UP TO A POINT

For some technologies, small improvements can have a big impact at first. In the early days of recorded music, listeners had few pieces to choose from, so the utility of increasing the selection even a small amount was high. Today consumers have virtually unlimited choices, so the additional utility of increasing selection is low.

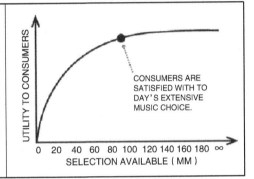

CONSUMERS ARE SATISFIED WITH TODAY'S EXTENSIVE MUSIC CHOICE.

THE CAR-SPEED SWEET SPOT

Some technology improvements have little appeal early on and then quickly grow in value before their utility levels off. The first cars were too slow to be very useful. As they became faster and roads improved, consumers valued ever-greater top speeds—up to about 90 miles per hour. Beyond that, extra speed makes no difference to most drivers.

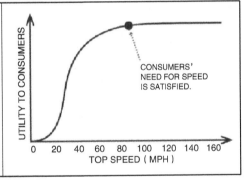

CONSUMERS' NEED FOR SPEED IS SATISFIED.

HIGH DEMAND FOR DRUGS THAT WORK

For some technologies, consumers prize even modest advances. Only one of the approved treatments for the neurodegenerative disease ALS extends life span—and only by a few months. Patient demand for effective drugs won't be satisfied until efficacy is 100%, but any improvement up to that point has high utility.

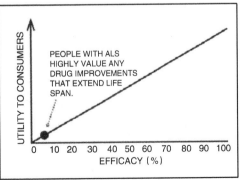

PEOPLE WITH ALS HIGHLY VALUE ANY DRUG IMPROVEMENTS THAT EXTEND LIFE SPAN.

STEP TWO: LOCATE YOUR POSITION

For each dimension, you next want to determine the shape of its utility curve—the plot of the value consumers derive from a technology according to its performance—and establish where on the curve the technology currently sits. This will help reveal where the greatest opportunity for improvement lies.

For example, the history of audio formats suggests that the selection of music available has a concave parabolic utility curve: Utility increases as selection expands, but at a decreasing rate, and not indefinitely (see the exhibit "More Music, More Value—Up to a Point"). When there's little music to choose from, even a small increase in selection significantly enhances utility. Consider that when the first phonographs appeared, there were few recordings to play on them. As more became available, customers eagerly bought them, and the appeal of owning a player grew. Increasing selection even a little had a powerful impact on utility. Over the ensuing decades, selection grew exponentially, and the utility curve ultimately began to flatten; people still valued new releases, but each new recording added less additional value. Today digital music services like iTunes, Amazon Prime Music, and Spotify offer tens of millions of songs. With this virtually unlimited selection, most customers' appetites are sated—and we are probably approaching the top of the curve.

Now let's consider the fidelity dimension, the primary focus of Super Audio CD and DVD-Audio. It's likely that fidelity also has a concave parabolic utility curve. The first phonographs had awful fidelity: Music sounded thin and tinny, though it was still a remarkable benefit to be able to hear any recorded music at all. The early improvements in fidelity that records offered made a big difference in people's enjoyment of music, and sales took off. Then along came compact discs. The higher fidelity they offered was not as widely appreciated—many people felt that vinyl records were good enough, and some even preferred their "warmth". For most consumers, further improvements in fidelity provided little additional utility. The fidelity curve was already leveling out when Sony, Philips and the DVD-Audio consortium introduced their new formats in the early 2000s.

Both formats offered higher fidelity, by certain technical measures, than the compact disc. For example, whereas CDs have a frequency range up to about 20,000 cycles per second, or 20 kHz, the new formats offered ranges that reached 50 kHz. That's an impressive high end—but because human hearing peaks out at about 20 kHz, only the family dog was likely to appreciate it. In 2007 the Audio Engineering Society released the results of a yearlong trial assessing how well subjects (including professional recording engineers) could detect the difference between Super Audio and regular CDs. Subjects correctly identified the Super Audio CD format only half the time—no better than if they'd been simply guessing.

Had the companies introducing the new formats created even a back-of-the-envelope utility curve for fidelity, they could have seen that there was little room for improvement that customers would appreciate. Meanwhile, even a cursory look at the portability curve would have suggested opportunity on that dimension. Sony, of all companies, should have recognized the importance of portability in the evolution of audio formats. Back in 1979, the company had introduced one of the most successful consumer electronics products ever created—the Sony Walkman. The device, a lightweight cassette player that could be held in one hand, was a runaway hit not because it cost less or offered greater fidelity or selection than other formats but because it was portable. Similarly, MP3 was successful because it made music much more portable; MP3 files were small enough to be easily stored on a computer and shared with friends.

Fast-forward to today. Although music lovers now take portability and selection for granted, there's still lots of room for improvement on the customizability dimension. Pandora offers primitive customizability (you can create a channel where all the songs sound more or less like Taylor Swift), but artificial intelligence may get us much further up that utility curve in the future. It's plausible (likely, in fact) that a program could identify elements of your preferred music style and then create music for you. Perhaps it would produce an endless stream of "Beatles songs", nearly indistinguishable from the real thing but not written or played by the Beatles (or by any human performer). Machine-learning programs already compose music for advertisements and video games, and in 2016 Sony released two songs composed by an artificial intelligence system called Flow Machines. The first, "Daddy's Car", is reminiscent of the Beatles, and the second, "Mr Shadow", emulates the styles of Duke Ellington, Irving Berlin, and Cole Porter. While neither quite hits the mark, both suggest what's to come—and where music companies might sensibly invest.

Parabolic utility curves like those for audio fidelity and selection show that for some technology performance dimensions, small improvements can have a dramatic impact on utility from the start. Of course, not all technologies follow such utility curves. Many dimensions have S-shaped curves: Below some threshold of performance there is no utility, but utility increases quickly above that threshold and then maxes out somewhere beyond that. Consider the utility of a car's speed for an average customer (see the exhibit "The Car-Speed Sweet Spot"). The first motor vehicles, such as Richard Trevithick's 1801 Puffing Devil, were steam-powered. They offered a proof of concept and were sometimes purchased by wealthy technophiles, but they were too slow and unreliable to be worth the cost to the average family. Horses traveled farther and faster and rarely broke down. For the next hundred years, inventors sought to develop an automobile that was more useful than a horse-drawn wagon. During this time, the utility curve for speed remained flat; increasing a car's top speed by a few miles an hour offered no additional utility if the car was still slower than a horse—particularly if it was also less reliable, as was typically the case. It wasn't until the early 20th century, when passenger automobiles started to routinely offer speeds over 15 miles per hour, that they began to be adopted in serious numbers. By the 1990s most passenger cars had a top speed of about 120 mph, and today for many it's near 150 mph. It's uncommon, however, for drivers to exceed 90 mph; for most drivers, the utility curve for speed flattens out at that point. Improvements in other dimensions, such as fuel efficiency, acceleration, safety and reliability, offer more utility to most customers.

The utility curve for speed reveals that the point at which improvements in a dimension are of little value can change with shifts in the environment or in enabling technologies. Forty miles per hour probably seemed more than fast enough, for example, when the Model T was introduced, since most roads at the time weren't paved. As roads improved and highways appeared, the top speeds desired by customers shifted upward. The move to autonomous vehicles may make even higher speeds safe, comfortable, and desirable. If so, the lat top of the current utility curve for speed may slope upward once again.

FROM EXERCISE TO INNOVATION			
By examining the evolution of key technology dimensions, teams across industries have conceived and launched an array of promising new products.			
TECHNOLOGY AREA	KEY TECHNOLOGY DIMENSIONS	RESULTING PRODUCT CONCEPT (DIMENSION SELECTED FOR DEVELOPMENT)	STATUS
GLUCOSE MONITORING	Reliability, comfort, ease of use, cost	Noninvasive glucosemonitoring skin patch streams data to mobile device. (COMFORT, EASE OF USE)	In development by industry and university teams
SPORTS TELEVISION	Selection, social interactivity, immersiveness, cost	Virtual reality platform allows separated viewers to watch games in a shared virtual space. (SOCIAL INTERACTIVITY, IMMERSIVENESS)	2017 launch expected
FINANCIAL DATA	Speed, accuracy, breadth, usability, portability, cost	Mobile app provides instant access to proprietary high-value content and analytics. (USABILITY, PORTABILITY)	App released in 2013 is now among the top three in financial services
ACADEMIC PUBLISHING	Reach, access, impact, searchability, cost	Online portal enhances research discoverability and collaboration. (IMPACT, SEARCHABILITY)	Launched in early 2017

STEP THREE: DETERMINE YOUR FOCUS

Once you know the dimensions along which your firm's technology has (or can be) improved and where you are on the utility curves for those dimensions, it should be straightforward to identify where the most room for improvement exists. But it's not enough to know that performance on a given dimension can be enhanced; you need to decide whether it should be. So first assess which of the dimensions you've identified are most important to customers. Then assess the cost and difficulty of addressing each dimension.

For example, of the four dimensions that have been central to automobile development—speed, cost, comfort, and safety—which do customers value most, and which are easiest or most cost-effective to address? On the speed dimension, cars are already at the top of the utility curve, and top speed is relatively difficult and expensive to increase: Higher speed requires more power, which requires a bigger engine, which reduces fuel efficiency and increases cost. Comfort is probably the easiest dimension to address, but is it as important to consumers as safety? And how much does it cost to improve performance on these dimensions?

Tata Motors' experience with the Nano is instructive. The Nano was designed as an affordable car for drivers in India, so it needed to be cheap enough to compete with two-wheeled scooters. The manufacturer cut costs in several ways: The Nano had only a two-cylinder engine and few amenities—no radio, electric windows or locks, antilock brakes, power steering, or airbags. Its seats had a simple three-position recline, the windshield had a single wiper, and there was only one rearview mirror. In 2014, after the Nano received zero stars for safety in crash tests, analysts pointed out that adding airbags and making simple adjustments to the frame could significantly improve the car's safety for less than $100 per vehicle. Tata took this under advisement—and placed its bets on comfort. All 2017 models include air-conditioning and power steering but not airbags.

To assess which technology investments are likely to yield the biggest bang for the buck, managers can use a matrix like the one in the exhibit "How to Improve Glucose Monitoring?" First, for the technology being examined, list the performance dimensions you've identified as most important. (For cars, for example, that might be cost, safety, and comfort.) Then score each dimension on a scale of 1 to 5 in three areas:

- Importance to customers (1 = "not important" and 5 = "very important")
- Room for improvement (1 = "minor opportunity" and 5 = "major opportunity")
- Ease of improvement (1 = "very difficult" and 5 = "very easy")

The exhibit shows a manufacturer's scores on four dimensions of blood-glucose monitors: reliability, comfort, cost, and ease of use. The team identified reliability as most important to customers; having accurate glucose measures can be a matter of life and death.

However, existing devices (most of which require a finger prick) are already very reliable and thus scored low on the "room for improvement" measure. They are also fairly easy to use and reasonably low in cost—but they are uncomfortable. Comfort is highly valued yet has much room for improvement. Both comfort and ease of use are moderately difficult to improve (scoring 3s), but because comfort is more important to customers and has more room for improvement, this dimension received the higher total score. So comfort became the focus for innovation efforts; the company began to develop a patch worn on the skin that would detect glucose levels from sweat and would send readings via Bluetooth to the user's smartphone.

Notably, with a simple manipulation, the weight of the matrix scores can be adjusted to reflect any organization's particular situation. For example, if a company is cash-strapped or under other duress, it may want to prioritize easy-to-improve dimensions rather than pursue those that have the greatest potential but are harder to address. If the scale for ease of improvement is switched to 1–10 (while the other scales are kept at 1–5), ease-of-improvement scores can be expected to roughly double and thus have a greater influence on total scores. Alternatively, a company seeking breakthrough innovation might extend the scale for importance to buyers, the scale for room for improvement, or both.

HOW TO IMPROVE GLUCOSE MONITORING?

To prioritize their innovation efforts, the makers of a blood-sugar-monitoring device listed the technology dimensions they knew customers cared about most and scored each one according to how important it was, how much improvement was possible, and how easily improvements could be made. The high total score for comfort led the company to develop a noninvasive device.

DIMENSION	IMPORTANCE TO CUSTOMERS (1–5 SCALE)	ROOM FOR IMPROVEMENT (1–5 SCALE)	EASE OF IMPROVEMENT (1–5 SCALE)	TOTAL SCORE
RELIABILITY	5	1	1	7
COMFORT	4	4	3	11
COST	4	2	2	8
EASE OF USE	3	2	3	8

Similarly, a company's competitive positioning may affect which technology dimensions it emphasizes. For example, safety may be a key differentiator for an automaker such as Volvo, while speed (or, more broadly, driving performance) may be the differentiator for BMW. So although the companies make the same technology (cars), they market to different customer segments and thus emphasize different dimensions.

(For more on competitive analysis, see the sidebar "Getting an Edge on Competitors".)

> GETTING AN EDGE ON COMPETITORS
>
> The technology assessment exercise can help companies anticipate competitors' moves. Because competitors may differ in their capabilities (making particular technology dimensions harder or easier for them to address), or because they may focus on different segments (influencing which dimensions seem most important or have the most room for improvement), they are likely to come up with different rankings for a given set of dimensions.
>
> For example, managers at a financial technology company realized that for some of their product offerings, Google could be considered a potential competitor. The company had identified speed, accuracy, breadth, usability, and portability as key financial-data dimensions. By considering how Google might rank those dimensions—probably giving greatest weight to speed and breadth (areas where it had particular strength)—the firm determined that Google would be likely to continue directing its focus there. The firm also realized that usability was an important differentiator and a dimension where it had a significant advantage over potential competitors. Whereas Google and others could provide large amounts of searchable, nonproprietary data, the financial technology company was better positioned to provide proprietary algorithms that would transform data into meaningful metrics and graphs. With this understanding, the managers decided to emphasize proprietary analytics in their mobile offering, rather than data feeds alone.

SHIFTING THE FOCUS

The three-part exercise I recommend can help managers broaden their perspective on their industry and shift their focus from "This is what we do" to "This is where our market is (or should be) heading". It can also help overcome the bias and inertia that tend to keep an organization's attention locked on technology dimensions that are less important to consumers than they once were. For example, at a large financial services firm I worked with, data-transfer speed had long been a key dimension where the leadership expected to see regular improvements. At its founding, the firm had developed technology to deliver financial data more rapidly than anyone else could. Being faster than competitors was, and remained, central to the company's strategy and a matter of organizational pride. However, when I used this exercise with the firm's managers, they realized that concentrating on data-transfer speed (which was now in the nanoseconds) was diverting their attention away from technology dimensions where there was greater opportunity to make improvements that customers would actually value.

For this firm, data-transfer speed had become what fidelity was to Super Audio CD: It could be improved upon year after year, but it offered diminishing utility to users. Furthermore, speed no longer provided a competitive advantage; technology to move data quickly had become ubiquitous and commoditized. The firm's proprietary algorithms for transforming raw data into strategically useful information were far more defensible. The exercise revealed much greater opportunity for delivering this information on demand.

Following the workshop, a group of managers made plans to shift resources into ensuring that their most highly used and differentiated analytics-based products could be effectively delivered on phones and tablets. The result was an award-winning mobile application that is now among the top three financial services applications worldwide.

New product ideas are not the only—or even the most important—outcome of this exercise. Perhaps more valuable is the big-picture perspective it can give managers—shedding new light on market dynamics and the larger-scale or longer-term opportunities before them. Only then will they be able to lead innovation in their industries rather than scramble to respond to it.

Words and Expressions

anticipate	vt.	预期,期望,占先,抢先,提前使用
fidelity	n.	保真度,忠诚,精确,尽责
consortium	n.	财团,联合,合伙
counterattack	n.	反击,反攻
	vi.	反击,反攻
	vt.	反击,反攻
algorithm	n.	算法,运算法则
disruptive	adj.	破坏的,分裂性的,制造混乱的
trajectory	n.	轨道,轨线,弹道
redirect	n.	再直接询问
	vt.	使改方向,重新寄送
	adj.	再直接的
tandem	n.	串联,串座双人自行车
	adj.	串联的
	adv.	一前一后地,纵排地
portability	n.	可移植性,轻便,可携带性
customizability	n.	可定制性
phonograph	n.	留声机
	vt.	用留声机灌音,用留声机放音
cylinder	n.	圆筒,汽缸,柱面,圆柱状物
cumbersome	adj.	笨重的,累赘的,难处理的
cartridge	n.	弹药筒,打印机的墨盒,暗盒,笔芯,一卷软片
durability	n.	耐久性,坚固,耐用年限

Unit Nine Innovation

magnification	n.	放大,放大率,放大的复制品
instantaneous	adj.	瞬间的,即时的,猝发的
efficacy	n.	功效,效力
curve	n.	曲线,弯曲,曲线球,曲线图表
	adj.	弯曲的,曲线形的
	vt.	弯,使弯曲
derive from		源自,来自,得自,衍生于
concave	n.	凹面
	adj.	凹的,凹面的
	vt.	使成凹形
exponentially	adv.	以指数方式
parabolic	adj.	抛物线的,比喻的,寓言似的
vinyl	n.	乙烯基(化学),黑胶唱片
plausible	adj.	貌似可信的,花言巧语的,貌似真实的,貌似有理的
reminiscent	n.	回忆录作者,回忆者
	adj.	怀旧的,回忆往事的,耽于回想的
threshold	n.	入口,门槛,开始,极限,临界值
technophile	n.	技术爱好者,爱好技术的
flatten	vt.	击败,摧毁,使……平坦
	vi.	变平,变单调
scooter	n.	小轮摩托车,速可达,单脚滑行车,小孩滑板车
windshield	n.	挡风玻璃
duress	n.	强迫,监禁
differentiator	n.	微分器,微分电路,区分者
ubiquitous	adj.	普遍存在的,无所不在的
shed	n.	小屋,棚,分水岭
	vt.	流出,摆脱,散发,倾吐
	vi.	流出,脱落,散布

Notes to the Text

1. Toshiba:东芝,是日本最大的半导体制造商,也是第二大综合电机制造商,隶属于三井集团。公司创立于1875年7月,原名"东京芝浦电气株式会社",1939年由东京电气株式会社和芝浦制作所合并而成。东芝业务领域包括数码产品、电子元器件、社会基础设备、家电等。20世纪80年代以来,东芝从一个以家用电器、重型电机为主体的企业转变为包括通讯、电子在内的综合电子电器企业。进入90年代，东芝在数字技术、移动通信技术、网络技术等领域取得了飞速发展，成功从家电行业的巨人转变为IT行业的先锋。

2. HITACHI：日立，是来自日本的全球500强综合跨国集团，1979年便在北京成立了第一家日资企业的事务所。日立在中国已经发展成为拥有约150家公司的企业集团。事业领域涉及能源系统、保障人们安全舒适出行的铁路等交通系统、运用大数据进行创新的信息系统，以及通过健康管理、诊断、医疗技术等提供健康生活的医疗保健等。

3. Time Warner Inc.：时代华纳，是美国一家跨国媒体企业，成立于1990年，总部位于纽约。其事业版图横跨出版、电影与电视产业，包括时代杂志、体育画报、财富杂志、生活杂志、特纳电视网、CNN、HBO、DC漫画公司、华纳兄弟等具有全球影响力的媒体皆为旗下事业。

4. Sony Corporation：索尼，是日本一家全球知名的大型综合性跨国企业集团。总部设于日本东京都。索尼是世界视听、电子游戏、通信产品、信息技术等领域的先导者，是世界最早便携式数码产品的开创者，是世界最大的电子产品制造商之一、世界电子游戏业三大巨头之一、美国好莱坞六大电影公司之一。其旗下品牌有Xperia、Walkman、Sony music、哥伦比亚电影公司、PlayStation等。

5. Philips：飞利浦，1891年成立于荷兰，主要生产照明、家庭电器、医疗系统方面的产品。2011年7月11日，飞利浦宣布收购奔腾电器(上海)有限公司，金额约25亿元。

Unit Ten

Economic Equality

Gain and Pain

Cuts in corporate tax may come with some unpleasant side-effects

December 17, 2016, *The Economist*

American corporate tax

Since Donald Trump won America's presidential election investors have salivated over the prospect of lower taxes. Mr Trump has promised to cut corporation tax, a levy on firms' profits, from 35% to 15%. Republicans remain in charge of both houses of Congress; Paul Ryan, the speaker of the House of Representatives, wants to cut the levy to 20%. The coming reforms, though, are about more than just lower rates. Republicans want to overhaul business taxes completely. Unfortunately, this task is far from straightforward.

America's corporate-tax rate, which reaches 39.6% once state and local levies are included, is the highest in the rich world. But a panoply of deductions and credits keeps firms' bills down. These include huge distortions, such as a deduction for debt-interest payments, as well as smaller scratchings of pork like special treatment for NASCAR racetracks. After all the deductions are doled out, corporate tax revenues are roughly in line with the average in the rest of the G7, according to economists at Goldman Sachs.

Still, a high tax rate and a narrow tax base is a glaringly inefficient combination. Politicians of all stripes have sought to improve things. For instance, since 2012 Barack Obama has proposed cutting the rate to 28%, while doing away with (mostly unspecified) tax breaks. That idea never got a look in. But analysts are poring excitedly over Mr Ryan's plan, which is for now the most detailed Republican offering. It pro-clutches to expand the tax base in two main ways. The first is to kill off the deduction for debt interest, putting a welcome end to the incentive for companies to binge on debt. The savings from this would be spent on letting businesses deduct the full cost of their investments when they make them, however they are financed.

The second concerns geography. Uniquely in the G7, America taxes firms' global profits (net of any payments to foreign taxmen). But companies need pay only when they bring profits home, so they keep cash overseas—some $2.6trn-worth, by one estimate. Some escape Uncle Sam's pro-clutches altogether by merging with a foreign company and moving to its tax jurisdiction (although the Obama administration has penned rules making such "inversions" harder).

Mr Trump wants to offer a one-time tax rate of 10% to firms that repatriate their cash. To put an end to the barmy incentives, Mr Ryan, adopting a pet cause of Kevin Brady, chairman of the influential House Ways and Means Committee, would stop taxing foreign profits. In fact, he wants to ignore foreign activity altogether, including profits made selling American goods abroad. Meanwhile, firms would no longer be able to knock off the cost of imported goods when adding up their profits. In combination, these two changes are dubbed "border adjustment".

This would make America's corporate tax very similar to a value-added tax (VAT), a kind of border-adjusted sales tax, says Kyle Pomerleau of the Tax Foundation, a think-tank. Most rich countries have both a VAT and a corporate tax (see the following table). When, say, Rolls-Royce exports a jet engine from Britain to France, it pays French VAT on the sale and British corporate tax on its profits. But while America levies the corporate tax on exporters' profits, it imposes no VAT on imported goods (except for state and local sales taxes). Mr Ryan's proposal would more or less reverse this.

Unit Ten　Economic Equality

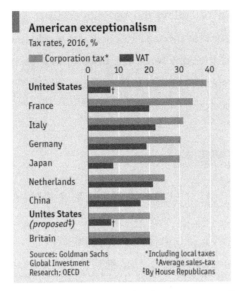

Border adjustment penalizes imports and subsidies exports. So some hope it would help to close the trade deficit. Mr Trump has often complained about the VAT Mexico imposes on American goods, when Mexican exports flowing north incur no such levy. America is "the only major country that taxes its own exports", lamented Mr Brady in June.

Economists are suspicious of these complaints. In theory, border adjustments do not affect trade, because export subsidies and import taxes both push up the dollar. So imports are taxed more, but get cheaper. Exports escape tax, but get pricier. In combination, the currency and tax effects should balance exactly.

In reality, it might take time for the dollar to rise. If so, American exporters would benefit in the interim. But big importers would take a hit. The Retail Industry Leaders Association, a trade group, is already campaigning against the change.

However long the dollar took to appreciate, it would be no small adjustment. To offset a border-adjusted tax of 20%, the greenback would have to rise by a staggering 25%, according to Goldman. It is already up by 24% on a trade-weighted basis since mid-2014; repeating that appreciation would hammer those emerging markets with sizeable dollar-denominated debts and threaten the health of the world economy. It would also reduce the dollar value of American investments abroad.

Despite the plan's appealing simplicity, it seems unlikely that Congress will pass a proposal that would cause such volatility in currency markets. Senate Republicans have been largely mum on the House plan. And unless America switches to a full fledged VAT, border adjust ability may also be judged to breach World Trade Organization rules.

That bodes ill for the size of the overall corporate-tax cut. Since America imports much more than it exports, border adjust ability would raise fully $1.2trn over a decade, covering almost two-thirds of the cost of cutting the tax rate to 20%, according to the Tax Policy Centre, a think-tank. Without that money, Republicans would have to scale back their plans, disappointing investors. And it might force the government to borrow more, widening the budget deficit, and putting short-term upward pressure on the dollar. Either way, markets could be in for a few surprises yet.

Words and Expressions

salivate	vi.	（尤指看到或嗅到食物时）垂涎,流口水
prospect	n.	可能性,希望,前景
levy	n.	征收额,（尤指）税款
	vt.	征收,征(税)
overhaul	vt.	彻底检修
	n.	检修,大修,改造
straightforward	adj.	简单的,易懂的,不复杂的
panoply	n.	巨大的数量（或收藏品）,（尤指令人印象深刻的）一整套,全套
pork scratchings		炸脆猪皮（一种流行的小吃食品）
special treatment		特别的待遇
racetrack	n.	跑道,赛道
dole out		（少量地）发放,发给
glaring	adj.	显眼的,明显的,易见的
of all stripes		各种类型的
do away with		消除,终止,废除
unspecified	adj.	未说明的,不明确的
get a look-in		受应有的关注
pore over		钻研,仔细阅读
pore	vi.	专心阅读,钻研,沉思
	n.	（皮肤上的）毛孔,（植物的）气孔,孔隙
offering	n.	主动提出,自愿给予,提供（东西或机会）
clutch	n.	控制,掌握,势力范围
pro-clutch	n.	专门的掌握、控制
kill off		使停止,毁灭,破坏,扼杀
binge	vi.	放纵,不加节制
deduct	vt.	（从总量中）扣除,减去

Unit Ten Economic Equality

finance	vt.	提供资金
net of tax		纳税后净额,纳税后净收入额
net of payment		支付费用后的净收入额
taxmen	n.	税务部门,税务机关,收税员
jurisdiction	n.	司法权,审判权,管辖权
pen	vt.	起草,规定
one-time tax rate		一次性税率
repatriate	vt.	遣送回国,遣返,寄(钱)回国,将(利润)调回本国
barmy	adj.	傻乎乎的,疯疯癫癫的
pet cause		热门原因,热门事件
tax	vt.	对……征税,课税
knock off		使减少,使降低,从(名单或文件中)删除
add up		积累,集聚
dub	v.	把……戏称为,给……起绰号
exceptionalism	n.	美国例外论,例外主义
penalize	vt.	处罚,惩罚
subsidize	vt.	资助,补助
close the deficit		消除赤字
lament	vt.	对……感到悲痛,对……表示失望
push up		强使(物价等)上升
pricy	adj.	价格高的,昂贵的
interim	n.	间歇,过渡期间
take a hit		受到影响
Retail Industry Leaders Association		美国进出口商协会
campaign against		与……对抗
appreciate	vi.	(货币)升值
offset	vt.	抵消,弥补,补偿
staggering	adj.	令人难以相信的
hammer	vt.	(因税收政策变化、经济不景气等)使(企业)受到打击
sizeable	adj.	相当大的
denominate	v.	以(某种货币)为单位
appealing	adj.	有吸引力的,有感染力的
simplicity	n.	简单(性),容易(性)
mum	adj.	沉默的,无言的

full fledged		完全成熟的
fledged	adj.	能飞翔的,羽翼已丰的
breach	n.	(对法规等的)违背,违犯
bode ill		预示恶兆
bode	vt.	预示(好事或坏事),是……的兆头
scale back		缩小,缩减,减弱
be in for		肯定会很快就经历,注定将遭受

Notes to the Text

1. Congress, United States：美国国会,是美国最高立法机构,由参、众两院组成。两院议员由各州选民直接选举产生。美国国会是行使立法权(legislative authority)的地方。美国国会由参议院(Senate)及众议院(House of Representatives)组成,因此有两个议院(chamber), chamber 一词有时也指参议院或众议院举行全体会议的会议厅。参、众两院共有 535 名议员,全部由选民直选选出,其中参议员每州 2 名,共 100 名,任期 6 年,每两年改选 1/3。众议员按各州的人口比例分配名额选出,共 435 名,任期 2 年,期满全部改选。两院议员均可连任,任期不限。参众议员均系专职,不得兼任政府职务。

2. NASCAR：全国运动汽车竞赛(National Association for Stock Car Auto Racing)的简称,是一项在美国流行的汽车赛事。每年有超过 1.5 亿人次现场观众观看比赛,电视收视率更是远远超过棒球、篮球、橄榄球等体育运动,因此有人称它为美国人的"F1"比赛。NASCAR 每年组织约 2000 场比赛。这些比赛分为十二个独立的系列,在全国的 100 多个赛场举行。NASCAR 的成员人数超过 50000 人,其中包括一部分全世界最出色的车手、机械师和车队老板。这个"在椭圆形赛道上一圈一圈傻跑"(前 F1 车手阿莱西语)的纳斯卡赛事也许正是美国赛车运动的缩影。

3. G7：七国集团,是主要工业国家会晤和讨论政策的论坛,成员国包括美国、英国、德国、法国、日本、意大利和加拿大。20 世纪 70 年代初,在第一次石油危机重创西方国家经济后,在法国倡议下,1975 年 11 月,美、英、德、法、日、意六大工业国成立了六国集团。此后,加拿大在次年加入,七国集团(简称 G7)就此诞生。1997 年俄罗斯的加入使得 G7 转变为 G8。七国集团是八国集团(Group-8, G8)的前身。2014 年 6 月 4 日,由欧盟主持的七国集团(G7)领导人的会晤在比利时布鲁塞尔开幕,这是俄罗斯自 1997 年加入这一集团后首次被排除在外。

4. tax base：课税基础,被称为"税基",指建立某种税或一种税制的经济基础或依据。它不同于课税对象,如商品课税的课税对象是商品,但其税基则是厂家的销售收入或消费的货币支出;也不同于税源,税源总是以收入的形式存在,但税基可能是支出。

5. Uncle Sam：山姆大叔（英文名字首字母缩写为 US），是美国的绰号和拟人化形象，是美国政府或美国的国家化身。一般被描绘成穿着蓝色燕尾服、头戴星条旗纹样的高礼帽、身材高瘦、留着山羊胡子、鹰钩鼻、精神矍铄的老人形象。此漫画形象由著名画家詹姆斯·蒙哥马利·弗拉格（James Montgomery Flagg）创作，他的灵感来源于 1914 年艾尔弗雷德莱特创作的英国征兵海报，海报上的基钦纳勋爵摆着同样的姿势，下面写着 Lord Kitchener Wants You。

6. tax inversion：税务倒置，又被称为"税收倒置"或"税负倒置"，是指企业通过改变注册地的方式（由高税率国家迁往低税率国家），将原本应适用的比较高的税率变为适用比较抵的税率，以达到避税的目的。此外税务倒置也可通过海外并购后的业务转移来完成。奥巴马在 2014 年准备发起法案支持税负倒置，恰逢美国与其他地区税赋差距越来越大（如下图，黑色实线为美国税率）。因此，税负倒置的并购交易在 2014 年发生了井喷。2016 年 4 月 4 日，美国大选如火如荼，靶子纷纷对准了企业并购的税负倒置。美国财政局发布对于税务倒置的最新政策，无数追求税负倒置的并购交易就此告吹。

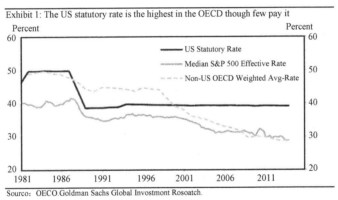

7. Border Tax Adjustment：边境税收调节（简称 BTA），是在国际贸易领域产生的一种较为普遍的税收体制，又被称为"边境调节税"或"边境调节"，是指任何全部或部分采纳目的地原则征税的财政措施，它使一国出口产品与那些在进口国国内市场销售的相似国内产品相比，能够全部或部分地免除其在出口国已经征收过的税费，同时进口国对销售给消费者的进口产品征收与对国内相似产品所征的税负一样的税收。例如，从上海出口运往美国的钢材可以被免除在中国的钢材税，而是在纽约的税收水平下在纽约交纳钢材税，主要应用在消费税、增值税和营业税上。

8. American Exceptionalism：美国例外主义，又译为"美国卓异主义""美国优越主义"，为亚历西斯·托克维里于 1831 年所杜撰之词组。在历史上，此词组意指美利坚合众国因具独一无二之国家起源、文教背景、历史进展以及突出的政策与宗教体制，故世上其他发达国家皆无可比拟。美利坚合众国有多项特征在政治学上独一无二，如个人主义、美洲大陆与世界其他地区在地理上的区隔、受到宗教（尤其是基督教）等的大力影响。这些特征和开发程度相近的西欧与斯堪的那维亚半岛（Scandinavia，即北欧）等国家或影响拉丁美洲大量人口的马克思主义国家全不相类。若干评论家指责美国例外主义不过是"民族优越感"（ethnocentrism）的一种形式。

9. border-adjusted tax：特朗普政府提出的"一揽子进口税政策"，对零售行业产生重要影响。这一政策主要是为了补贴出口，并对国内企业的进口征收 20% 关税。根据 RBC Capital Markets 的分析师 Scot Ciccarelli 预计，征收 20% 关税将使美国国内六大零售商的营收缩减 130 亿美元，这些零售商包括沃尔玛、Costco 等。然而 Ciccarelli 列出的六大零售商名单中并没有大型零售企业亚马逊的身影。这一部分原因在于亚马逊是一家电商，把进口商品的成本转移到了平台卖家身上，由卖家负责购买并发送库存至亚马逊的物流中心。作为对比，沃尔玛则是美国最大的进口商。根据美国经济政策研究所（Economic Policy Institute）2015 年的一份分析显示，沃尔玛在 2013 年从中国进口了 490 亿美元的商品。沃尔玛需要负担这些商品的进口税，Ciccarelli 估计，特朗普提出的一揽子进口税政策将导致沃尔玛纳税额从 60 亿美元增长到 166 亿美元。亚马逊因产品利润低而闻名，近几年亚马逊不断推出自有品牌，包括 Amazon Basics、时装品牌等。亚马逊有望在电子产品和时装品类上增加它的市场份额，并在年底成为最大的时装零售商。亚马逊并不是完全不受这一关税政策的影响。《华尔街日报》援引一位 Instinet 的分析师称，在这一政策下，海外商品比例高以及产品利润低的商家都会面临更大的压力。据了解，亚马逊平台上，多个自有品牌制造商都在中国制造商品。比如，Amazon Basics 的优秀卖家 Anker 就在中国制造商品。Anker 面临的税收压力将对它平台产品的零售价产生累积效应。

10. greenback：绿币，又被称为"林肯绿币"，是林肯在美国南北战争前为筹集战争资金而又要避免向其他银行贷款而带来的巨额债务而发行的一种债券，由 13 个殖民地的联合政权"大陆会议"批准发行，被称为"大陆币"。1863 年，财政部被授权开始发行钞票，背面印成绿色，被称为"绿币"。另根据宋鸿兵的《货币战争》一书所述，林肯绿币在美国货币系统中一直流通到 1994 年。

11. trade-weighted exchange rates：贸易加权，是指用来描述一个国家货币相对于与其有贸易往来国家的货币的价值指数，其计算会参考每一个国家的贸易量以确定其在指数的比重。根据一国各贸易伙伴的相对贸易量，给它的币值进行加权，这是一种评估该国货币是否坚挺的方法。举例来讲，如果一国的大部分贸易是与日本进行的，那么该国货币对日元的比值变动在计算总体汇率价值时将占有较大的比重。这个总体价值一般用一个指数水平表示，每天都在变化。

(Averages of daily figures. A weighted average of the foreign exchange value of the US dollar against the currencies of a broad group of major US trading partners.)

A Field Day for America's One Per Cent

Edward Luce
February 27, 2017, *Financial Times*

He was supposed to be leading a revolt against America's elites. In practice Donald Trump is laying out a banquet for their delectation. The Trump White House is drawing up plans for across-the-board deregulation, tax cuts and a new generation of defence contracts. The only question is at what speed.

In contrast, Mr Trump's middle-class economic plans, such as they were, are already receding. The chances of a big infrastructure bill are rapidly dimming. In marketing they call this bait and switch. The effect of Mr Trump's economic agenda will be to deepen the conditions that gave rise to his candidacy.

The biggest winners will be on Wall Street, in the fossil fuel energy sector and defence. Stephen Bannon, Mr Trump's most influential adviser, last week described the bonfire of regulations as the "deconstruction of the administrative state". For every new regulation, two will be scrapped. The first clutch will come this week with executive orders undoing Barack Obama's "clean power plan" that limits carbon dioxide emissions and a separate one on clean water. Anticipation of this has helped to fuel the boom in energy stocks since Mr Trump was elected. The Dow Jones Industrial Average rose more in Mr Trump's first month than for any president since Franklin Roosevelt.

Financial stocks have also over-performed since the election. Many, if not most, of the protections included in the Dodd-Frank law after the collapse of Lehman Brothers are in Mr

Trump's sights. These include the Volcker rule that restricts banks from speculating with other people's money, and possibly protections designed to shield the consumer—what Mr Trump called the "forgotten American"—from reckless marketing. Such rules have inhibited Mr Trump's Wall Street friends from lending money, he said earlier this month.

Elsewhere the open season is well under way. Mr Bannon's "deconstruction" is already touching most areas of US federal activity. Last week the stocks of private prison companies soared after the Department of Justice scrapped an Obama rule that ended the outsourcing of federal incarceration. They had already jumped after the announcement the Trump administration would detain illegal immigrants infederal centres rather than release them.

Likewise, the new head of the Federal Communications Commission has purged key parts of the net neutrality rules put in place to shield consumers from discrimination. The FCC also scrapped plans to open the cable box market to competition. Expect similar field days in the for-profit higher education sector, defence industrial stocks and public housing contractors.

The scale of Mr Trump's tax cuts are more vague. Steven Mnuchin, the Treasury secretary, wants them enacted by August. It is unclear whether it will include a "border adjustment tax" that would hit importers but supposedly incentivise manufacturers to bring production back home. The import tax would raise roughly $1bn over the next decade and finance a much larger tax cut than otherwise. Unsurprisingly, the only stocks that have done badly since Mr Trump was inaugurated are big retailers, such as Walmart, who would be hardest hit by a 20 per cent border tax. Their customers are the forgotten Americans whose grocery bills would soar. It matters little to them whether Mr Trump pushes through a large or a medium sized tax cut. Simple arithmetic ensures the gains would go disproportionately to the top one per cent.

How will Mr Trump keep the forgotten Americans happy? His only concrete promises were to boost infrastructure and protect entitlements such as social security and Medicare. Only the second is likely. Plans to raise infrastructure spending were more apparent than real—most of the supposed new money was in tax credits rather than spending. But even this is unlikely to pass Congress this year.

The answer lies instead in Mr Trump's grander promise to pursue a "buy American and hire American" agenda. The beauty is that he can define the art of this deal any way he wants. Talking up the "big mess" Mr Trump says he inherited from Mr Obama is a part of it. Deporting illegal immigrants counts as hiring Americans. Cajoling companies to announce new jobs in the US, or to bring them back, will also fuel that narrative—even if they are simply repackaging existing plans. Expect a flood of fake job announcements.

The darker side is who Mr Trump will blame when people start to complain.

His administration's perennial enemy is what Mr Bannon calls the "big opposition"—the media. Bad news will be dismissed as globalist propaganda.

Mr Bannon has also reiterated the case for "economic nationalism". Mexico and others are ready scapegoats. Expect large anti-dumping actions in the coming months. Then there are illegal immigrants and so on. They are soft targets.

Will Mr Trump's tactics be enough to make the forgotten American feel remembered? Possibly. The president has a knack of sounding off against the elite while lining their pockets. The rule with Mr Trump, as in life, is to watch what he does, not what he says. They are often two different things.

Words and Expressions

revolt	n.	(尤指针对政府的)反抗,违抗,起义,叛乱
	v.	反抗,反叛(当权者),叛逆,违抗,使惊骇,令人厌恶
lay out		(整齐地)铺开,展开,摊开,阐述,讲解,说明,规划,布置,设计(场地或建筑),花(大钱)
dim	adj.	暗淡的,微弱的
	v.	(使)变暗淡,(使)变微弱

deconstruction	n.	解构(文本不可能只有一个固定含义,强调读者在意义产生过程中的作用)
detain	v.	拘留,扣押,耽搁,留住,阻留
deport	v.	把(违法者或无合法居留权的人)驱逐出境,递解出境
cajole	v.	劝诱,诱骗
perennial	adj.	长久的,持续的,反复出现的,多年生的
	n.	多年生植物
reiterate	v.	反复地说,重申
knack	n.	(天生的或学会的)技能,习惯,癖好

Notes to the Text

1. Lehman Brothers:雷曼兄弟公司,是为全球公司、机构、政府和投资者的金融需求提供服务的一家全方位、多元化投资银行。自1850年创立以来,已在全球范围内建立起了创造新颖产品、探索最新融资方式、提供最佳优质服务的良好声誉。雷曼兄弟公司雄厚的财务实力支持其在所从事的业务领域的领导地位,并且是全球最具实力的股票和债券承销和交易商之一。同时,公司还担任全球多家跨国公司和政府的重要财务顾问,并拥有多名业界公认的国际最佳分析师。雷曼兄弟是《商业周刊》评出的2000年最佳投资银行,整体调研实力高居《机构投资者》排名榜首,是《国际融资评论》授予的2002年度最佳投行。北京时间2008年9月15日,在次级抵押贷款市场(次贷危机)危机加剧的形势下,美国第四大投行雷曼兄弟最终丢盔弃甲,宣布申请破产保护。

2. Volcker rule:沃尔克规则,是奥巴马在2010年1月时公布的,由奥巴马政府的经济复苏顾问委员会主席保罗·沃尔克(Paul Volcker)提出,内容以禁止银行业自营交易为主,将自营交易与商业银行业务分离,即禁止银行利用参加联邦存款保险的存款,进行自营交易、投资对冲基金或者私募基金。奥巴马批准了沃尔克提出的这个建议,并把这项政策称为"沃尔克规则"。

3. FCC(Federal Communications Commission):美国联邦通信委员会,于1934年根据《通信法案》(Communications Act)建立,是美国政府的一个独立机构,直接对国会负责。FCC通过控制无线电广播、电视、电信、卫星和电缆来协调国内和国际的通信。涉及美国50多个州、哥伦比亚以及美国所属地区为确保与生命财产有关的无线电和电线通信产品的安全性。FCC的工程技术部(Office of Engineering and Technology)负责委员会的技术支持,同时负责设备认可方面的事务。许多无线电应用产品、通信产品和数字产品要进入美国市场,都要求得到FCC的认可。FCC委员会调查和研究产品安全性的各个阶段以找出解决问题的最好方法,同时FCC也负责无线电装置、航空器的检测等。

Miners Warn ANC Over Black Ownership Plan

Joseph Cotterill in Johannesburg
February 26, 2017, *Financial Times*

Corporate speeches usually avoid talk of a "difficult and dark" past. But this month Mark Cutifani, head of Anglo American, defended the South African mining industry's record on opening up ownership to the country's black majority.

With the government planning to shore up black participation in mining, the next few months were the most critical in the sector's 150-year history, Mr Cutifani said. Many "still don't understand" that the modern owners of South African mines are no longer the "Randlords", he said, referring to the white industrialists who exploited black labour to establish the country as one of the world's leading miners.

His speech was widely seen as a warning to the ruling African National Congress.

Increasingly reliant on populist rhetoric as its support wanes and the economy stagnates, the government wants to consolidate black ownership in an industry that was once the country's economic bedrock but is now declining.

The ANC introduced black economic empowerment (BEE) to address the historic apartheid-led exclusion of blacks from South Africa's economy and it encompassed far more than just mining. Companies had to bring black ownership up to a stipulated level.

But its implementation has been criticized for enriching a politically connected elite, such as Cyril Ramaphosa, the deputy president, and Tokyo Sexwale, another ANC veteran. As a result, empowerment had been seen as a narrow "self-enrichment scheme for a few people" connected to policymakers, said William Gumede, chair of the Democracy Works Foundation.

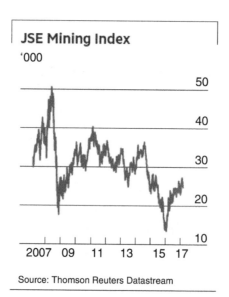
Source: Thomson Reuters Datastream

In March the government is to update the 2002 mining charter, the social compact designed to accelerate the industry's racial transformation. It now wants companies to maintain black ownership at 26 per cent—even if the original BEE beneficiaries sell out.

Miners—who say they met the original target three years ago and that the level of black ownership is now at 38 per cent—fear this is financially unsustainable.

Already struggling to attract capital as corruption scandals and policy uncertainty tarnish South Africa's reputation, companies warn they would have to dilute existing shareholders repeatedly to sell enough shares to a relatively small base of black capital.

Miners also fear that under the amended charter their mining rights could be confiscated if they fail to comply. This reflects wider concerns that under President Jacob Zuma, the ANC is redistributing shrinking resources to its political allies.

"The original thinking behind the charter was that it was meant to be a social compact, one very corporatist in philosophy," said Peter Leon, a mining lawyer at Herbert Smith Freehills' Africa practice. "What's happened is, frankly put, rent-seeking."

The government counters that "radical economic transformation" is overdue. Mosebenzi Zwane, mining minister, has said the charter changes "will talk to the workers of this country who have worked in the industry for decades. And go back and live in shacks."

The conversation needed to move from "rigid, reductive and restrictive ideas about fixed black equity in white companies" as a measure of empowerment, said Mxolisi Mgojo, chief executive of Exxaro, South Africa's biggest black-owned miner.

Even for the black investors it was meant to benefit, empowerment had often proved a "recipe for tears and frustration", he said.

The frustration is based on what analysts say is one of the flaws of the empowerment model—black investors have often had to borrow against their shares to buy the stakes.

Given the sharp drop in miners' share prices during the last commodities downturn, many empowerment transactions "collapsed" because of their structure, said Mr Mgojo.

In recent years, there has been a shift to other models of empowerment, such as share trusts for black employees.

One scheme at Kumba, an iron ore miner owned by Anglo American, increased so much in value in the previous decade's commodities boom that workers bought flashy cars and houses with their dividends.

But Mr Gumede said the ANC was only "tinkering" with empowerment so that most benefits continued to flow to its elite supporters. "We can be so much more imaginative."

Words and Expressions

shore up		支撑,稳住
populist	n.	民粹派,平民主义者
	adj.	民粹主义的,平民主义的
wane	v.	衰落,衰败,(月)缺,亏
	n.	衰退,月亏,缺损
consolidate	vt.	使加强,使巩固,使结成一体,合并
bedrock	n.	牢固基础,基本事实,基本原则,基岩(松软的沙土层下的岩石)
apartheid	n.	种族隔离(前南非政府推行的政策)
veteran	n.	经验丰富的人,老手,退伍军人,老兵
empowerment	n.	许可,授权
compact	adj.	小型的,袖珍的,紧凑的,紧密的,坚实的,(人)矮小而健壮的
	n.	协定,契约,合约
	v.	把……紧压在一起
tarnish	vt.	使失去光泽,使暗淡,玷污,败坏(名声)
	n.	(金属表面的)暗锈
dilute	vt.	稀释,冲淡,削弱,降低
	adj.	稀释的,冲淡的
stake	n.	桩,标桩,股份,(在公司中的)重大利益,重大利害关系,赌注

	v.	(就某事)以……打赌,用桩支撑
tinker	n.	(旧时走街串巷的)小炉匠,补锅匠
	vi.	(尤指不起作用地)小修补,小修理

Notes to the Text

1. ANC (African National Congress):南非非洲人国民大会,现为南非执政党,简称"非国大",是南非最大的黑人民族主义政党,也是南非唯一跨种族的政党。1912年1月7日,非国大在布隆方丹成立,最初叫"南非土著人国民大会",1923年改称现名,现有约100万党员。2017年11月18号,南非执政党非国大第54届全国代表大会选出新一届非国大主席——南非现任副总统,65岁的西里尔·拉马福萨最终胜出,接替现任主席、南非总统祖马。

The Board View: Directors Must Balance All Interests

A Conversation with Corporate Governance
Expert Barbara Hackman Franklin

Sarah Cliffe

May–June, 2017, *Harvard Business Review*

The 29th US secretary of commerce and chair emerita of the National Association of Corporate Directors, Barbara Hackman Franklin has served on the boards of 14 public and four private companies. She has been cited by the American Management Association as one of the 50 most influential corporate directors in America. She is the president and CEO of Barbara Franklin Enterprises, a consulting firm that advises American companies doing business in international markets.

HBR: Do you agree that an excessive focus on shareholders has become a problem?

FRANKLIN: The short answer is yes. But let me first tell you how I think about corporate governance. I have always viewed it as a tripartite system of checks and balances. Shareholders own shares and elect the board of directors. The board of directors sets policies and hires and fires the CEO. The CEO and management run the company. The power balance among those three parties ebbs and flows over time, but there's always some balance. When I first joined boards of large public companies, three decades ago, CEOs were dominant. Then boards began to assert themselves, and the balance shifted toward them, particularly after Sarbanes-Oxley was passed, in 2002. The balance has shifted again in the past five or six years, toward shareholders.

But there's an added complication, which is activist shareholders, and their increased presence seems to me different from the normal ebb and flow among the three parties. Different and more worrying. This has been a new thing over the past few years. So I agree that the power should now shift back from shareholders and more toward boards and management.

What impact do you see?

The hedge fund activists have affected how other investors behave. I see an increase in pressure from the investment community generally for quarterly earnings, for pushing up the stock price. There's some impact perhaps on strategy development and how resources are being allocated. The idea that we should "think like an activist" pops up from time to time in boardroom conversations.

When Joseph Bower and Lynn Paine sent their article around for comments, one person said that corporate centricity wouldn't be possible unless boards made some substantive changes in how they do their job. Does that sound right to you? If so, what changes?

One thing I like about that article: It defines some of the things that boards should have been doing all along. And some boards are doing them, but maybe not enough. (It's hard to do them if you're experiencing unrelenting pressure for short-term performance.) For example, boards need to have strategy discussions with management and the CEO all year long. It can't be a "once and done" event—strategy needs to be discussed at literally every meeting.

If strategy is on the docket every time, then you can discuss all aspects of it—short-term versus long-term decisions, of course, and whether any decisions need to be revisited. Resource allocation is a part of that. Risk management is a part of that. And underlying the ability to tackle those questions is how the culture in the boardroom works. Is there respect for all voices? Is the CEO willing to listen, interact, and respond? Is there just one agenda: the future well-being of the corporation and its stakeholders, always with an eye to how that will create value for shareholders?

A focus on the short term has led some boards to neglect core responsibilities, such as succession planning. That, too, needs to happen continuously. Board members need to be sure there's a viable bench of CEO candidates, and that means knowing them really well. That way, when you need to make a decision about the next leader, you can match the right candidate to the strategic direction. Another piece that gets neglected—but is hugely important to this discussion—is good communication. The board and the company need to give shareholders and other stakeholders accurate, timely information. Some shareholders get unnerved when they don't know enough about what's really going on or about the thought process that led to a collective decision. A lot of times when things come unglued, it's the result of poor communication.

Compensation is another big part of the board's job. How should the thinking on that change, if at all?

People talk a lot about "pay for performance". But what does that mean? I think boards need to develop a balanced scorecard for assessing performance, which will then help to determine compensation. If you have a performance scorecard that covers an array of issues, both long term and short term, it's another hedge against short-termism.

Regardless of whether there's a shift away from shareholder centricity, I think boards are going to have to step up because of changes in the business environment that are happening now, as often occurs when we have a new administration and a new Congress.

Bower and Paine believe that extreme shareholder centricity turns boards and executives into order takers rather than fiduciaries and that boards and CEOs must keep the health of the organization—rather than wealth maximization—front and center.

Yes, I agree with that. I have always believed that my fiduciary responsibility was to the corporation, and that includes its stakeholders. The article calls them constituencies, but we're talking about the same thing. You have to include stakeholders as well as shareholders.

There are interesting variations among state-level statutes. In the first place, most state corporation statutes do not require directors to put shareholders first. Rather, it is the body of case law accumulated over several decades that has caused the focus on maximizing shareholder value. And it's worth noting that there are now 28 states whose statutes allow directors to consider the interests of "other constituencies". I believe this is a good thing.

What do you hear CEOs saying about how they balance pressures from various constituencies?

I think there is concern about balancing longer term and short term. Some of us have signed on to these pronouncements claiming that there's too much emphasis on short-termism, whether it's a focus on stock price or on TSR. Too much focus on any single measure is really detrimental to the long-term purposes of a company. Finding the right balance is on all our minds—CEOs as well as board members.

But it's the global business environment that is keeping us up at night.

You've spent a lot of time in boardrooms—is there anything big that you wish Bower and Paine had addressed?

For me, what's missing is a discussion of the appropriate power balance between management and the board. That's easy to define on paper but really difficult in practice. A topic for another day. Maybe once we get the problem of activist investors sorted out, the authors can tackle that.

Words and Expressions

tripartite	adj.	三重的,分成三部分的,一式三份的
hire	n.	雇用,租用,租金,工钱
	vt.	雇用,出租
	vi.	雇用,租用,受雇
docket	n.	摘要,记事表,(待判决的)诉讼事件表
	vt.	在……上附加摘要
tackle	n.	滑车,装备,用具,扭倒
	vi.	扭倒,拦截抢球
	vt.	处理,抓住,固定,与……交涉
viable	adj.	可行的,能养活的,能生育的
candidate	n.	候选人,候补者,应试者
unnerved	adj.	气馁的,烦恼不安的
	vt.	使失去气力,使焦躁(unnerve 的过去分词形式)
array	n.	数组,阵列,排列,列阵,大批,一系列,衣服
	vt.	排列,部署,打扮
detrimental	adj.	不利的,有害的

Notes to the Text

1. Sarbanes-Oxley Act:《萨班斯-奥克斯利法案》,始创于 2002 年,由美国证券交易委员会(SEC)提交,经美国总统小布什签署,是继安然公司(Enron)和世界通信公司(WorldCom)曝出财务破产的丑闻之后的一部为消除企业欺诈和弊端的历史性典型法规。

Unit Eleven

Payment

Decoding CEO Pay

*The truth is buried in the fine print—and that's a problem

Robert C. Pozen and S. P. Kothari

July – August, 2017, *Harvard Business Review*

(Robert C. Pozen is the former executive chairman of MFS Investment Management and a senior lecturer at the MIT Sloan School of Management. S. P. Kothari is the Gordon Y. Billard Professor of Accounting and Finance and a former deputy dean at the Sloan School.)

IN BRIEF

The Problem

More than 95% of the time, a firm's shareholders approve the recommendations of its compensation committee. Yet committees often adjust performance numbers in complex and obscure ways to justify overly generous pay.

How It Happens

Many committees add some costs and charges back into earnings, arguing that they don't affect operating performance. Many also create a misleading picture of performance by using non-GAAP numbers and benchmarking against inappropriate companies. It's not feasible for most shareholders to quantify all the nonstandard criteria used by the committee.

The Solution

Compensation committees need to explain the basis of their decisions more clearly in their reports. For their part, investors need to develop a set of best practices for compensation design and reporting.

Each year most public companies issue reports on the pay packages of their top executives, describing how their compensation committees arrived at the numbers. These reports are part of the proxy statements sent to all shareholders, who vote on the packages.

The votes are advisory or binding, depending on the country where a company is chartered.

More than 95% of the time, shareholders overwhelmingly approve the pay recommendations. Yet our research suggests that investors should be more skeptical. Compensation committees frequently adjust company performance numbers in complex and even obscure ways, for a variety of reasons. Sometimes, for example, they want to focus on the performance of a company's core or continuing operations. Whatever the motive, the upshot is all too often inflated numbers, calculated on a nonstandard basis, that rationalize overly generous compensation.

Given that reality, compensation committees need to explain the basis of their decisions more clearly in their reports. For their part, investors need to develop standards and best practices for compensation design and reporting, around which they can build a meaningful dialogue with companies. Such a dialogue is critical today in view of the public's concerns over the rising ratio of CEO pay to the average worker's wages and of shareholders' growing insistence that high pay be justified by superior managerial performance.

ONE CEO'S PAY PACKAGE

Here's how the compensation committee report of one multinational company broke down its CEO's pay package. Much of it was skewed in the CEO's favor: Large portions of the cash bonus and long-term stock awards were based on nonstandard criteria (non-GAAP earnings and adjusted operating income) that are very difficult for investors to evaluate. Furthermore, the part of the long-term awards tied to TSR was overly generous, given that the company performed in the bottom quartile of its peer group.

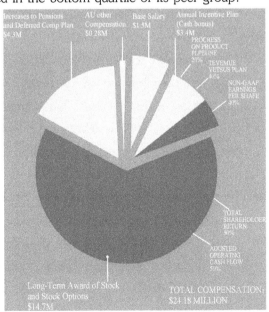

In the following pages we'll review the common shortcomings of compensation committee reports, especially the use of nonstandard accounting measures and the selection of inappropriate peer companies. We'll also propose ways in which companies and shareholders can improve their approach to determining top management's compensation. Let's begin by looking at an example of the problem.

GENEROUS TO A FAULT

In their reports, most compensation committees identify the criteria used to award both annual cash bonuses and longer-term stock grants—usually the two largest components of executive pay. But even at the most upstanding companies, those criteria are seldom well explained.

Take the 2015 compensation committee report of a well-known Fortune 500 company (which you'll find summarized in the exhibit "One CEO's Pay Package"). Running 15 single-spaced pages, it makes a serious effort to delineate the components of the $24 million this CEO received for the year and the criteria behind them. But, like most such reports, it doesn't provide enough information to allow the reader to make an informed judgment on the merits of the pay package without doing a lot of extra work. So we dug a bit deeper:

The cash bonus. The committee tied 40% of this to a revenue target and 20% to a goal for the company's product pipeline. Its report provides clear numbers for the revenue target and specific milestones for the pipeline.

But shareholders would struggle to understand the criterion for the other 40% of the bonus: non-GAAP EPS, or earnings per share calculated on a basis other than generally accepted accounting principles. Companies often use such earnings figures, arguing that GAAP numbers don't provide a fair picture of performance.

Let's examine that a little. The report discloses that the CEO's goal for 2015 was a non-GAAP EPS of $3.40 a share and describes in general terms the categories of GAAP expenses that were excluded in arriving at that number. The committee concluded that the company's non-GAAP EPS for 2015 was $3.59, which was adjusted down to $3.56 to eliminate currency effects. According to those numbers, the CEO exceeded his goal by 16 cents a share.

What the report doesn't make clear is the considerable disparity between the company's GAAP and non-GAAP earnings. Instead, a footnote refers the reader to the company's 10-K report. There the curious reader learns that this difference is approximately $7.5 billion, which constitutes more than 100% of this company's GAAP earnings for 2015. In plain English, the company's earnings under GAAP were $1.56 a share, versus $3.56 under the non-GAAP criterion used by the committee.

Why such a big difference? A review of the 10-K reveals that most of it came from eliminating charges for acquisition and divestiture costs in 2015 and earlier years. While that move may have helped the committee focus on the continuing business, the reader has no good way to evaluate whether the huge costs of these transactions were outweighed by their benefits.

In addition, the non-GAAP earnings exclude a charge of \$680 million for settling litigation that began when the current CEO was the company's general counsel. The report, however, makes no attempt to distinguish between litigation charges related to decisions made by the current CEO and those for which he did not have responsibility.

Long-term incentives. The compensation committee based 50% of the CEO's grant of stock and options on "adjusted operating cash flow". This term is not explained in the company's proxy statement for 2015. All we could find is an exhibit in the company's 10-K providing the following definition:

"Adjusted Operating Cash Flow" means the Company's after-tax non-GAAP income (attributable to the Company) less the change in working capital (working capital includes Trade Accounts Receivables and Inventory—including Trade Accounts Receivables and Inventory included in Other Assets—net of Accounts Payable) plus non-GAAP depreciation and amortization for each calendar year of the Award Period.

We could not find any quantification of adjusted operating cash flow in the proxy statement or the company's 10-K for 2015. So it would be extremely difficult for any shareholder to understand the implications of relying on this complex definition.

The other 50% of the long-term incentive award was tied to total shareholder return over the previous three years. TSR is the increase or decrease in share price plus dividends, and the report compares the company's annualized TSR to that of 11 peers—an appropriate group of large international companies.

This comparison shows that the company's annualized TSR was 10.6%—lower than that of nine of its peers, whose TSRs ranged from 12.4% to 32.2%. Although the report notes that the company's annualized TSR ranked 10th in the peer group of 12, the committee awarded the CEO 80% of his target payout on this measure. The only explanation in the report is a small chart showing that the payout was set by the committee at 80% if the company's TSR came in 10th, 11th, or 12th in the peer group.

Reasonable investors might ask why the CEO should get a large award for such lackluster performance. To give him 80% of his payout for a TSR in the lowest quartile of the irm's peers does not seem to qualify as pay for performance. In our view, if a company's TSR ranks in the lower half of its peer group, its CEO should receive less than half the base payout.

What would have been reasonable compensation for this CEO? To estimate that, we applied the model described by John Core, Wayne Guay and David Larcker in their 2008 *Journal of Financial Economics* article "The Power of the Pen and Executive Compensation". Although regression-based models typically aren't used by companies and their consultants, the one Core, Guay, and Larcker proposed is the most academically reputable way to calculate appropriate CEO compensation. Its main inputs are the firm's TSR, revenue and GAAP earnings, the length of the CEO's tenure, and the ratio of the company's book to market value. This model indicates that the CEO should have received total compensation of roughly $12 million—half what he actually got.

MIND THE GAAP

The company used as our example is by no means the only one to make big adjustments to GAAP earnings. In 2015, 36 companies in the S&P 500 announced adjusted earnings that were more than 100% higher than their GAAP income, and another 57 announced adjusted earnings that were 50% to 100% higher.

All told, roughly two-thirds of S&P 500 companies reported adjusted earnings exceeding their GAAP income in 2015. And most compensation committees in firms with substantial differences between GAAP and non-GAAP numbers used the non-GAAP ones to set CEO pay. At those companies adjusted earnings or adjusted operating cash flow determined at least 40% of either annual cash bonuses or long-term stock awards, or both.

To be sure, there are often good reasons for adjusting GAAP figures. But a more nuanced analysis suggests that in many cases, compensation committees are too quick to exclude certain items or make inconsistent exclusions. Let's review the GAAP expense items most commonly involved:

External events. Compensation committees often exclude items related to events beyond management's control, and this is usually a reasonable practice. The best illustration is a shift in currency values. Committees legitimately factor these out so that they can compare this year's income to last year's on a constant currency basis. To be credible, however, a compensation committee should be evenhanded, excluding the upside as well as the downside. For example, many compensation committees at energy companies excluded losses due to the sharp drop in oil prices in 2015. But in earlier years few of them excluded windfall gains from high oil prices.

Extraordinary or nonrecurring expenses. Compensation committees typically exclude onetime losses associated with extraordinary events—such as restructuring costs after acquisitions. But they also omit onetime losses resulting from poor management or executive misbehavior, such as plant closures for safety reasons or legal settlements for alleged misstatements. Indeed, management has considerable discretion in deciding what items will be labeled extraordinary or nonrecurring. An overwhelming majority tend to be losses, and their recurrence is not so infrequent. (For more on that practice, see "Do Stock Prices Fully Reflect the Implications of Special Items for Future Earnings?" by David Burgstahler, James Jiambalvo and Terry Shevlin, *Journal of Accounting Research*, 2002.)

Taxes and interest. Some committees exclude interest and taxes when calculating non-GAAP earnings. The typical rationale is that these items represent fiscally mandated charges, not operating expenses. But much of the money companies borrow goes into plant and equipment needed to produce goods and services. Moreover, efficient management of financing and taxes is directly relevant to the functions of the CFO and other executives.

Noncash expenses. Compensation committees may also exclude depreciation and amortization on the grounds that they aren't operating expenses. But this argument is thin: Both types of expenses represent the economic wear and tear on plant and equipment involved in generating operating income on an annual basis. Still other compensation committees exclude depreciation and amortization because they're noncash subtractions. Yet both these items represent the actual future investment required for rebuilding or replacing tangible or intangible property.

Stock grants and options. In our view the most problematic exclusions are expenses for grants of restricted shares or stock options. The Financial Accounting Standards Board, after years of extensive discussions, has ruled that these expenses should be included in calculating GAAP net income. So it is questionable for a compensation committee to undermine this accounting rule. The impact of this expense can be considerable.

LinkedIn provides a good illustration of the problem. A company press release projected that the firm would have adjusted earnings of $950 million for calendar year 2015. The accompanying table revealed that under GAAP the company's net income would be minus $240 million. The biggest reason for the difference was the exclusion of $630 million in GAAP expenses for stock options and restricted shares awarded to the company's top executives. We fundamentally question whether it's legitimate for compensation committees to use a criterion for CEO compensation that excludes large expenses for awards they themselves have granted to the CEO.

Given the lack of uniform definitions for non-GAAP measures, most shareholders cannot understand the amounts involved in GAAP adjustments simply by reading compensation committee reports. Though the reports typically describe the adjustments in general terms, they usually do not quantify the differences between GAAP and non-GAAP figures. Instead, they refer readers to the company's 10-K—a large and complex filing that is hard to digest.

TSR: RELATIVE TO WHAT?

The Fortune 500 company's overly generous treatment of weak performance on relative TSR is not an isolated case. Although CEO compensation is indeed higher for superior-TSR firms and lower for inferior-TSR firms over extended time periods, empirical evidence demonstrates that the difference is skewed: CEOs get large rewards for outperforming a peer group's average but modest penalties for underperformance.

Much of the problem stems from the choice of peers. The typical compensation committee compares the TSR of its own company with the TSRs of its peers over the previous three years as well as the current pay packages for its top executives with those of its peers. To provide a fair comparison, the peer group should consist of companies with similar revenues and market capitalizations and from similar industries. A biased peer group totally undermines its utility in setting compensation.

Unfortunately, the peer groups of many firms are packed with much larger enterprises, in order to provide a high benchmark for compensation comparisons. In 2010 the IRRC Institute found that S&P 500 companies with high CEO pay, relative to that at companies of similar size, were 25% smaller than their self-selected peers by revenue and 45% smaller by market capitalization. A study of the 2015 proxy statements of companies in the Russell 3000 found that they most frequently chose as peers 13 large manufacturers, such as 3M and Honeywell. But most companies in the Russell 3000 are not primarily engaged in manufacturing and are considerably smaller than such huge companies.

One office-supplies company we examined illustrates the point well. It reported revenue of $13 billion for 2015 and a market capitalization of $2.6 billion at the end of that year. But the 20 companies in the peer group the compensation committee chose all had higher market capitalizations, and eight of the 20 had market caps above $10 billion. Thirteen had higher revenues. Moreover, several of the larger companies in the group were outside the business of office supplies.

To mitigate bias in the composition of peer groups, we urge every compensation committee to choose comparison companies before the start of the period for measuring TSR rather than at the end, as now often happens. Before the start date, the committee would not know the TSR or CEO pay of any peers. In addition, the SEC should require the committee report to disclose the market capitalizations, revenues and industry codes of all companies in the peer group.

To be fair, the SEC has made efforts to highlight the relationship between CEO compensation and TSR: In 2015 it proposed that the compensation committee report include a graph mapping the company's TSR over the prior five years against the compensation of its CEO in each of those years. Such a graph would be helpful because it would extend the typical measurement period from three to five years, but it would still highlight only the performance of the company. So we think the report should also include a table listing, from highest to lowest, the annualized TSR of the company and its peers over the five years. That move would help the committee and shareholders align the CEO's stock awards more closely with the firm's relative TSR.

CREATING A CONSTRUCTIVE DIALOGUE

Although large asset managers typically have a unit responsible for recommending proxy votes, it's usually small and hard-pressed to review more than 1,000 proxies it might be sent during proxy season. Staffers in such units readily admit they lack the time and expertise to conduct in-depth analyses of complex issues like non-GAAP criteria and peer group composition. That's why most asset managers subscribe to proxy advisory services, such as Institutional Shareholder Services (ISS) and Glass Lewis (GL).

But shareholders should not automatically follow the recommendations of proxy advisers on compensation votes. Take GL, which screens compensation reports against a company's GAAP financial statements. While GL does in a few cases express concerns about adjustments that it believes are not well justified and that result in much higher payouts, it did not do so with the compensation report of the Fortune 500 company analyzed earlier.

ISS employs relative TSR as its primary screen for compensation reports, using its own methodology for creating peer groups. If this screen reveals serious concerns, ISS will assign a staffer to do an in-depth analysis of the report. However, according to ISS, its screen did not raise any major questions about the report of the company in our example, although the company's relative TSR was in the lowest quartile of its self-selected peer group.

The bottom line is that even institutional shareholders with subscriptions to proxy advisers don't have access to the data or the expertise to make a meaningful assessment of the executive pay packages that companies propose. It is incumbent, therefore, on compensation committees, which do have access, to do a better job of explaining their rationales. As we have suggested, more-transparent reporting of GAAP adjustments, pre-selection of a TSR peer group, and less tolerance for relatively poor TSR performance would be major advances.

But even if compensation committees do take steps to improve their reports, institutional investors still need to set standards and monitor compliance. Instead of relying on proxy advisers, investors should take matters into their own hands. The best way to do so would be to support a US association dedicated to creating long-term corporate value through shareholder engagement on compensation resolutions. It could be formed under the umbrella of an existing association, such as FCLT (Focusing Capital on the Long Term) Global.

The new association could develop and promote a nonbinding set of best practices for compensation committees, which could include very basic guidelines about the use of non-GAAP criteria. (See the sidebar "Guidelines for Non-GAAP Adjustments".) The committee at each company would either apply these practices or explain its reason for departing from them. This approach would resemble the model successfully adopted in the UK, where regulators frequently impose rules—such as limits on the tenure of independent directors—but allow a company to deviate from them if it explains why to shareholders.

> **GUIDELINES FOR NON-GAAP ADJUSTMENTS**
>
> We suggest that investors create an association that asks compensation committees to comply with the following guidelines:
>
> Committees should generally use GAAP measures of financial performance in determining both long-term and short-term compensation. Departures from GAAP may be permitted to exclude the consequences of events beyond the control of management, provided the exclusion applies to both positive and negative changes. Committees may also exclude GAAP expenses for onetime events such as restructuring charges, provided such charges do not recur each year. Committees should not exclude expenses for stock-related awards to executives. All exclusions of GAAP expenses should be justified and quantified in the compensation committee's report.

To further promote engagement, each company should hold a public conference call, a few weeks before its annual meeting, in which compensation committee members explain major variations from the association's best practices and respond to shareholders' questions. Pre-vote discussions with large shareholders have prompted companies to revise compensation plans and head of adverse votes on resolutions in the past. (One company we looked at dropped a plan to pay certain taxes for its CEO after such a call.)

As more countries mandate shareholder votes on executive pay, compensation committee reports could play an important role in enhancing the relationship between company boards and shareholders. Properly designed and prepared, these reports could help educate shareholders about the objectives of companies and the ways they measure success. More broadly, clear, unambiguous explanations of how the various components of pay are linked to reasonable metrics of company performance would help the business community respond more effectively to growing public concerns about excessive CEO compensation.

Unit Eleven Payment

 Words and Expressions

proxy	n.	代理人,委托书,代用品
upshot	n.	结果,结局,要点
delineate	vt.	描绘,描写,画……的轮廓
disparity	n.	不同,不一致,不等
divestiture	n.	脱衣,剥夺
exclude	vt.	排除,排斥,拒绝接纳,逐出
depreciation	n.	折旧,贬值
amortization	n.	分期偿还
dividend	n.	红利,股息,奖金,被除数
lackluster	adj.	无光泽的,平凡的
	n.	无光泽,暗淡
quartile	n.	四分位数,四分点
tenure	n.	(尤指重要政治职务的)任期,任职,(尤指大学教师的)终身职位,长期聘用,(房地产的)保有权,保有期
substantial	n.	本质,重要材料
	adj.	大量的,实质的,内容充实的
windfall	n.	意外之财,被风吹落的果子,意外的收获
non-recurring	adj.	一次性的,不重现的
omit	vt.	省略,遗漏,删除,疏忽
empirical	adj.	经验主义的,完全根据经验的,实证的
skewed	adj.	歪斜的,曲解的
capitalization	n.	资本化,资本总额,用大写
biased	adj.	有偏见的,结果偏倚的
mitigate	vt.	使缓和,使减轻
	vi.	减轻,缓和下来
graph	n.	图表,曲线图
	vt.	用曲线图表示
annualize	vt.	按年计算,按年折算
subscription	n.	捐献,订阅,订金,签署
compliance	n.	顺从,服从,承诺
excessive	adj.	过多的,极度的,过分的

Notes to the Text

1. non-GAAP（non-generally accepted accounting principles）:非公认会计原则。GAAP 与 non-GAAP 的区别:一方面是最直观的差异,即来自财报公布准则 GAAP 和 non-GAAP 之间的差异。通俗点说,GAAP 就是通用会计准则,在美国上市,接受的是用 GAAP 来做账和出具 GAAP 式的财务报告。而 non-GAAP 则指企业在 GAAP 基础上自行加工后的财务报表,为的是更好地体现公司业务经营状况。

2. TSR（Total Shareholder Return）:股东总回报,为一种股票对投资者的总回报,等于上市公司在一定时期内(通常为 1 年或更长)的资本收益加股息,在数值上表现为一个或正或负的百分比。(期末股票价格 − 期初股票价格 + 股息)/期初股票价格 = 股东总回报（TSR）。

3. LinkedIn:领英,全球最大职业社交网站,是一家面向商业客户的社交网络（SNS）,成立于 2002 年 12 月并于 2003 年启动,于 2011 年 5 月 20 日在美上市,总部位于美国加利福尼亚州山景城。网站的目的是让注册用户维护他们在商业交往中认识并信任的联系人,俗称"人脉"。用户可以邀请他认识的人成为"关系"（Connections）圈的人。

Some Lenders Demand $10,000 for Single Phone Call with Most Senior Analysts

Outrage over Cost of Bank Research

Madison Marriage

February 27, 2017, *Financial Times*

Asset managers and banks are locked in fierce negotiations over how much fund companies should pay for investment research, with some lenders demanding $10,000 for a single phone call with their most senior analysts.

Banks have put forward quotes of as much as $10m a year to provide fund companies with complete access to their research, according to several asset managers and consultants that are involved in the negotiations.

Fund managers who want additional services, such as face to face meetings with analysts or invitations to events with companies, are being asked to pay more on top of the annual subscription fee to access banks' research platforms.

A research expert at a large European asset manager, speaking on condition of anonymity, said his company had been asked to pay "mid single-digit millions" of dollars annually to access some banks' research platforms.

He described the negotiations as a "phoney war" between sellside analysts and their asset management clients, with both sides waiting for the other to concede on price.

"The figures are all over the place at the moment. Some [quotes] are fair and reasonable, and [with others] we thought: there is no way we are paying that—they will have to re-calibrate their business models or part ways with us altogether."

The tense discussions over how much analyst research is worth have intensified since the start of the year as the investment industry readies itself for the introduction of new European rules, known as Mifid II, in 2018.

The rules will force fund companies to explain clearly to investors how much of their money is spent on research. Previously research was sent to fund managers for free in return for the business asset managers provided to banks and brokerages when they placed trades. The cost of the research was included in the price of trading.

The head of a boutique fund company, which has a yearly research budget of £1.1m, said brokers were now asking for $300,000 for an annual subscription to their research. "As a global house covering emerging and global markets, you might need a dozen brokers. That's a huge bill," he said.

"For smaller managers this is a big problem. They just don't have the scale to put a cheque of that size through. We had one broker say it might be $500,000 [to access their research annually], but that's a nonsense starting negotiation position."

Brijesh Malkan, a former Legal & General fund manager and senior consultant at BCA Research, an independent research provider, said some of his clients have been asked to pay up to $10,000 for phone calls with top bank analysts.

Banks have also requested a $30,000 annual fee to provide an individual with access to their research platforms, and up to $10m to provide a fund company with the same level of access across its workforce, according to Mr Malkan, who has more than 2,200 fund management clients.

The new European rules have made fund managers question the true value of the vast quantity of broker notes and analyst reports they have received for free for decades. Many investment houses have already made drastic cuts to their external research spend.

Henderson, the FTSE 250 asset manager, has cut its external research spend by 50 per cent over the past three years.

Schroders, the UK's largest listed fund company, said: "Our spend on external research has reduced substantially over the past five years and we continue to reduce the external research budgets."

Globally asset managers are forecast to reduce their external research budgets by a third, although the cuts are likely to be much deeper in Europe. This is expected to force banks to make heavy cuts to their analyst workforce, although some lenders are fighting back in an attempt to protect their research departments.

Benjamin Quinlan, chief executive of Quinlan & Associates, the consultancy, and former head of Asia-Pacific equities strategy at Deutsche Bank, said some banks were adopting a "bait and hook" strategy: offering a lower annual subscription rate of around $300,000, in the expectation of raising the fee once asset managers are signed up.

The prices being put to asset managers are varied and very flexible at this stage, and often depend on the size of the fund company and the amount of trades they place with the bank, according to Mr Quinlan.

"This is the biggest problem," he said. "It will cause a lot of problems in 2018 because no one has worked out how much the research is worth."

"There will be a lot of c**p that clients won't pay for and that is when the big cuts [to the analyst workforce] at the global banks will come. The feedback from many [in asset management] is that the price of research is too high and not granular enough."

Words and Expressions

lender	n.	贷款机构
outrage	vt.	使震怒,激怒
asset manager		资产管理人,资产经理
fierce	adj.	激烈的
subscription fee		订购费,申购费,订阅费,会员费
anonymity	n.	匿名,不知姓名,名字不公开
phoney war		(战争时期并未真正交战的)假战争
concede	v.	(尤指勉强地)让与,让步,允许
all over the place		糊涂,一团糟
re-calibrate	v.	重新校正
part ways		分开,分道扬镳
ready for		为……做好准备
brokerage	n.	经纪业务,经纪人佣金(或回扣)
place a trade		进行交易

broker	n.	经纪人
cheque	n.	支票
put through		实施,完成
nonsense	n.	谬论,胡扯
broker note		经纪人的进出交易单据
forecast	n.	预测,预报
equities	n.	(在优先股之后享受红利的)股票,普通股
sign up		(和……)签约,报名(参加课程)
work out		解(谜),通过计算得出
granular	adj.	详细的

Notes to the Text

1. MiFID（Markets in Financial Instruments Directive）：欧盟金融工具市场法规,通常指修订后的欧洲金融工具市场指令。它的影响范围非常大,只要在欧盟地区经营的外汇经纪商都得受到它的监管,不管这些服务商的客户是不是在欧洲,这影响到欧洲大陆金融服务体系的每一个角落。

2. Legal & General Group：英国法通保险公司,是英国50大公司之一,被标准普尔公司评定为AAA级,公司拥有大量超过20年的长期保单。2018年7月19日,《财富》世界500强排行榜发布,英国法通保险公司位列172位。

3. Schroders Group：施罗德集团,在香港被称为"宝源",国际知名资产管理集团,于1804年成立,拥有逾200年的金融服务经验,是全球最大的上市资产管理公司之一。

4. Deutsche Bank：德意志银行,即德意志银行股份公司,是一家私人拥有的股份公司,是德国最大的银行和世界上最主要的金融机构之一,总部设在莱茵河畔的法兰克福。2018年7月19日,《财富》世界500强排行榜发布,德意志银行位列223位。

5. Bait and Hook："饵与钩"模式,也被称为"剃刀与刀片"（Razor and Blades）模式,或"搭售"（Tied Products）模式,出现在20世纪早期。在这种模式里,基本产品的出售价格极低,通常处于亏损状态;而与之相关的消耗品或服务的价格则十分昂贵。比如说,剃须刀（饵）和刀片（钩）,手机（饵）和通话时间（钩）,打印机（饵）和墨盒（钩）,相机（饵）和照片（钩）,等等。这个模式还有一个很有趣的变形:软件开发者们免费发放他们文本阅读器,但是对其文本编辑器的定价却高达几百美金。

Infighting Hobbles Efforts to Curb Bumper Bonuses

Chris Newlands

February 27, 2017, *Financial Times*

(Chris Newlands is asset management editor at the FT and editor of FT fm@ newlands_chris)

There appears to be a mood shift among large investors when it comes to how much they want the top people to earn at the companies they invest in.

Several of the world's most powerful shareholders say they intend to take even tougher action on excessive bonuses for company bosses this year, after investor protests over executive pay reached a five-year high in 2016.

Fidelity International, Aberdeen Asset Management, Calpers, the $300bn California pension fund, Standard Life and Henderson Global Investors have all told the Financial Times they plan to increase the pressure on boards to reduce excessive pay and introduce greater transparency in 2017.

Investor protests over executive pay reached a five-year high in 2006 —FT montage

This is commendable. What would be useful, however, is if investors were more joined up in their thinking.

In submissions to the UK government's green paper on corporate governance reform, born out of Prime Minister Theresa May's promise to tackle a situation where FTSE 100 bosses are typically paid more than 120 times the wage of their average employee, investors offered a bewildering range of measures to curb high executive pay.

Proposals backed by asset managers include forcing the chairs of remuneration committees to stand down in the face of shareholder disapproval, implementing annual binding votes on pay, and publishing pay ratios between executives and lower ranking workers.

But while Fidelity disliked the idea of publishing pay ratios because, in its words, different industries have differing ratios that make it difficult to make meaningful comparisons, Old Mutual Global Investors believes pay ratios should be disclosed.

The two fund houses also clashed over whether having annual binding votes on pay as opposed to the current system of binding votes every three years was a good idea. Fidelity thinks it is; Old Mutual not.

There were further disputes among Hermes Investment Management and Fidelity; the Pension and Lifetime Savings Association, which represents 1,300 UK retirement schemes, and Old Mutual; and again between Old Mutual and Fidelity on whether remuneration chairmen, who sign off on a company's salary and bonus plans, should face consequences if there is a shareholder protest.

Fidelity believes remuneration committee chairmen should step down if a company fails to get 75 per cent support from shareholders; Old Mutual thinks they should be left alone.

And the Local Authority Pension Fund Forum, which represents 72 local government pension schemes overseeing £175bn of assets, clashed with everyone.

It went further than other investor groups in calling for companies to put forward a maximum level of annual pay for senior executives that would be approved by shareholders. "We felt some drastic proposals needed to be discussed," an LAPFF spokesperson said.

David Pitt-Watson, executive fellow of finance at the London Business School, believes the cacophony of voices is harmful and does little more than hamper efforts to address the spectacular rise of executive pay.

"Given the incentives and conflicts that surround this issue, it is difficult to formulate a sensible policy to curb what most accept is a system that is not working," he says.

If they are serious about tackling the widening wealth gap between bosses and workers, large investors should work together. They have shown they can. Just last week Calpers and more than 120 other investors collectively called on banks funding US president Donald Trump's Dakota Access pipeline to get it rerouted away from Native American land.

Not working together would enliven cynics to believe the amount fund managers pay themselves is the real stumbling block. The long-held argument is that once a chief executive or any other senior executive at an asset management company receives a multi-million pound salary, which many do, it effectively stops them from opposing excessive pay at the companies in which they invest.

Asset managers state this is not the case. Working together would prove it.

Words and Expressions

commendable	adj.	值得赞美的,很好的,可推荐的
submission	n.	投降,提交(物),服从,(向法官提出的)意见,谦恭
tackle	n.	滑车,装备,用具,扭倒
	vt.	处理,抓住,固定,与……交涉
	vi.	扭倒,拦截抢球
bewilder	vt.	使迷惑,使不知所措
remuneration	n.	报酬,酬劳,赔偿
implement	vt.	实施,执行,实现,使生效
	n.	工具,器具,手段
formulate	vt.	规划,用公式表示,明确地表达
disclose	vt.	公开,揭露
dispute	n.	辩论,争吵
	v.	辩论,怀疑,阻止,抗拒,争论
leave alone		不打扰,不干涉,不管,不理
drastic	adj.	激烈的,猛烈的
cacophony	n.	刺耳的音调,不和谐音
hamper	vt.	妨碍,束缚,使困累
	n.	食盒,食篮,盛脏衣服的大篮子
spectacular	adj.	壮观的,惊人的
	n.	壮观的场面,精彩的表演
enliven	vt.	使活泼,使生动,使有生气,使活跃
stumble	vi.	~(over/on sth) 绊脚,跌跌撞撞地走,(不顺畅地)说,读,演奏
	n.	绊脚,失足,差错,失误,失败

Notes to the Text

1. Aberdeen Asset Management Limited PLC:安本资产管理有限公司,成立于1876年,总部位于英国。近年来在海外基金市场快速窜起,以黑马之姿频频荣获国际媒体机构评比奖励,知名的史坦普尔公司亦评选安本集团为最佳英国投资管理集团第二名,是近来扩展最迅速的跨国投资集团之一。安本资产管理集团旗下之分公司及行政枢纽遍及全球各主要金融中心,如伦敦、爱丁堡、都柏林、新加坡、芝加哥、福特劳德等。

Shareholders Demand Right to Cap Bosses' Pay

The ability to approve or deny a mandatory pay cap would expand
shareholders' power significantly—Jeff Brass/Getty Images
Group of UK pension funds is concerned about the moral defensibility of big bonuses
Chloe Cornish and Jim Pickard
February 27, 2017, *Financial Times*

An influential group of large UK pension funds has urged the British government to allow shareholders to limit pay for company bosses, amid rising public concern that executive remuneration has reached unjustifiable levels.

The Local Authority Pension Fund Forum, which represents 72 local government pension schemes overseeing £175bn of assets in total, has gone further than other investor groups in calling for "binding upper thresholds for total annual pay" for executives.

The retirement funds want companies to put forward a maximum level of annual pay for senior executives that would be approved by shareholders.

"We felt some drastic proposals needed to be discussed," says a LAPFF spokesperson.

The call came in the LAPFF's submission, seen by FTfm, to the UK government's green paper on corporate governance reform that underpins Prime Minister Theresa May's promise to create a fairer economy.

The LAPFF made the policy suggestion in an attempt to address the debate among companies and shareholders over what constitutes appropriate "quantum"—the total amount of money paid to executives, including salary, bonuses and share payments.

"Everyone is complaining about how much directors get paid, but there is no single measure to give shareholders control over it," the spokesperson says.

Shareholders have complained that a company's pay policy, which is voted on every three years and sets out how much executives might earn in future share awards, provides little insight into the potential value of those stock options.

This means companies that have experienced sharp share price rises can legitimately award huge payouts to executives under the shareholder approved pay policy, even if investors believe the value of that payout is excessive.

The ability to approve or deny a mandatory pay cap would expand shareholders' power significantly by enabling them to "restrict the absolute amounts that can be paid out", the

LAPFF spokesperson says.

He adds that the pension body did not have a view on the level at which pay should be capped. "At this stage, debate about the idea is the goal," he says.

129x	231x
The number of times the average total pay for FTSE 100 chief executives exceed that of the average worker	The number of times the average total pay of American chief executives exceed that of the average worker

Shareholders have been worried by rising rewards for chief executives that largely failed to reflect company performance during the stock market downturn that followed the financial crisis.

The widening wealth gap between bosses and workers has also raised questions about the moral defensibility of big bonuses, when workforces face falling average earnings. The average total pay for FTSE 100 chief executives is 129 times that of the average worker, according to the High Pay Centre, a think-tank.

However, David Pitt-Watson, executive fellow of finance at the London Business School, warned that past attempts to curb pay have aggravated the situation.

He highlighted the decision by former US president Bill Clinton to make chief executive salaries in excess of $1m non-tax deductible as an example of a well-intentioned policy that had the opposite effect.

The tax changes, which were introduced in 1992 in an attempt to clamp down on high chief executive pay, inadvertently encouraged companies to find alternative ways to pay their top executives, enabling the performance-linked bonus culture to take off.

"Anyone making new rules about executive pay should remember the reforms passed by the Clinton administration to curb runaway pay for corporate chieftains, but [which] instead ended up encouraging excessive bonus payments," Mr Pitt-Watson says.

The LAPFF believes the government will consider the idea of a shareholder-approved pay cap, as politicians on both the left and right increasingly attack excessive pay packages as symptomatic of the widening gulf between bosses and workers.

In July, Mrs May tore into "an irrational, unhealthy and growing gap between what these companies pay their workers and what they pay their bosses".

On Tuesday, Vince Cable, the UK's former business secretary, also slammed pay for bosses, accusing top chief executives of a "narcissistic obsession" with pay.

Speaking at an event in parliament organised by ResPublica, the thinktank, Mr Cable said that even during the height of the banking crisis, bosses were worrying about their remuneration. "I was getting reports back from chairs that all the conversations with their chief executives were about pay," he said.

The LAPFF spokesperson says: "We think that a cap on total pay is an idea worth discussing. Hopefully that is the way the prime minister is looking at it as well."

Many of the world's largest asset managers told the Financial Times earlier this month that 2017 promises more shareholder uprisings over pay in the US and UK.

But the cacophony of voices has yet to give rise to a clear consensus on how to tackle the problem, according to Mr Pitt-Watson.

"Given the incentives and conflicts that surround this issue, it is difficult to formulate a sensible policy to curb what most accept is a system that is not working," he says.

Words and Expressions

mandatory	adj.	强制的,法定的,义务的
cap	vt.	限定金额
defensibility	n.	防卫能力
remuneration	n.	报酬,酬劳,赔偿
unjustifiable	adj.	不可原谅的,无法接受的,无正当理由的
pension scheme		(同 pension plan)退休金计划,养老金计划
oversee	v.	监督,监视
bind	v.	约束,限制
upper threshold		上限阈值
drastic	adj.	极端的,急剧的
submission	n.	提交(或呈递)的文件、建议等
underpin	v.	加强,巩固,构成(……的基础等),加固(墙)基
share-based payment		以股份为基础的支付
insight	n.	洞察力,领悟,洞悉
legitimate	adj.	正当合理的,合情合理的,合法的
excessive	adj.	过多的,极度的,过分的
payout	n.	付出的巨款
downturn	n.	(商业经济的)衰退,下降,衰退期
aggravate	v.	使严重,使恶化

clamp down		取缔,压制,管制
inadvertent	adj.	无意的,并非故意的,因疏忽造成的
alternative	adj.	可供替代的,非传统的,另类的
	n.	可供选择的事物
runaway	adj.	失控的
chieftain	n.	首领,酋长
pay package		工资待遇,薪酬方案
symptomatic	adj.	作为症状的,(有)症状的,作为征候的
tear into		怒斥,强烈批评
business secretary		商务大臣
slam	vt.	猛烈抨击
narcissistic	adj.	自我陶醉的,自我欣赏的
obsession	n.	痴迷,着魔
remuneration	n.	酬金,薪水
chair	n.	主席席位,委员长职位,(会议或委员会的)主席,委员长
promise	vt.	使很可能,预示
uprising	vi.	起义,奋起反抗
have yet to		尚未,有待
give rise to		造成,引起,导致

Notes to the Text

1. Getty Images：盖帝图像,于1995年成立于美国西雅图,作为全球数字媒体的缔造者首创并引领了独特的在线授权模式——在线提供数字媒体管理工具以及创意类图片、编辑类图片、影视素材和音乐产品。华盖创意(北京)图像技术有限公司是Getty Images在中国的合资公司,成立于2005年,公司总部设于北京。

2. FTSE 100：英国富时100指数,它是在伦敦证券交易所上市的100家最高度资本化的公司的股票指数,是目前为止使用最广泛的英国股市指标。它由世界级的指数计算金融机构FTSE(富时指数有限公司)所编制,自1984年起,特别挑选在伦敦证券交易所交易的100种股票,由很多行业组成,从航空航天和国防到烟草公司,其成分股涵盖欧陆9个主要国家,以英国企业为主,其他国家包括德国、法国、意大利、芬兰、瑞士、瑞典、荷兰及西班牙。指数中最大的5家公司是：必和必拓公司、荷兰皇家壳牌集团、汇丰银行、沃达丰集团、英国石油公司。它是为世界投资人欢迎的金融商品之一,和法国的CAC-40指数、德国的法兰克福指数并称为欧洲三大股票指数,是当前全球投资人观察欧股动向最重要的指标之一。

3. FTSE Group：富时集团,是一家英国股票市场指数和相关数据服务供应商,它由伦敦证券交易所全资控股。富时集团是由《金融时报》和伦敦证券交易所共同持有的独立公司。富时集团经营著名的英国富时 100 指数、罗素 2000 指数和许多其他指数。富时集团于 1995 年由《金融时报》前母公司 Pearson 和伦敦证券交易所集团共同创立。

4. LBS（London Business School）：伦敦商学院，是一所国际化商学院，为伦敦大学的两个研究生院之一，不提供本科教学，只提供金融和管理学方向的研究生课程。学院坐落于伦敦市中心，紧靠皇家公园摄政公园。伦敦商学院历来被认为是欧洲最顶尖的商学院，同时也是全球最顶尖的 10 所商学院之一。2011 年，该校连续第三年被金融时报、全球商学院排行榜评为世界第一，与沃顿商学院并列第一。

5. Theresa May：特雷莎·梅，全名为"特雷莎·玛丽·梅"（Theresa Mary May），英国现任首相兼首席财政大臣、文官大臣。1956 年 10 月 1 日生于英国伊特斯本，毕业于牛津大学圣休学院。

The Clintons' Financial Affairs Bill and Hillary Inc.

New York

Oct 1, 2016, *The Economist*

The Clintons' activities outside politics are both inspiring and worrying

Several years ago your correspondent attended a talk that Bill Clinton gave to the rich and powerful of a megacity in Asia. On a sweltering night the former president discussed his philanthropic foundation and the global battle against AIDS, climate change and poverty. The host, the boss of a local bank, then asked Mr Clinton to give the audience a special insight into whether his wife would run again for president. Mr Clinton sidestepped the question—while trying to give the star-struck crowd a sense that they really had a window into American power. His financial disclosures later indicated he was paid $500,000 for the speech, one of hundreds of talks he has done for his personal benefit, not for his charity.

The mix of politics, profit and philanthropy evident that evening has become a problem for the Clintons. Their foundation and financial affairs are now a liability: a swirl of truth, innuendo and crazed conspiracy theories. What shortcomings there are, it is true, pale into insignificance compared with Donald Trump's empire of lies and misconduct. But Mrs Clinton has been repeatedly forced to defend her own financial affairs, weakening her campaign.

Scrambling to limit the damage, the Clintons say they will wind down part of their activities, including the Clinton Global Initiative (CGI), a philanthropic event that operates as a division of the Clinton Foundation, their charity. In New York on September 21st, at the

CGI's final gathering, Mr Clinton croaked that it had "turned out better than I ever dreamed". The crowd, including the actor Ben Affleck, New Zealand's prime minister, activists and weepy billionaires, hugged to John Lennon's "Imagine". Yet a review of the Clintons' affairs suggests there are things to worry about as well as admire.

You may say I'm a dreamer

The Clintons' activities have three pillars. First, their role as politicians and the holders of public office. Second, their private income generating activities, mainly "for profit" speeches that they give for their own gain rather than for the foundation or other causes. The Economist estimates that, based on their tax returns and other disclosures, the couple have given 728 such talks since Mr Clinton left office in 2001, making $154m of fee income. Of this, 86% came from Mr Clinton. Mrs Clinton gave no for profit speeches while in office, but because of Mr Clinton's speaking tours, $49m, or 32% of the couple's for-profit speech revenue, was made while she was secretary of state in 2009–2013. Some gigs echoed the banality of the campaign trail—try the American Camping Association in Atlantic City. Others were far-flung, with visits to Moscow, Jeddah and Beijing. About 43% of total revenue came from events abroad.

After the crisis of 2008–2010 concerns rose about banks "capturing" regulators and politicians, so payments from these firms are controversial. The frequency of the Clintons' for-profit speaking appearances at some banks does raise eyebrows: 13 talks for Toronto Dominion, 12 for Goldman Sachs and ten for UBS. Of the 23 Western banks that regulators classify as systemically important, 12 have paid the Clintons on a for-profit basis. Still, overall only 15% of the Clintons' cumulative speech income came from financial firms. Mrs Clinton's campaign declined to comment on the figures in this article.

The third pillar is the Clinton Foundation, a sprawling philanthropic conglomerate. It was formed in 1997 to fund Mr Clinton's presidential library and then morphed into something bigger. Mr Clinton says the inspiration came just after he left office, in 2001, when he was based in Harlem and helped local firms there. He realised the benefits of partnerships. After the attacks of September 11th, 2001, he raised funds to help the victims' children. In 2002 the foundation took on HIV in the emerging world. Since then, new divisions have been added to respond to new problems. Today it has 12 divisions, including its health activities abroad, the CGI events and its work in Haiti.

The foundation's expansion and operating performance have been impressive. But its governance, sources of capital and approach to related parties are flawed.

Revenues from donations and grants rose from $10m in 2001 to $338m in 2014, the last year for which accounts are available. Assets rose from $21m to $440m. Unlike many foundations, the Clinton Foundation operates projects on the ground and employs 2,000 staff. It runs a fairly tight ship, with 64% of revenues in 2014 spent on its projects rather than on overheads.

The foundation is surrounded by hyperbole, so judging the outcomes it has delivered is difficult. It claims to have helped 100m people, and if you include the activities by participants at CGI events, this number rises to 535m, or one in every 14 people on Earth. Even if you discount this figure by 90%, it would be a major achievement. About two-thirds of the foundation's spending is by the division that works on HIV. Here its record is indisputably good, particularly in working to reduce the price of antiretroviral drugs.

The foundation's governance shows little sign of independence from the family or their political careers. Chelsea Clinton acts as vice-chairman. (Dynastic appointments are common in American philanthropy: Michael Bloomberg's daughters are on his foundation's board, for example.) The chairman, president and several senior executives worked for the Clintons in government or on their political campaigns.

Mr Clinton wanted a philanthropic empire, but unlike America's tycoons he had to do it with other people's money. The foundation is mainly financed by the pillars of society, for example the Gates Foundation. But an estimated $181m, or 9%, of its cumulative revenues has come from foreign governments and $54m of that, or 3% of the total, from autocratic states such as Saudi Arabia and Kuwait. A further 40% has come from other foreign sources, including multilateral bodies and companies. Donations are either earmarked for specific projects, or go into a general kitty.

An obvious question is what ancillary benefits donors thought they were getting, and here the Clintons' sloppy approach to conflicts of interest is evident, with the three pillars of their activities—public, private and charitable—colliding. Donors to the foundation attempted to get, and on occasion may have got, favours from Mrs Clinton while she was secretary of state. Most of these requests appear to have been for meetings with her. There was a flow of communication between donors, aides and Mrs Clinton's government office.

The $154m that the Clintons have made from for-profit speeches also involves potential conflicts of interest. You might expect the cost of hiring an ex-president for an evening to atrophy over time as his proximity to power declines. But Mr Clinton's for-profit speaking fees have risen since Mrs Clinton became a big political figure in her own right, especially for events abroad (see the following chart). The benign explanation is that there has probably been a general inflation in the fees famous speakers get over the past decade. But the Clinton Foundation has sustained Mr Clinton's profile. And some customers may have perceived that Mr Clinton's marriage gave him an insight into the government while Mrs Clinton was secretary of state.

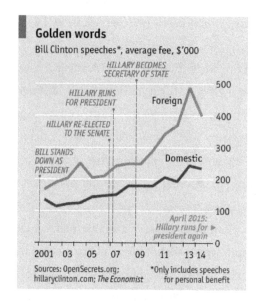

Belatedly the Clintons have realised how damaging their arrangements are. If Mrs Clinton becomes president, Mr Clinton says he will step down from the foundation and that it will stop taking donations from foreigners and private firms. In a similar effort to resolve potential conflicts of interest, Tony Blair, who seems to have mimicked the Clintons' business model, said this month that he would cease much of his commercial work and focus on his charitable activities. It seems likely that the Clinton Foundation will eventually be broken up, with each division having to secure its own donors.

The foundation has done many good works. But it grew in an innocent phase of globalisation, when the public were a little more forgiving of politicians getting rich while simultaneously seeking office, helping the needy and raising funds from business people and foreign governments. After the financial crash, and at a time when a majority of Americans feel the economy is rigged by an elite, the collision of politics, power, money and suffering seems tawdry. It will become tragic if the Clintons' financial affairs assist the election of a demagogue.

Unit Eleven Payment

 Words and Expressions

megacity	n.	大城市
sweltering	adj.	酷热难耐的
philanthropic	adj.	(人或机构)乐于助人的,慈善的
sidestep	vt.	回避,规避(问题等),横跨一步躲过,侧移一步闪过
innuendo	n.	暗指,影射
conspiracy	n.	密谋策划,阴谋
weepy	adj.	悲伤欲哭的,眼泪汪汪的,动不动就哭的
	n.	催人泪下的电影(或戏剧),令人伤感的电影(或戏剧)
pillar	n.	(组织、制度、信仰等的)核心,基础,支柱,台柱子
echo	n.	回响,回声,共鸣,附和
	v.	回响,回荡,重复,附和(想法或看法)
banality	n.	平凡,陈腐,陈词滥调
cumulative	adj.	(在力量或重要性方面)聚积的,积累的,渐增的
conglomerate	n.	联合大公司,企业集团,合成物,聚合物
morph	v.	(使)变化,(使)改变
	n.	(动植物的)变种,变体,语素形式
hyperbole	n.	夸张
indisputably	adv.	不容置疑地
antiretroviral	adj./n.	抗反转录病毒的,抗反转录病毒的药
tycoon	n.	(企业界的)大亨,巨头
autocratic	adj.	独裁的
ancillary	adj.	补充的,辅助的,附属的,附加的
	n.	助手,随从
sloppy	adj.	马虎的,凌乱的,草率的,肥大而难看的,庸俗伤感的
atrophy	n.	萎缩
	vi.	萎缩,衰退
proximity	n.	(时间或空间)接近,邻近,靠近
benign	adj.	善良的,和善的,慈祥的,良性的
mimic	vt.	模仿(人的言行举止)
	n.	会模仿的人(或动物)
rig	vt.	~ sth (up) (with sth) (以不正当的手段)操纵,控制,(给船只)装帆,提供索具,(秘密地)安装

tawdry	adj.	俗丽而不值钱的,花里胡哨的,下流的
demagogue	n.	蛊惑民心的政客

 Notes to the Text

1. CGI (Clinton Global Initiative):克林顿全球倡议,由美国前总统比尔·克林顿(Bill Clinton)于2005年创立,是独立于克林顿基金会的非政府组织,旨在聚集全球各界领军人物的智慧和资源,致力于推动人们探讨世界性问题,促进世界各地共同承担责任,尤其强调变想法为行动,应对一系列全球化挑战,解决全球性的问题。

Unit Twelve

Career Development

Millennial Women See No Glass Ceiling

High achievers believe nothing stands between them and the C-suite. Are they right?

Emma Jacobs

February 27, 2017, *Financial Times*

Sian Cleaver's childhood ambitions to become an astronaut did not fade with age. The 27-year-old simply adapted them as she grew up. Her teachers at her all-girls' school encouraged her to study maths and science and aim for a career in the space industry, despite the fact it was a male-dominated world. Today she works as a systems engineer at Airbus, the aerospace and defence company, helping to develop future missions to explore our solar system.

Ms Cleaver says she has never encountered outright sexism at work, and is cautiously optimistic about her future, insisting "it's about proving yourself".

She has every right to feel confident. Ms Cleaver is part of a generation of women who are better educated than their male peers. According to the OECD, women's academic achievements in G20 countries have "advanced to a degree that gender gaps in educational attainment are now most often reversed".

Millennial women such as Ms Cleaver have higher expectations of achieving equal pay and career progression than their mothers and grandmothers did. Whether they will achieve parity with their male colleagues in the decades to come remains a matter for debate.

In terms of equal pay, women in their twenties have never done better in some countries. In the UK, the Resolution Foundation, a think-tank, found they earn 5 per cent less than men on an hourly basis. Their baby boomer grandmothers, by contrast, faced a gender pay gap of 16 per cent in their 20s.

"Young women face relatively little disadvantage in terms of their pay packets," says Laura Gardiner, senior policy analyst at the foundation. But this does not necessarily mean that young men and women have equal chances of making it to the top of their professions.

Generations of young women started out as optimistic about avoiding a glass ceiling, says Nancy Kelley of NatCen, a UK social research group—only to be stymied by reality as they grew older.

"Women [generally] downplay the expectation of sexism in their careers," she says. "They are massively hopeful."

When they look upwards, millennial women do not see much to be optimistic about. "Here's what's not hopeful," says Brigid Schulte of New America, a US think-tank. "In every industry, in every profession, in virtually every field, women are stuck at the bottom and middle layers."

Older women, to use Sheryl Sandberg's phrase, are used to reading that they do not "lean in" enough—in other words, speak up or seek promotion. Their younger colleagues may feel the same. A 2017 survey by Deloitte, the professional services firm, found women of the millennial generation were not as confident as their male colleagues. "Men consistently believe they have more influence in the workplace," it said.

This may not only indicate that women hold themselves back, but also that their managers curtail them. Researchers at Stanford University scrutinised performance evaluations of men and women in three high-tech companies and a professional services firm. They found that women received less constructive feedback on their work from their bosses.

By contrast, "men are offered a clearer picture of what they are doing well and more specific guidance of what is needed to get to the next level".

The finding was backed in a 2016 report by McKinsey covering 132 companies. The consultancy found that women received less access to—and feedback from—their managers.

It also found women who tried to negotiate promotions or higher pay were 30 per cent more likely than men to be told they were "aggressive" or "bossy".

As for salaries, while the gender pay gap is relatively low for people in their twenties, millennials are finding it does not always stay that way.

According to data from Britain's Office for National Statistics, female managers and directors in financial institutions earned 34 per cent less than their male counterparts in 2016. The earnings deficit was 29 per cent for female medics and 8 per cent for people in public relations and advertising.

And while millennial women believe this will not be the case for them, some data suggest the gap is opening already.

The Resolution Foundation found the pay gap for millennials rose steeply, from 5 per cent in their twenties to 9 per cent when they hit 30. That is only marginally lower than the gender pay disparity experienced by the previous generation at the same age.

This is likely to be largely because young women step back from the workplace as they get married and have children.

Millennial couples who assumed their careers would be equal are slipping into traditional gender roles once children arrive, according to research published in the American Sociological Review in 2015. The reason, according to authors David Pedulla, then at Princeton University, now at Stanford, and Sarah Thébaud of the University of California, is "the constraints of current workplaces".

Will such constraints endure? There are reasons to be optimistic.

Alexandra Beever, a 24-year-old who works in the tax division of Deloitte, believes her company's commitment to flexible working will be good for her if she does have children. "It's not just geared to women," she says. "Men can spend more time at home, too."

But she and her female peers have yet to discover whether their employers' emphasis on flexible working will help them scale the career ladder.

A 2013 survey of 1,000 part-time workers—mostly female—by Time wise, a UK consultancy, found 77 per cent feel trapped in their jobs and unable to get promoted.

Women starting their careers should know that "it's about so much more than merit and talent," says Ms Schulte. "It's [also] about so much more than asking, negotiating, or being confident. Lean in, sure. But lean into what?"

Engineer Sian Cleaver says she has never encountered sexism at work

The gender pay gap for UK women in their twenties compared with men and measured on an hourly basis
Resolution Foundation

The gender pay gap for UK women aged 30 compared with men and measured on an hourly basis
Resolution Foundation

Proportion of part time workers, mostly women, who feel trapped and denied promotion
Timewise

Shortfall in salaries of female managers and directors in UK financial services compared with male colleagues
ONS

Words and Expressions

millennial	adj.	一千年的,千禧年的
high achiever		成就卓越者,成功者
aerospace	n.	航天航空工业,航空航天技术
encounter	vt.	遭遇,遇到(尤指令人不快或困难的事)
outright	adj.	完全的,彻底的,绝对的,公开的
optimistic	adj.	乐观的,抱乐观看法的
reverse	v.	颠倒,彻底转变,使完全相反
parity	n.	(薪金或地位)平等,相同,对等,(两国货币的)平价
pay packet		所得工资
start out		开始,最初
stymie	vt.	阻挠,阻碍
downplay	vt.	对……轻描淡写,使轻视,贬低
hopeful	adj.	(人)抱有希望的,满怀希望的
lean in		往桌前坐,跻身领导层
speak up		大胆地说,公开表态,大声说
workplace	n.	工作场所
hold back		(使)犹豫,(使)退缩
curtail	vt.	限制,缩短
scrutinise	vt.	审查,详细检查
bossy	adj.	好指挥人的,专横的
Office for National Statistics		(英国)国家统计局
counterpart	n.	职位(或作用)相当的人
deficit	n.	(比预期或者要求少的)差额
medics	n.	医科学生,医生
steep	adj.	陡峭的,突然的,急剧的

hit	vt.	达到某个水平、程度
marginally	adv.	轻微地,微不足道地
disparity	n.	差异,悬殊
largely	adv.	在很大程度上,多半,主要地
step back from		后退,退出
slip into		不知不觉地进入
constraint	n.	限制,限定
endure	v.	持续,持久
flexible working		弹性工作制
gear to		调整(某物)使其适合……
scale	v.	攀登,到达……顶点
career ladder		职业晋升阶梯
trap	vt.	使落入险境,使陷入困境
merit	n.	优点,美德
shortfall	n.	缺口,差额

Notes to the Text

1. baby boom:婴儿潮,指的是在某一时期及特定地区出生率大幅度提升的现象。历史上有记载的几次婴儿潮通常是起因于有振奋人心的因素,如农作物丰收、打赢战争、赢得体育竞赛等,但也有因为迷信的因素。英文中把在婴儿潮时期出生的婴儿称为 baby boomer。"婴儿潮"首次出现主要是指美国第二次世界大战后的"4664"现象——从 1946 年至 1964 年,这 18 年间婴儿潮人口高达 7800 万人。

2. glass ceiling:玻璃天花板。1999 年出版的《英汉大词典补编》是国内最早收录这个新词的双语词典,当时词典中给出的译名是"玻璃天花板,无形封顶(指视若无形而实际存在的妇女、少数族裔成员在职业岗位升迁的极限)"。

根据《牛津英语大词典》的解释,glass ceiling 源于美国英语,首现于 1984 年 3 月 15 日的《广告周刊》(*Adweek*),即"Women have reached a certain point—I call it the glass ceiling. They're in the top of middle management and they're stopping and getting stuck."(女性已经到达一定的极限——我把这种极限称作"玻璃天花板"。这些女性位居中间管理层的顶部,已经无法升迁,只好困在原处。)

"玻璃天花板"出现于 1986 年 3 月 24 日的《华尔街日报》的"企业女性"的专栏当中,用来描述女性试图晋升到企业或组织高层所面临的障碍。"天花板效应"是莫里森等人在 1987 年的一篇文章——《打破天花板效应:女生能够进入美国大企业的高层吗?》

("Breaking the Glass Ceiling: Can Women Reach the Top of America's Largest Corporations?")中首先使用的概念。一年以后,玛里琳·戴维森和加里·库珀在其《打碎天花板效应》(Shattering the Glass Ceiling)一书中也讨论了这个问题。

4. Airbus:空中客车公司(又被称为"空客""空中巴士"),是欧洲一家飞机制造、研发公司,1970年12月于法国成立。空中客车公司的股份由欧洲宇航防务集团公司(EADS)100%持有。空中客车A380(Airbus A380)是欧洲空中客车工业公司研制生产的四发550座级超大型远程宽体客机,投产时也是全球载客量最大的客机,有"空中巨无霸"之称。

5. sexism:性别歧视主义,一般是指基于他人的性别差异而非他人优缺点所造成的厌恶或歧视,但也可用来指称任何因为性别所造成的差别待遇。

6. OECD(Organization for Economic Co-operation and Development):经济合作与发展组织,简称"经合组织",是由36个市场经济国家组成的政府间国际经济组织,旨在共同应对全球化带来的经济、社会、政府治理等方面的挑战,并把握全球化带来的机遇。成立于1961年,目前成员国总数36个,总部设在巴黎。

7. G20:20国集团,是一个国际经济合作论坛,于1999年9月25日由八国集团(G8)的财长在德国柏林成立,于华盛顿举办了第一届G20峰会,属于非正式对话的一种机制,由原八国集团及其余12个重要经济体组成,包括中国、阿根廷、澳大利亚、巴西、加拿大、法国、德国、印度、印度尼西亚、意大利、日本、韩国、墨西哥、沙特阿拉伯、南非、土耳其、英国、美国、俄罗斯及欧盟。

8. Deloitte:德勤,是世界四大会计师事务所之一。遍布全球的分支机构和会员,总部设立在英国。其主要业务集中在四个领域:审计、税务规划、咨询和财务顾问。

9. Stanford University:斯坦福大学,全名小利兰·斯坦福大学(Leland Stanford Junior University),简称"斯坦福"(Stanford),位于美国加州旧金山湾区南部的帕罗奥多市(Palo Alto)境内,临近世界著名高科技园区硅谷,是世界著名的私立研究型大学、环太平洋大学联盟成员。斯坦福大学与旧金山北湾的加州大学伯克利分校共同构成了美国西部的学术中心。

10. University of California:加州大学,是位于美国加州的一个由10所公立大学组成的大学行政系统,也是世界上最具影响力的公立大学系统,被誉为"公立高等教育的典范"。美国加州大学是世界上最大的公立大学系统,拥有10所相互独立的校区(大学)、4所法学院、5所医学院和教学医院。加州大学还管理3个国家实验室。加州大学在伯克利(Berkeley)、戴维斯(Davis)、尔湾(Irvine)、洛杉矶(Los Angeles)、河滨(Riverside)、圣地亚哥(San Diego)、旧金山(San Francisco)、圣塔巴巴拉(Santa Babara)和圣克鲁兹(Santa Cruz)的校区均是世界级的教育和科研机构。

Long Lives Mean Demand for Endless Coaching

Alumni expect business schools to support them over their careers—even during retirement

Miranda Green

February 27, 2017, *Financial Times*

After 25 years working in the City of London, Bruce Rigal has gone back to college. Now in his fifties, the former senior Deutsche Bank director is the oldest student on his behavioural and economic science course at Warwick university.

He has returned to class for this joint MSc, offered by the business school and the economics and psychology departments, to pick up where his 1980s business education left off. But in order to make the leap back into education, he needed a nudge.

"The decision to actually do it was very difficult," he says. "To jump back in and be in a classroom with a bunch of much younger people."

So he turned to his former business school for help. In the 1980s, he had studied for an MBA at Chicago Booth. For Mr Rigal, life-long access to unlimited coaching offered by the business school was invaluable as he decided how and whether to re-enter education.

With extended lifespans and dwindling pensions, careers are likely to get longer—sometimes running into seven decades—so business schools are finding new ways to support alumni through mid- and late-career changes. The perk is valuable: private coaching sessions with top consultants can start at nearly $300 per session.

Mr Rigal appreciated the "structured approach" of the business school's careers service: "With a life-long career, there aren't that many places where you get that continuity."

Spain's jobless MBAs

Spain's brutal rates of unemployment since the financial crisis have worsened the plight of older workers, according to Ana Herranz of the careers services at IE business school. "I serve anyone who is struggling," she says. After a rise in requests for help from former students in their forties and fifties, Ms Herranz offers annual intensive career coaching for older alumni, with an emphasis on building consulting practices or portfolio careers.

Chris Lecatsas-Lyus, director of career management for Chicago Booth in Europe, is a psychotherapist and career coach. Alongside colleagues in Chicago and Hong Kong, she offers coaching to alumni facing career dilemmas at the business school's three global campuses and for any age up to retirement—even beyond, in some cases.

Using a range of counselling techniques, Ms Lecatsas-Lyus says her coaching sessions find solutions to career problems, leading the client to decide on action—and a better understanding of how to tackle a problem or challenge. "[Coaching] is not a chat," she says. "We use questions to dig down through whatever uncertainties or discomfort they are feeling."

Most Chicago Booth alumni, she says, come for one of three reasons: a desire to change career, guidance on how to move from corporate roles to entrepreneurial ventures, or how to advance in their organisation or industry.

Often they are struggling: "Some have a desire to move from their more regimented career to search for more value in what they do," she says.

Others are at what she calls "transitional stages" in a longer career path: "When they take an MBA, students are on structured courses where the next step is visible. Several years on, they are more senior and the next step is less obvious."

Chicago Booth's unlimited coaching offer is unusual, but other business schools are adapting to longer working lives.

Insead's 50,000 alumni spread across the world provide "a steady stream of demand" for career coaching, according to Steven Burton, managing director of executive degrees. The school limits its free sessions to two hours per former student. "A lot of our coaches are former Insead grads themselves," he says.

"A lot of our coaches are former Insead grads themselves," he says.

At London Business School, coaching is one of the most popular resources for former students, according to Natalie Simpson, manager of the alumni career centre. Coaching sessions, limited to two per year for alumni, are provided in London, New York and Dubai, with the school picking up the tab for more than 400 hours annually.

At twice-yearly reunions, sessions are booked in advance and demand outstrips supply. "It's usually when they are thinking about a career shift or change," says Ms Simpson.

Lynne Allen, who coaches LBS alumni in the US, often sees professionals in their forties or fifties facing redundancy and forced into new careers, or those who want to find away to get on corporate boards.

She says many top business schools are choosing to subsidise this personal service: "It's a competitive advantage, and if you give, hopefully they will give back—it makes sense to support their success because it also enhances the reputation of the school."

But LBS, like other business schools, is braced for even more demand from older alumni on non-traditional career paths. "Over time," says Chicago Booth's Ms Lecatsas-Lyus, "we'll begin to notice much more of them working longer—if the need is there, we will respond."

For Mr Rigal, who enjoys being a pioneering older learner, the hope is that others will follow, and soon. "I would like to see more of a trend, because I would like a few other older people in my class to keep me company," he says.

Words and Expressions

leave off		停止(做某事),中断
nudge	n.	轻推,渐渐推动,用肘轻推(朝某方向)
invaluable	adj.	极有用的,极宝贵的
life span		(人、动植物的)寿命,预期生命期限
dwindle	vi.	减少,变小
	vt.	使缩小,使减少
run into		(费用或数量)高达,达到
perk	n.	(工资之外的)补贴,津贴,额外待遇
structured approach		结构化方法
brutal	adj.	残酷无情的,难以忍受的
plight	n.	苦难,困境
continuity	n.	连续性,持续性
portfolio career		组合式职业生涯
psychotherapist	n.	心理治疗医师
dilemma	n.	(进退两难的)窘境,困境
dig down through		追究,探寻
entrepreneurial	adj.	富于企业家精神的
regimented	adj.	非常严格的,死板的,严格规划的,排列整齐的
transitional stage		过渡阶段,过渡期
senior	adj.	级别(或地位)高的
managing director		总经理,常务董事
grad	n.	(同 graduate)毕业生
coaching	n.	(体育运动、工作或技能的)培训,指导
pick up the tab		(替一群人)付账,承担费用
venture	vt.	敢于
	vi.	冒险,投机
	n.	企业,风险,冒险
outstrip	vt.	超过,胜过,比……跑得快

Notes to the Text

1. **The University of Warwick**:华威大学,是英国顶尖研究型大学,在英国主流媒体排名中,除牛津、剑桥之外唯一未跌出过排名前十的英国大学。华威大学位于英格兰中部华威郡和考文垂市的交界处,创立于1965年。华威大学以严苛的招生、高水准的学术研究和教学质量而闻名。

2. **Master of Science**:理学硕士,是指对于硕士研究生阶段专攻理科方向(如数学、物理、力学、化学、生物学、天文学、地学等专业)的学生的一种专业上的称谓。

3. **University of Chicago Booth School of Business**:芝加哥大学商学院,创建于1898年,是美国最好的商学院之一,多次跻身于商学院排行榜前三名。芝加哥大学商学院以其多位荣获诺贝尔经济学奖的学者而著称于世。

4. **instituto de Empresa**:西班牙IE商学院,1973年创办于西班牙,被公认为世界领先的商学院。IE商学院坐落在西班牙首都马德里。IE商学院的学生非常享受学习和使用西班牙语——这个世界上第二大商业语言所带来的乐趣。国际化是IE商学院的一大特征。目前IE商学院的毕业生在全世界100多个国家坐拥管理职位。学校的管理学硕士项目(Master in Management)在2014年*Financial Times*的全球管理学硕士排名中列第9位。

5. **INSEAD**:欧洲工商管理学院,是一所世界一流的商学院。INSEAD在2018年和2019年QS世界大学排名商业与管理学领域名列全球第2,连续多年位于全球前三位置,其在学术声誉(Academic Reputation)一栏更是取得了满分100分的评级。它汇聚世界各地的人才、文化和思想,其全球视野和文化多样性体现在研究和教学的各个环节之中,被誉为"欧洲的哈佛商学院"。

6. **Dubai**:迪拜,是阿拉伯联合酋长国人口最多的城市,2018年被GaWC评为年度世界一线城市第九位。迪拜是中东地区的经济金融中心,它也是中东地区旅客和货物的主要运输枢纽。迪拜拥有世界上最高的人工建筑哈利法塔,还有世界上面积最大的人工岛项目棕榈岛。

Neurodiversity as a Competitive Advantage

Why you should embrace it in your workforce
Robert D. Austion and Gary P. Pisano
May – June, 2017, *Harvard Business Review*

Robert D. Austin is a professor of information systems at Ivey Business School and a coauthor of *The Adventures of an IT Leader* (Harvard Business Review Press, 2016). Gary P. Pisano is the Harry E. Figgie Professor of Business Administration and a member of the US Competitiveness Project at Harvard Business School.

IN BRIEF
The Problem

Many people with neurological conditions such as autism spectrum disorder, dyspraxia and dyslexia have extraordinary skills, including in pattern recognition, memory, and mathematics. But the neurodiverse population remains largely untapped.

The Cause

Conventional recruitment and career-development methods (for example, job interviews) and the belief that scalable work processes require absolute conformity to standardized approaches screen out neurodiverse people who could be valuable employees.

The Solution

A growing number of companies—among them SAP, Hewlett Packard Enterprise, Microsoft, Willis Towers Watson, and EY—have reformed HR practices to capitalize on the talents of neurodiverse people. In the process, they are becoming better able to fully leverage the skills of all workers.

Meet John. He's a wizard at data analytics. His combination of mathematical ability and software development skill is highly unusual. His CV features two master's degrees, both with honors. An obvious guy for a tech company to scoop up, right?

Until recently, no. Before John ran across a firm that had begun experimenting with alternative approaches to talent, he was unemployed for more than two years. Other companies he had talked with badly needed the skills he possessed. But he couldn't make it through the hiring process.

If you watched John for a while, you'd start to see why. He seems, well, different. He wears headphones all the time, and when people talk to him, he doesn't look right at them. He leans over every 10 minutes or so to tighten his shoelaces; he can't concentrate when they're loose. When they're tight, though, John is the department's most productive employee. He is hardworking and never wants to take breaks. Although his assigned workplace "buddy" has finally persuaded him to do so, he doesn't enjoy them.

"John" is a composite of people whose privacy we wanted to protect—people with autism spectrum disorder. He is representative of participants in the programs of pioneering companies that have begun seeking out "neurodiverse" talent.

A lot of people are like John. The incidence of autism in the United States is now 1 in 42 among boys and 1 in 189 among girls, according to the Centers for Disease Control and Prevention. And although corporate programs have so far focused primarily on autistic people, it should be possible to extend them to people affected by dyspraxia (a neurologically based physical disorder), dyslexia, ADHD, social anxiety disorders, and other conditions. Many people with these disorders have higher-than-average abilities; research shows that some conditions, including autism and dyslexia, can bestow special skills in pattern recognition, memory, or mathematics. Yet those affected often struggle to it the profiles sought by prospective employers.

Neurodiverse people frequently need workplace accommodations, such as headphones to prevent auditory overstimulation, to activate or maximally leverage their abilities. Sometimes they exhibit challenging eccentricities. In many cases the accommodations and challenges are manageable and the potential returns are great. But to realize the benefits, most companies would have to adjust their recruitment, selection, and career development policies to reflect a broader definition of talent.

A growing number of prominent companies have reformed their HR processes in order to access neurodiverse talent; among them are SAP, Hewlett Packard Enterprise (HPE), Microsoft, Willis Towers Watson, Ford, and EY. Many others, including Caterpillar, Dell Technologies, Deloitte, IBM, JPMorgan Chase and UBS, have start-up or exploratory efforts under way. We have had extensive access to the neurodiversity programs at SAP, HPE and Specialisterne (the Danish consulting company that originated such programs), and have also interacted with people at Microsoft, Willis Towers Watson and EY.

Although the programs are still in early days—SAP's, the longest running among major companies, is just four years old—managers say they are already paying off in ways far beyond reputational enhancement. Those ways include productivity gains, quality improvement, boosts in innovative capabilities, and broad increases in employee engagement. Nick Wilson, the managing director of HPE South Pacific—an organization with one of the largest such programs—says that no other initiative in his company delivers benefits at so many levels.

Perhaps the most surprising benefit is that managers have begun thinking more deeply about leveraging the talents of all employees through greater sensitivity to individual needs. SAP's program "forces you to get to know the person better, so you know how to manage them," says Silvio Bessa, the senior vice president of digital business services. "It's made me a better manager, without a doubt."

Why Neurodiversity Presents Opportunities

"Neurodiversity is the idea that neurological differences like autism and ADHD are the result of normal, natural variation in the human genome," John Elder Robison, a scholar in residence and a cochair of the Neurodiversity Working Group at the College of William & Mary, writes in a blog on Psychology Today's website. Robison, who himself has Asperger's syndrome, adds, "Indeed, many individuals who embrace the concept of neurodiversity believe that people with differences do not need to be cured; they need help and accommodation instead." We couldn't agree more.

Everyone is to some extent differently abled (an expression favored by many neurodiverse people), because we are all born different and raised differently. Our ways of thinking result from both our inherent "machinery" and the experiences that have "programmed" us.

Most managers are familiar with the advantages organizations can gain from diversity in the backgrounds, disciplinary training, gender, culture and other individual qualities of employees. Benefits from neurodiversity are similar but more direct. Because neurodiverse people are wired differently from "neurotypical" people, they may bring new perspectives to a company's efforts to create or recognize value. At HPE, neurodiverse software testers observed that one client's projects always seemed to go into crisis mode before a launch. Intolerant of disorder, they strenuously questioned the company's apparent acceptance of the chaos. This led the client company to realize that it had indeed become too tolerant of these crises and, with the help of the testers, to successfully redesign the launch process. At SAP, a neurodiverse customer-support analyst spotted an opportunity to let customers help solve a common problem themselves; thousands of them subsequently used the resources he created.

Nevertheless, the neurodiverse population remains a largely untapped talent pool. Unemployment runs as high as 80% (this figure includes people with more-severe disorders, who are not candidates for neurodiversity programs). When they are working, even highly capable neurodiverse people are often underemployed. Program participants told us story after story of how, despite having solid credentials, they had previously had to settle for the kinds of jobs many people leave behind in high school. When SAP began its Autism at Work program, applicants included people with master's degrees in electrical engineering, biostatistics, economic statistics, and anthropology and bachelor's degrees in computer science, applied and computational mathematics, electrical engineering, and engineering physics. Some had dual degrees. Many had earned very high grades and graduated with honors or other distinctions. One held a patent.

Not surprisingly, when autistic people with those sorts of credentials do manage to get hired, many turn out to be capable, and some are really great. Over the past two years HPE's program has placed more than 30 participants in software-testing roles at Australia's Department of Human Services (DHS). Preliminary results suggest that the organization's neurodiverse testing teams are 30% more productive than the others.

Inspired by the successes at DHS, the Australian Defense Department is now working with HPE to develop a neurodiversity program in cybersecurity; participants will apply their superior pattern detection abilities to tasks such as examining logs and other sources of messy data for signs of intrusion or attack. Using assessment methods borrowed from the Israeli Defense Forces (IDF), it has found candidates whose relevant abilities are "off the charts". (The IDF's Special Intelligence Unit 9900, which is responsible for analyzing aerial and satellite imagery, has a group staffed primarily with people on the autism spectrum. It has proved that they can spot patterns others do not see.)

The case for neurodiverse hiring is especially compelling given the skills shortages that increasingly afflict technology and other industries. For example, the European Union faces a shortage of 800,000 IT workers by 2020, according to a European Commission study. The biggest deficits are expected to be in strategically important and rapidly expanding areas such as data analytics and IT services implementation, whose tasks are a good match with the abilities of some neurodiverse people.

Why Companies Don't Tap Neurodiverse Talent

What has kept so many companies from taking on people with the skills they badly need? It comes down to the way they find and recruit talent and decide whom to hire (and promote).

Especially in large companies, HR processes are developed with an eye toward wide application across the organization. But there is a conflict between scalability and the goal of acquiring neurodiverse talent. "SAP focuses on having scalable HR processes; however, if we were to use the same processes for everyone, we would miss people with autism," says Anka Wittenberg, the company's chief diversity and inclusion officer.

In addition, the behaviors of many neurodiverse people run counter to common notions of what makes a good employee—solid communication skills, being a team player, emotional intelligence, persuasiveness, salesperson-type personalities, the ability to network, the ability to conform to standard practices without special accommodations, and so on. These criteria systematically screen out neurodiverse people.

But they are not the only way to provide value. In fact, in recent decades the ability to compete on the basis of innovation has become more crucial for many companies. Innovation calls on firms to add variety to the mix—to include people and ideas from "the edges", as SAP put it in the press release announcing its program. Having people who see things differently and who maybe don't it in seamlessly "helps offset our tendency, as a big company, to all look in the same direction," Bessa says.

You might think that organizations could simply seek more variety in prospective employees while retaining their traditional recruiting, hiring, and development practices. Many have taken that approach: Their managers still work top down from strategies to capabilities needed, translating those into organizational roles, job descriptions, and recruiting checklists. But two big problems cause them to miss neurodiverse talent.

The first involves a practice that is almost universal under the traditional approach: interviewing. Although neurodiverse people may excel in important areas, many don't interview well. For example, autistic people often don't make good eye contact, are prone to conversational tangents, and can be overly honest about their weaknesses. Some have confidence problems arising from difficulties they experienced in previous interview situations. Neurodiverse people more broadly are unlikely to earn higher scores in interviews than less-talented neurotypical candidates. SAP and HPE have found that it can take weeks or months to discover how good some program participants are (or, equally important, where their limitations lie). Fortunately, as we'll see, interviews are not the only way to assess a candidate's suitability.

The second problem, especially common in large companies, derives from the assumption that scalable processes require absolute conformity to standardized approaches. As mentioned, employees in neurodiversity programs typically need to be allowed to deviate from established practices. This shifts a manager's orientation from assuring compliance through standardization to adjusting individual work contexts. Most accommodations, such as installing different lighting and providing noise-canceling headphones, are not very expensive. But they do require managers to tailor individual work settings more than they otherwise might.

How Pioneers Are Changing the Talent Management Game

The tech industry has a history of hiring oddballs. The talented nerd who lacks social graces has become a cultural icon, as much a part of the industry mythos as the company that starts in a garage. In his book *NeuroTribes*, Steve Silberman points out that the incidence of autism is particularly high in places like Silicon Valley (for reasons not completely understood). He and others have hypothesized that many of the industry's "oddballs" and "nerds" might well have been "on the spectrum", although undiagnosed. Hiring for neurodiversity, then, could be seen as an extension of the tendencies of a culture that recognizes the value of nerds.

In recent years a few pioneering companies have formalized and professionalized those tendencies. Although their programs vary, they have elements in common, not least because they draw on the body of knowledge developed at Specialisterne. Thorkil Sonne founded the irm in 2004, motivated by the autism diagnosis of his third child. Over the next several years it developed and reined noninterview methods for assessing, training and managing neurodiverse talent, and demonstrated the viability of its model by running a successful for-profit company focused on software testing.

Dissatisfied with the rate at which his own company could create jobs, Sonne established the Specialist People Foundation (recently renamed the Specialisterne Foundation) in 2008 to spread his company's know-how to others and persuade multinationals to start neurodiversity programs. Most companies that have done so have worked with the foundation to deploy some version of the Specialisterne approach. It has seven major elements:

Team with "social partners" for expertise you lack. Managers in, say, a tech company know a lot about many things but usually are not experts in autism or other categories of neurodiversity. Also, for many good reasons, companies hesitate to extend their activities into employees' private lives, where neurodiverse people may need extra help.

To fill these gaps, the companies we studied entered into relationships with "social partners"—government or nonprofit organizations committed to helping people with disabilities obtain jobs. SAP has worked with California's Department of Rehabilitation, Pennsylvania's Office of Vocational Rehabilitation, the US nonprofits EXPANDability and the Arc, and overseas agencies such as EnAble India, while HPE has worked with Autism SA (South Australia). Such groups help companies navigate local employment regulations that apply to people with disabilities, suggest candidates from lists of neurodiverse people seeking employment, assist in prescreening, help arrange public funding for training, sometimes administer training, and provide the mentorship and ongoing support (especially outside work hours) needed to ensure that neurodiverse employees will succeed. In Germany, recognition of the benefits of moving people of public assistance and into jobs that generate tax revenue has led to publicly funded positions to support the retention of neurodiverse employees. Although estimates of the benefits a government gains by turning such people into taxpaying tech workers vary, they often are on the order of \$50,000 per person a year.

Use nontraditional, noninterview-based assessment and training processes. To this end, Specialisterne created "hangouts"—comfortable gatherings, usually lasting half a day, in which neurodiverse job candidates can demonstrate their abilities in casual interactions with company managers. At the end of a hangout, some candidates are selected for two to six weeks of further assessment and training (the duration varies by company). During this time they use Lego Mindstorms robotic construction and programming kits to work on assigned projects—first individually and then in groups, with the projects becoming more like actual work as the process continues. Some companies have additional sessions. SAP, for example, established a "soft skills" module to help candidates who have never worked in a professional environment become familiar with the norms of such a setting. These efforts are typically funded by the government or nonprofits. Trainees are usually paid.

Despite the social difficulties experienced by many neurodiverse people, candidates often display complex collaborative and support behaviors during the project-based assessment period. At HPE, for example, groups were asked to devise a reliable robotic pill-dispensing system. During the presentation of solutions, one candidate froze. "I'm sorry, I can't do it," he said. "The words are all jumbled up in my head." His neurodiverse teammates rushed to his rescue, surrounding and reassuring him, and he was able to finish.

By extending the assessment process, such programs allow time for candidates' capabilities to surface. There are, of course, other ways to do this. HPE has begun using internships that include similar elements.

Train other workers and managers. Short (some are just half a day), low-key training sessions help existing employees understand what to expect from their new colleagues—for example, that they might need accommodations and might seem different. Managers get somewhat more-extensive training to familiarize them with sources of support for program employees.

Set up a support ecosystem. Companies with neurodiverse programs design and maintain simple support systems for their new employees. SAP defines two "support circles"—one for the workplace, the other for an employee's personal life. The workplace support circle includes a team manager, a team buddy, a job and life skills coach, a work mentor, and an "HR business partner", who oversees a group of program participants. Buddies are staff members on the same team who provide assistance with daily tasks, workload management, and prioritization. Job and life skills coaches are usually from social partner organizations. Other social partner roles include vocational rehab counselor and personal counselor. Usually, families of employees also provide support.

HPE takes a different approach. It places new neurodiverse employees in "pods" of about 15 people, where they work alongside neurotypical colleagues in a roughly 4:1 ratio while two managers and a consultant are tasked with addressing neurodiversity related issues.

Tailor methods for managing careers. Employees hired through these programs need long-term career paths, just as other workers do. This requires serious thought about ongoing assessment and development that will take the special circumstances of neurodiverse employment into account. Fortunately, over time supervisors usually get a good sense of program employees' talents and limitations. Participants undergo the same performance evaluations that other employees do, but managers work within those processes to set specific goals. Although some goals may relate to participants' conditions, no allowances are made for unsatisfactory performance. If anything, neurodiverse employees must satisfy more requirements than others, because they must meet program objectives in addition to the performance objectives expected of anyone in their role.

Some participants quickly demonstrate potential to become integrated into the mainstream organization and go further in their careers. HPE's pods are designed to provide a safe environment in which participants can build skills that will allow them to perform well and eventually to transition out of their pods into more-mainstream jobs.

Scale the program. SAP has announced an intention to make 1% of its workforce neurodiverse by 2020—a number chosen because it roughly corresponds to the percentage of autistic people in the general population. Microsoft, HPE and others are also working to enlarge their programs, although they have declined to set numerical targets. It's easiest to expand employment in those areas, such as software testing, business analytics, and cyber security, in which tasks are a good it with neurodiverse talent. SAP, however, has placed its more than 100 program employees in 18 roles. "The original expectation, as I understood it, was that these colleagues would be mostly focused on repetitive work, such as software testing," one manager told us. "But in practice they have been able to add value in a much broader range of tasks." Those include product management, which involves coordinating the development of new SAP offerings; HR service associate, which entails organizing and planning HR activities; associate consultant, which requires helping customers apply SAP solutions to business problems; and customer support, which means working with customers on the phone to help them use SAP software. The latter two defy the assumption that people with autism can't hold jobs that require social skills.

HPE is deploying neurodiverse specialists nine at a time, in pods, to client organizations—in effect, selling packages of the advanced capabilities derived from neurodiversity. The model has intriguing scale possibilities, both because many workers are placed at once and because client demand enlarges the domain of possible placements.

Mainstream the program. The success of neurodiversity programs has prompted some companies to think about how ordinary HR processes may be excluding high-quality talent. SAP is conducting a review to determine how recruiting, hiring, and development could take a broader view. Its stated goal is to make its mainstream talent processes so "neurodiversity friendly" that it can ultimately close its neurodiversity program. Microsoft has similar ambitions.

Companies have experienced a surprising array of benefits from neurodiversity programs. Some are straightforward: Firms have become more successful at finding and hiring good and even great talent in tough-to-ill skills categories. Products, services and bottom lines have profited from lower defect rates and higher productivity. Both SAP and HPE report examples of neurodiverse employees' participating on teams that generated significant innovations (one, at SAP, helped develop a technical fix worth an estimated $40 million in savings).

Other benefits are subtler. One executive told us that efforts to make corporate communications more direct, in order to account for the difficulties autistic employees have with nuance, irony and other fine points of language, have improved communication overall. The perfectionist tendencies of some HPE software-testing pods have caused client organizations to raise their game and stop viewing certain common problems as inevitable. In addition, employee engagement has risen in areas the programs touch: Neurotypical people report that involvement makes their work more meaningful and their morale higher. And early indications suggest that program employees, appreciative of having been given a chance, are very loyal and have low rates of turnover.

Last but not least, the programs confer reputational benefits. The companies that pioneered them have been recognized by the United Nations as exemplars of responsible management and have won global corporate citizenship awards.

Challenges of a Neurodiverse Workforce

To be sure, companies implementing neurodiversity programs have encountered challenges. Although there are plenty of potential candidates, many are hard to identify, because universities—sensitive to issues of discrimination—do not classify students in neurodiversity terms, and potential candidates do not necessarily self-identify. In response, HPE is helping colleges and high schools set up nontraditional "work experience" programs for neurodiverse populations. These involve video gaming, robotic programming, and other activities. Microsoft, too, is working with universities to improve methods of identifying and accessing neurodiverse talent.

Another common difficulty involves the dashed hopes of candidates who are not chosen for placement—an inevitable circumstance that must be handled carefully. At one company, parents whose son did not qualify for a job wrote to the CEO; the program had raised their hopes that he would finally achieve meaningful employment, and they were understandably disappointed. Executives fretted about a potential PR problem. In the end, compassionate discussions between the parents and managers of the program—some of whom had families that had experienced similar issues—calmed the situation.

Issues related to fairness and norms of interaction might arise as well. In one case we encountered, a program participant who had overstimulation difficulties was given his own office while four people in a nearby department were crowded into a similar space, generating complaints. Those subsided after an explanation was offered. We also heard of instances in which the excessive honesty typical of autistic people raised hackles. One concerned a program employee who told a colleague, "You stink at your job." Coaching by managers and mentors can help address such situations.

Some supervisors reported that the program generated extra work for them. For instance, the perfectionist tendencies of some participants made it difficult for those employees to judge which defects were worth fixing, which were not, and which required them to seek additional direction.

Managing neurodiverse employees' stress presents another challenge. We heard reports that unexpected and uncontrollable events, such as systems outages that interfered with work routines, caused unusually high levels of anxiety among participants. Many people we interviewed emphasized the need to be sensitive to program employees' stress. To keep it under control, some participants work only part-time—a limitation that may create problems, especially when deadlines loom.

To handle such situations, organizations need people in place who can spot and address issues before they escalate. Many managers said that with these and other supports, they could perform their jobs in a fairly normal fashion. And contrary to their initial assumptions, SAP managers found they could even supervise program participants remotely, as long as buddies and mentors provided support locally.

A Major Shift in Managing People

Neurodiversity programs induce companies and their leaders to adopt a style of management that emphasizes placing each person in a context that maximizes her or his contributions. SAP uses a metaphor to communicate this idea across the organization: People are like puzzle pieces, irregularly shaped. Historically, companies have asked employees to trim away their irregularities, because it's easier to fit people together if they are all perfect rectangles. But that requires employees to leave their differences at home—

differences firms need in order to innovate. "The corporate world has mostly missed out on this [benefit]," Anka Wittenberg observes.

This suggests that companies must embrace an alternative philosophy, one that calls on managers to do the hard work of fitting irregular puzzle pieces together—to treat people not as containers of fungible human resources but as unique individual assets. The work for managers will be harder. But the payoff for companies will be considerable: access to more of their employees' talents along with diverse perspectives that may help them compete more effectively. "Innovation," Wittenberg notes, "is most likely to come from parts of us that we don't all share."

Words and Expressions

neurological	adj.	神经病学的,神经学上的
autism	n.	孤独症,自闭症
autism spectrum disorder		自闭症谱系障碍
dyspraxia	n.	运用障碍
dyslexia	n.	诵读困难,阅读障碍
capitalize on		利用
leverage	vt.	为……融资,使借贷经营,充分利用(资源、观点等)
	n.	影响,杠杆作用,杠杆力量
Curriculum Vitae (CV)		简历,履历表
eccentricity	n.	古怪行为,反常行为,古怪的想法,怪异的动作
strenuous	adj.	艰苦的,费力的,费劲的,积极的,坚决的
subsequently	adv.	随后,后来,接着
credential	n.	证书,凭据
electrical engineering		电气工程
biostatistics	n.	生物统计学
anthropology	n.	人类学
bachelor degree		学士学位
dual degree		双学位
run counter to		违反,与……背道而驰
press release		新闻发布
oddball	n.	举止古怪的人
deploy	vt.	利用,调动(想法、论据等),部署,调度(士兵、军事装备等)

vocational rehab counselor		职业康复顾问
nuance	n.	细微差别
exemplar	n.	模范，典型
fungible	adj.	代替的，可取代的
	n.	可替代的物，(偿还债务用以)替代的财产，代替物

Notes to the Text

1. College of William & Mary：威廉与玛丽学院（简称 WM），又名"威廉玛丽学院"，创立于1693年，是全美历史第二悠久的高等院校，建校时间仅次于1636年建立的哈佛大学。威廉玛丽学院得名于英国国王威廉三世和玛丽二世，是一所有着"美国母校"美誉的一流高等学府，以精英教育著称，自美国建国以来一直享有非常高的名望。该校的硬件和软件环境都属一流，更是公立常春藤名校之一。威廉与玛丽学院拥有美国高等教育历史上的众多第一，是美国历史上第一所学院、美国第一所拥有完整教职员工的大学、美国第一个拥有选课制度的大学、美国第一所从学院成为大学的学校、美国第一个开设现代语言学、当代历史学和法学院的大学。

2. AS（Asperger's Syndrome）：亚斯伯格综合征，又名"艾斯伯格症候群""亚氏保加症"。20世纪40年代，来自维也纳的儿科医师汉斯·艾斯伯格研究一群和一般孩子不太一样的小男孩。这些男孩在社交和沟通上与自闭症的孩子有相似的问题。然而他们跟一般孩子一样聪明，甚至更聪明，并且具有很好的语言技能。艾斯伯格博士称这样的状态为"孤僻的精神病态"。亚斯伯格综合征是一种泛自闭症障碍，其重要特征是社交困难，伴随着兴趣狭隘及重复特定行为，但相较于其他泛自闭症障碍，仍相对保有语言及认知发展。亚斯伯格综合征患者经常出现肢体互动障碍、语言表达方式异常等状况，但并不需要接受治疗。

3. IDF（Israel Defense Forces）：以色列国防军，创立于1948年，是中东地区国防预算最高的军队之一，作为世界上富有战争经验的武装力量，在建国半个世纪以来参与了五场主要的大型战争和其他无数的小型冲突。在人员上，以色列国防军的主要优势是其人员训练的精良品质及完善的制度，而不是人员的数量。以色列国防军也大量依赖于高科技的武器系统，以色列国内也有一些专门替国防军生产和开发武器科技的机构或企业，其他的则进口自国外（大多来自美国）。

4. Silicon Valley：硅谷，位于美国加利福尼亚北部的大都会区旧金山湾区南面，是高科技事业云集的圣塔克拉拉谷（Santa Clara Valley）的别称。硅谷最早是研究和生产以硅为基础的半导体芯片的地方，因此得名。硅谷是当今电子工业和计算机业的王国，尽管美国和世界其他高新技术区都在不断发展壮大，但硅谷仍然是世界高新技术创新和发展的开创者和中心,该地区的风险投资占全美风险投资总额的1/3,硅谷的计算机公司已经发展到大约1500家。一个世纪前这里还是一片果园,但自从英特尔、苹果公司、谷歌、脸书、雅虎等高科技公司的总部在此落户之后,出现了众多繁华的市镇。在短短的几十年之内,硅谷走出了大批科技富翁。

Unit Thirteen

The Evolution of the CMO

Caren Fleit

July – August 2017, *Harvard Business Review*

As marketing channels and tools grew over the decades, so did the status and responsibilities of top marketing executives.

1950s

Marketing focuses largely on creating TV and print advertising to sell products to consumers. Top-level marketing executives are found almost exclusively in the consumer goods and automotive industries.

1960s

Advertising is still limited mainly to paid TV and print channels but moves away from exaggerated claims and aggressively pushing products and toward inventing creative and memorable approaches. The ad campaign is king.

1970s

Marketing adopts analytics and begins generating insights about customer choices and segmenting customers. Particularly in consumer goods, marketers become increasingly responsible for product management, pricing, promotion, and distribution.

ADVERTISING ARCHIVE

1980s

Cable TV, infomercials, and VCRs (which allow viewers to skip ads) make marketing's job more complex and ratchet up the pressure for advertising efficiency. Analytics become critical to precisely tracking performance in each sales channel. Consumer-goods marketers start to assume P&L responsibility and enterprise-wide roles. Other industries, like consumer finance, begin hiring top-level marketing executives, though those jobs focus more on branding and corporate communications.

1990s

A broader marketing function emerges in industries such as health care and technology, and B2B marketers appear. The role of the marketing leader becomes blurry, as companies struggle to find a balance between more-strategic responsibilities (brand positioning, segmentation, and business growth) and more-tactical ones (sales enablement, creating brochures, and manning trade shows). Marketing departments begin to set up matrix structures combining corporate functions with regional and business unit functions. Customer relationship management takes hold. The CMO title is first used.

2000s

The digital revolution changes the way companies and customers relate. As social media platforms take off, people rely more on one another for information about products. Marketers must manage omnichannel communications and both negative and positive messages about their brands. They begin focusing on building meaningful relationships with customers. The CMO title spreads but is used indiscriminately both for executives strictly focused on brand and communications and for true strategic business partners.

2010s

Big data and artificial intelligence swamp marketers with information. The focus shifts from telling and selling to customer engagement and dialogues and personalized communications and products. CMOs are expected to creatively apply insights to business challenges, validate decisions with data, create seamless customer experiences across media and revenue channels, and lead efforts to put the customer at the center throughout the organization. Most CMOs now sit on executive committees and report directly to the CEO. But there is confusion about the role, leading some to question the title and explore alternatives like chief customer officer, chief customer experience officer, and chief growth officer.

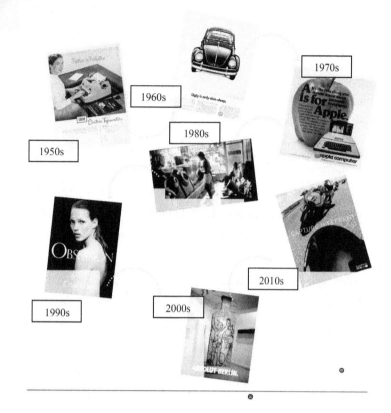

 Words and Expressions

paid TV		付费电视
memorable	adj.	值得纪念的,难忘的
analytics	n.	分(解)析学,逻辑分析法
segment	vt.	分割,划分
pricing	n.	定价,作价,计价
distribution	n.	(商品)运销,经销,分销
infomercial	n.	(电视上的)商业信息片,资讯广告节目
VCR (video cassette recorder)	n.	录像机
ratchet up		(使)有一定上升(或提高)
ratchet	vt.	朝某个固定的方向移动
track	vt.	跟踪,追踪
branding	n.	品牌创建

blurry	adj.	模糊不清的
tactical	adj.	战术上的
brochure	n.	资料(或广告)手册
man	vt.	配备(人员)
trade show		贸易展览会
take hold		站稳脚跟,开始发展
relate	v.	联系,使有联系,把……联系起来
indiscriminate	adj.	随意的,不加选择的,不加分析的
swamp	v.	淹没,使不堪承受,使应接不暇
personalized communication		个性化的交流
validate	vt.	证实,确认,确证
seamless	adj.	无(接)缝的,(两部分之间)无空隙的,不停顿的
Chief customer officer		首席客户官
chief customer experience officer		首席客户体验官
chief growth officer		首席发展官

Notes to the Text

1. CMO (Chief Marketing Officer): 首席营销官,是指企业中负责市场运营工作的高级管理人员,又被称作"市场部经理""营销总监""市场总监"。他们主要负责:在企业中对营销思想进行定位;把握市场机会,制定市场营销战略和实施计划,完成企业的营销目标;协调企业内外部关系,对企业市场营销战略计划的执行进行监督和控制;负责企业营销组织建设与激励工作。

2. CFO (Chief Financial Officer): 首席财务官,是企业治理结构发展到一个新阶段的必然产物。没有首席财务官的治理结构不是现代意义上完善的治理结构。从这一层面上看,中国构造治理结构也应设立 CFO 之类的职位。当然,从本质上讲,CFO 在现代治理结构中的真正含义不是其名称的改变、官位的授予,而是其职责权限的取得、在管理中作用的真正发挥。

3. CIO (Chief Information Officer): 首席信息官或信息主管,是负责一个公司信息技术和系统所有领域的高级官员。他们通过指导对信息技术的利用来支持公司的目标。他们具备技术和业务过程两方面的知识,具有多功能的概念,常常是将组织的技术调配战略与业务战略紧密结合在一起的最佳人选。CIO 原指政府管理部门中的首席信息官,随着信息系统由后方办公室的辅助工具发展到直接参与企业的有力手段,CIO 在企业中应运而生,成为举足轻重的人物。美国企业的首席信息经理相当于副总经理直接对最高决策者负责。

4. CHRO（Chief Human Resources Officer）：首席人力资源官。如今，竞争的优势要素已经从资金和硬件设备转到了智力上。因此，各个业务领导人在做关键决策的时候越发需要人力资源部门的协助。实质上，这就是把首席人力资源官（CHRO）推到了与 CEO、营销总监等高管层平起平坐的地位上。

5. NGO：非政府组织。20 世纪 80 年代以来，人们在各种场合越来越多地提及非政府组织（NGO）与非营利组织（NPO），把非政府组织与非营利组织看作在公共管理领域作用日益重要的新兴组织形式。

非政府组织是独立于政府体系之外的具有一定程度公共性质并承担一定公共职能的社会组织，这些组织活跃于人类社会生活的各个领域和层面，其形式、规模、功能千差万别，但一般都具有非政府性、非营利性、公益性、志愿性四个方面的基本属性。具体来说，非政府性指的是这些社会组织独立于政府机关及其附属机构之外，不是由政府出资成立，不具有自上而下的官僚体制，不具备排他性的垄断权力。

非营利性强调这些社会组织不是营利性的企业，它们不以营利为目的，不具有利润分红等营利机制，组织资产不得以任何形式为私人所占有；公益性强调这些社会组织在投入产出上更多地依赖社会和服务社会，它们往往以各种形式吸纳社会公益或共益资源，对公信力等社会资本有更强的依赖性，提供的是社会所需要的各种形式的公共产品或服务，并形成一定的公共空间；志愿性强调这些组织的参与者和支持者通常不存在外在的强制关系，而更多基于自愿、自主的奉献精神和不求回报索取的博爱精神，各种形式的志愿者成为其重要的人力资源。

6. R&D（research and development）：研究与开发，研究与发展，研究与试验性发展。R&D 指在科学技术领域为增加知识总量（包括人类文化和社会知识的总量）及运用这些知识去创造新的应用进行的系统的创造性的活动，包括基础研究、应用研究、试验发展三类活动。国际上通常采用 R&D 活动的规模和强度指标反映一国的科技实力和核心竞争力。一国的 R&D 水平体现了一国的政治经济实力，一个企业的 R&D 水平体现了一个企业的竞争力。国际上的著名企业都把 R&D 视为企业的生命，无不投巨资于 R&D。

7. corporate communication：企业传播，是如何加强公司内外沟通的一门学问。整合传播不仅包括广告和促销，而且还包括面向企业外部以企业广告、公共关系、企业宣传活动等为主要内容的对外企业传播（External Corporate Communication or Extracorporate Communication）与面向企业组织内部以提高组织成员士气、归属意识为目的的对内企业传播（Internal Corporate Communication or Intracorporate Communication），它反映出企业经营的整体水平，即企业面向内外部开展的所有形态的传播的整体化，也可被称为"整合营销传播"（Integrated Marketing Communications，IMC）。

8. market segmentation：市场细分，是指企业按照某种标准将市场上的顾客划分成若干个顾客群，每一个顾客群构成一个子市场，不同子市场之间需求存在着明显的差别。市场细分是选择目标市场的基础工作。市场营销在企业的活动包括细分一个市场并把它作为公司的目标市场,设计正确的产品、服务、价格、促销和分销系统"组合",从而满足细分市场内顾客的需要和欲望。

9. sales enablement:销售支持。销售支持能协助总经理(或相关负责人)进行日常销售工作的管理,配合销售团队做好后台支持工作,汇总销售数据及进行订单或项目信息的系统管理。国内某些外资企业又将销售支持按照职责和功能细分为销售技术支持(Sales Technical Support)、销售行政(Sales Admin)或商务行政(Business Admin)。

10. matrix organization:矩阵式组织,在一个机构之机能式组织形态下,为某种特别任务另外成立专案小组负责,此专案小组与原组织配合,在形态上有行列交叉之式,即为矩阵式组织。在组织结构上矩阵式组织可以将企业中各个办事处更有效地结为一体。矩阵组织结构可以解放各个职能部门经理间的限制,以达到职能部门经理间更好就资源进行全面的沟通。其次,矩阵式组织可以帮助企业暂时减少员工招聘的成本,特别是对一些刚刚建立的部门。各个部门中关键的人可以同时被企业中各个项目所使用,比如每个部门的经理。除此之外,当知识在一个平等的基础上,所有项目也是可以利用的。因此,矩阵式组织可以在项目管理过程中帮助企业在时间、成本和绩效上平衡。在组织结构上,它是把职能划分的部门和按产品(项目)划分的小组结合起来组成一个矩阵,一名管理人员既同原职能部门保持组织与业务上的联系,又参加项目小组的工作。职能部门是固定的组织,项目小组是临时性组织,完成任务以后就自动解散,其成员回原部门工作。

11. Omnichannel:全渠道,即通过覆盖全面的线上线下多种渠道和终端设备,无边界地为客户提供统一的、定制化的、持续的营销体验旅程,从而推动营销加速,同时运用系统和数据完善未知和已知客户的画像。

12. Big Data:大数据。大数据指无法在一定时间范围内用常规软件工具进行捕捉、管理和处理的数据集合,是需要新处理模式才能具有更强的决策力、洞察发现力和流程优化能力的海量、高增长率和多样化的信息资产。大数据的5V特点(IBM提出):Volume(大量)、Velocity(高速)、Variety(多样)、Value(低价值密度)、Veracity(真实性)。

13. Artificial Intelligence:人工智能,英文缩写为AI。它是研究、开发用于模拟、延伸和扩展人的智能的理论、方法、技术及应用系统的一门新的技术科学。人工智能是计算机科学的一个分支,它企图了解智能的实质,并生产出一种新的能以人类智能相似的方式做出反应的智能机器,该领域的研究包括机器人、语言识别、图像识别、自然语言处理和专家系统等。从诞生以来,人工智能理论和技术日益成熟,应用领域也不断扩大,可以设想,未来人工智能带来的科技产品将会是人类智慧的"容器"。人工智能可以对人的意识、思维的信息过程进行模拟。人工智能不是人的智能,但能像人那样思考,也可能超过人的智能。

14. Customer Engagement Selling:客户互动销售,是销售人员与客户之间的双赢销售理念和模型,可以真正形成与客户的互动,将销售过程与采购过程完美结合。销售团队的站位与配合关系到销售连续与有序、销售过程的评估管理。

The Power Partnership: CMO & CIO

Kimberly A. Whitler, D. Eric Boyd, and Neil Morgan

July – August 2017, *Harvard Business Review*

Historically, chief marketing officers and chief information officers have tended to see the world quite differently. Focused on generating demand, marketers place a high priority on speed and creativity and take risks to achieve aggressive goals. IT executives are often risk-averse, prizing stability, security, and accuracy. As marketing moves increasingly onto websites and mobile devices and into social media and e-mail, the two functions have come into conflict, in part because of shifts in power and resources. Here's one stark demonstration: This year, for the first time, CMOs will control more technology spending than IT departments do, according to a forecast by Gartner. "There's been a bleeding of responsibilities as CIOs get more involved in customer facing activities and CMOs get more involved in technology," says Anne Park Hopkins, a former recruiter at Korn Ferry who has placed executives in both roles. "The question is how to create better co-ownership to deal with growing ambiguity."

In our research, which includes in-depth interviews with successful CMO-CIO pairs, we've identified a useful technique for encouraging co-ownership: creating alignment through shared performance goals. This is not a common practice. In our surveys two-thirds of CMOs say their performance is measured against companywide financial results such as operating earnings or sales growth. We call those vertical alignment measures, since they match C-level executives' performance targets with the CEO's. In contrast, only 34% of CMOs (including most of those who are adept at collaborating with CIOs) are judged on metrics closely tied to the responsibilities they share with other C-suite colleagues, or using what we call horizontal alignment measures.

Regal Entertainment Group provides a good example of how horizontal alignment measures can spark collaboration. Digital marketing has become a strategic priority in the theater industry, so when CEO Amy Miles decided to replace Regal's CMO in 2012, she knew the next marketing chief would need to work closely with CIO David Doyle. She tied both executives' bonuses to shared goals they could hit only by collaborating. The metrics included the percentage of tickets sold on Regal's app or website, the percentage of customers visiting Regal's self-serve kiosks, the speed of ticket lines in theaters, and metrics related to customers' website experience (such as load times) and the relaunch of the Regal Crown Club loyalty program.

To fill the CMO role, Miles hired Ken Thewes, who'd studied engineering as an undergrad (and so had technical fluency). Miles had made it clear during the job interview process that effectively partnering with the CIO was a top priority. "Earlier in my career as a CMO, there wasn't much of a relationship at all" with the IT department, Thewes says. But when he arrived at Regal, the IT and marketing teams began holding twice-weekly joint department "scrums", coordinating their efforts to achieve their common goals. Says Thewes: "These relationships don't work just because you say you want them to—you have to really get folks engaged and make sure they collaborate."

The partnership has paid off: In the past five years, membership in Regal's loyalty program has more than doubled, hitting 14 million people. Digital commerce is up by 359% since 2013, and customer engagement has hit record levels. Improvements in all those areas have helped lift corporate results: Since 2011 Regal's revenue has increased by 20% and its shareholder value by 170%.

Words and Expressions

risk-averse	n.	厌恶风险,规避风险
prize	vt.	珍视,高度重视
stark	adj.	严酷的,赤裸裸的,真实而无法回避的
bleeding	n.	流血,流失
recruiter	n.	负责招聘的人员
co-ownership	n.	财产共同所有权,共有权
ambiguity	n.	歧义,模棱两可
identify	vt.	找到,发现,确认,认出,鉴定
alignment	n.	协调一致,(国家、团体间的)结盟
measure against		拿……和……比(长度)
vertical	adj.	竖的,垂直的,纵向的
be adept at		擅长于
metric	n.	衡量指标
horizontal	adj.	水平的,与地面平行的,横向的
app (application)	n.	(计算机)应用程序,(手机)应用程序
website	n.	网站
kiosk	n.	(出售报纸、饮料等的)小亭,售货亭

ticket line		排队购票的队伍
load time		(网页)加载时间长度
relaunch	n.	重新推出,(商品等的)重新投放市场,重新推向公众
loyalty	n.	忠诚,忠实
undergrad	n.	在校本科生,大学生
fluency	n.	(尤指外语)流利,熟练自如,流畅
scrum	n.	(橄榄球的)并列争球,(橄榄球)并列争球的全体前锋,相互拥挤的人群
engaged	adj.	忙于……的,从事于……的
pay off		成功,赢利

Notes to the Text

1. Korn Ferry:光辉国际,是一家全球化组织咨询公司。1969年成立于美国,1999年光辉国际在纽交所上市。2009年,光辉国际被《福布斯》评为高管搜寻行业CEO搜寻有效率排名第一。

2. Regal Entertainment Group:君豪娱乐,创立于2002年,总部位于田纳西州诺克斯维尔,是美国最大的连锁电影院公司(2016年,在万达集团旗下的AMC娱乐收购Carmike Cinemas后,已经超过君豪娱乐成为美国第一大电影院运营商)。它主要通过旗下子公司于美国境内从事电影放映,主要于大都会区中的中型都市和发展中的市郊地区开发、收购及营运多银幕戏院。

Unit Fourteen

Product Promotion

Finding the Platform in Your Product

Four Strategies That Can Reveal Hidden Value
Andrei Hagiu and Elizabeth J. Altman
July – August, 2017, *Harvard Business Review*

Andrei Hagiu is a visiting associate professor of technological innovation, entrepreneurship, and strategic management at the MIT Sloan School of Management. Follow him on Twitter: @ theplatformguy. Elizabeth J. Altman is an assistant professor of strategic management at the Manning School of Business at the University of Massachusetts Lowell and a visiting scholar at Harvard Business School. She was formerly a vice president of strategy and business development at Motorola. Follow her on Twitter: @ lizaltman.

Five of the 10 most valuable companies in the world today—Apple, Alphabet, Amazon, Facebook, and Microsoft—derive much of their worth from their multisided platforms (MSPs), which facilitate interactions or transactions between parties. Many MSPs are more valuable than companies in the same industries that provide only products or services: For instance, Airbnb is now worth more than Marriott, the world's largest hotel chain.

> **IN BRIEF**
>
> **The Problem**
> Many companies that sell products or services either don't realize they could turn their offerings into a platform business or struggle to do so.
>
> **The Opportunity**
> By becoming a multisided platform (MSP) that facilitates interactions between parties, a company may be able to provide new revenue sources while also preventing competitors from stealing market share from its product or service.
>
> **The Solution**
> Here are four scenarios whereby regular products or services can become MSPs. The authors take into account the advantages and pitfalls of each and the resources, relationships, and organizational changes that would be required.

However, companies that weren't born as platform businesses rarely realize that they can—at least partially—turn their products and services into an MSP. And even if they do realize it, they often wander in the dark searching for a strategy to achieve this transformation. Here we provide a framework for doing so. It lays out four specific ways in which products and services can be turned into platforms and examines the strategic advantages and pitfalls of each. These ideas are applicable to physical as well as online businesses.

Why seek to transform products and services into MSPs in the first place? As one Intuit executive told us, it comes down to "fear and greed". Greed, of course, refers to the potential for new revenue sources that could speed growth and increase a company's value. Fear refers to the danger that existing and incoming competitors will steal market share from your product or service. Transforming an offering into a platform might enhance your company's competitive advantage and raise barriers to entry via network effects and higher switching costs. We're not suggesting that every company should try to emulate Airbnb, Alibaba, Facebook, or Uber. But many companies would benefit from adding elements of a platform business to their offerings.

Our goal is to help managers discern how their products or services could become multisided platforms—and what challenges and opportunities might arise—so that they can decide whether or not to make the change. Our framework derives from our combined experience studying and advising more than a dozen companies (including several mentioned below) during product-to-MSP transformations. Managers might want to use this article as the basis for a corporate-strategy offsite at which everyone is given the task of articulating MSP strategies around existing company offerings. That assignment should include answering questions such as: (1) Are there benefits to turning some or all of our products and services into MSPs? (2) Are there risks involved in doing so? (3) What key resources, relationships (including how we interact with customers), and organizational changes would be required for such a transformation?

The reason regular products and services are not multisided platforms is that they do not serve multiple groups or facilitate interactions between customers or groups. In this article we discuss four ways in which regular products and services can bridge this gap and become MSPs.

1. Opening the Door to Third Parties

In this scenario your product or service has a big customer base that third-party sellers of other offerings are interested in reaching. You become an MSP by making it possible for those third parties to connect with your customers. "Connect with" can mean advertise or sell (or both) to them. The third party products may be independent of your product or service or may be apps or modules that work in combination with your offerings.

Consider three examples:

Intuit is the leading seller of financial management, accounting, and tax software products for consumers and small businesses in the United States. In the past six years or so it has taken significant steps to turn QuickBooks, its flagship financial-accounting product for small businesses, into an MSP. It opened up application-programming interfaces and introduced a developer program and an app store to allow third party developers to build and sell software products to QuickBooks' customer base. Those products leverage data about small-business finances provided by QuickBooks. Since 2013 QuickBooks has also enabled its customers to apply directly to several third-party financial institutions for loans through a service called QuickBooks Financing.

Health clubs are increasingly renting space inside their gyms to specialty studios so that the latter can serve health club members. This allows a club to offer a greater variety of classes, which helps it retain existing members and attract new ones. For instance, the Forum Athletic Club, in Atlanta, recently reached an agreement with Cyc Fitness, a national cycling-studio chain, which now operates a self-contained studio inside the Forum's 22,000-square-foot gym.

The lawson chain of convenience stores in Japan started in the 1990s to turn its shops into MSPs that facilitate transactions between its customers and third-party service providers. Today Lawson customers can pay utility bills and insurance premiums, ship and pick up parcels through postal service providers, and claim items ordered from e-commerce sites just by visiting their local convenience store.

For your product or service to become a true MSP in this scenario, at least some of the connection between your customers and third parties must be made through your product. Intuit could simply have sold aggregated (and anonymized) QuickBooks data to third-party developers and financial institutions. That would have added a potentially profitable new offering for Intuit, but it would not have turned QuickBooks into an MSP that could exploit network effects.

For this type of transition to make sense, your product or service must have an established brand and a large customer base—but that alone won't elicit interest from third parties. It must also meet one or both of the following conditions:

It serves a baseline need for many customers, yet leaves a large number of heterogeneous customer needs unserved. You can encourage and enable third parties to fill those gaps with products and services that are typically complementary to yours. Most third-party apps in Intuit's app store target market niches and customer needs not served by QuickBooks on its own.

It generates frequent customer interactions. That makes it a good candidate to become a one-stop shop for other, not necessarily complementary products and services. The third-party services that Lawson's customers can access are largely unrelated to its own products and services, but customers find it extremely convenient to access all of them in the same location.

It's important to be aware of several pitfalls associated with this approach to an MSP. One is that customers who come to you primarily for a product or service may object to the advertising of third-party offerings, especially if they are paying for yours. Intuit faced this when it started exploring services to offer through QuickBooks. As a result, the company is very careful to allow only offerings that align well with the needs and desires of QuickBooks customers and to obtain explicit consent to participate in tests for targeted third-party offers. In addition, Intuit has rebranded QuickBooks as "the operating system for small business" precisely to change customers' perceptions and to minimize potential backlash.

Another possible pitfall is that because you have an existing provider relationship with your customers, they may hold you responsible for the quality of their interactions with third parties. By enabling those parties to interact with your customers, you are implicitly endorsing their offerings—to a greater extent than does a company born as a multisided platform. For instance, a customer taking a spinning class offered by a third-party studio in a health club's gym is likely to blame the health club for a bad experience. As a result, you must curate third-party products and services much more carefully than a company born as an MSP has to.

Finally, some third-party products and services may cannibalize your offerings. The natural inclination would be to allow only those that are either complementary or unrelated to yours. But that approach can be misguided. In some cases it may make sense to coopt offerings that compete somewhat with yours and capture some of the resulting value to your customers. The Forum Athletic Club has replaced its own cycling classes with the Cyc Fitness classes offered at its gym. Cyc's spinning classes have proved more popular with members and allow the Forum to focus its resources on other services while converting Cyc from a competitor to a complementor.

The underlying logic is that if substitution from third parties is inevitable, bringing them onto your platform may expand its overall appeal to your customers, resulting in more demand and opportunities to sell your own services. It may also encourage you to reevaluate your offering's core competitive advantages and focus on them, which may mean ceding ground to third parties in some areas.

2. Connecting Customers

In this scenario you are selling a product or service to two distinct customer segments that interact or transact with each other outside your offering. You can become an MSP by modifying or expanding your offering so that at least some element of those interactions or transactions occurs through your product or service.

QuickBooks is used by both small businesses and accounting professionals. Intuit is in the process of adding a matchmaking function within QuickBooks that would enable small businesses to find and contact accountants with relevant expertise in their geographic area and would allow already-matched business-accountant pairs to exchange documents through the product.

Garmin and other fitness wearables are used by both consumers and personal trainers. Many companies that offer these products also host online systems (Garmin Connect, for example) to store fitness-training and health data. Garmin could enable users to share their data with personal trainers, thereby enhancing the interactions between those two groups. To further capture value from this strategy, Garmin could charge trainers for a "pro" subscription—software tools that would let them access clients' data to oversee activities and progress.

This scenario highlights how different customer segments of the same product or service can become customer groups on an MSP. For example, men and women are customer segments for a hair salon (no interaction between them is facilitated by the salon), but they are customer groups for a heterosexual dating service. An entrepreneurial hair salon that started offering matchmaking services to its customer segments could convert men and women into customer groups.

There are two pitfalls associated with this strategy. First, you run the risk of wasting resources on a feature that ultimately creates little additional value for your customers or your company. Worse, the MSP feature can be a detriment if customers perceive it as misaligned with the value of your underlying product or service. Some customers of a hair salon that provides matchmaking services might not want to risk encountering matches that didn't work out. Others might worry that offering a dating service means the salon isn't focused on giving the highest-quality haircuts.

Blizzard Entertainment's ill-fated Auction House for its popular Diablo video game provides a cautionary tale. Having noticed that Diablo players were routinely trading digital items on eBay and other external platforms, Blizzard created the Auction House in 2012 to make those transactions easier. It allowed players to buy and sell digital items in exchange for "gold" (digital currency in the Diablo game) as well as real dollars—and Blizzard was able to charge a transaction fee. It quickly became clear, however, that this feature created perverse incentives. Many players decided that buying items at the Auction House was an easier way to reach the game's advanced stages than devoting several hours to killing monsters and searching for loot inside the game. Other players strove to accumulate game items for the sole purpose of selling them in the Auction House. Realizing that this behavior was undermining the value of the game itself, Blizzard shut down the Auction House in 2014.

It is imperative that you conduct market research or run experiments to answer the following questions: Would significant proportions of our offering's various customer segments derive substantial benefits from interacting or transacting with one another? If yes, can our product or service enhance those interactions in a significant way? How will our customers react to the addition of an MSP feature, and how will that feature affect the way they interact with the original offering?

The second pitfall, as in scenario number one, is that although your offering is now simply facilitating a connection or a transaction between two parties, if one party is dissatisfied with the other, you may be held partly responsible. That means you need to put governance mechanisms in place to minimize (if not eliminate) the likelihood of unsatisfactory interactions. Intuit will have to carefully curate the accountants it recommends to QuickBooks customers through its matchmaking feature.

3. Connecting Products to Connect Customers

In this scenario you are selling two products or services, each to a different customer base, and the two customer bases interact outside your offerings. You can become an MSP by modifying or expanding your offerings so that at least part of those interactions occurs through one or both of your offerings.

Cards against humanity is a popular game in which players complete ill-in-the-blank statements with humorous (and often tasteless) words or phrases printed on physical playing cards. Its creators continue to sell the game and its numerous expansion packs to consumers, but they have also created Blackbox, a separate website through which they sell back-end fulfillment services (credit-card processing, customer service, shipping) to independent artists who want to sell their products—including third-party developers of other card games. Currently these are separate offerings, but the company could create an MSP by linking them. For instance, it could allow Blackbox customers to advertise their games to Cards Against Humanity's users with expansion packs. A more sophisticated implementation would allow Blackbox customers to test game concepts on willing Cards Against Humanity users, who would provide feedback.

Credit bureaus such as Equifax, Experian and TransUnion offer a suite of services for consumers (access to credit scores, identity theft protection, and so on) and a suite of services for financial institutions (credit reports on consumers and businesses). These suites are based on the same data, but the two types of customers interact outside the services (as when a consumer applies for a mortgage); the credit bureaus do not directly facilitate those interactions. Credit bureaus could create online MSPs where consumers could obtain their credit scores and receive targeted offers from financial institutions. (This is the business model of start-ups such as Credit Karma and Lendio.) These MSPs could go further and enable consumers to create and manage a digital data profile that they could then use to apply directly for financial products at participating institutions (similar to the way Intuit allows QuickBooks customers to apply for financial products through QuickBooks Financing).

Nielsen offers "watch" products to media companies (data on consumers' viewing habits) and "buy" products to consumer goods manufacturers (data on consumers' purchasing habits). One could easily imagine Nielsen's adding the ability for a consumer packaged-goods company to connect with relevant media companies for advertising purposes.

This scenario highlights how a multiproduct company can become a multisided platform that benefits from network effects. For example, by increasing sales of credit and identity-theft-protection products to consumers, credit bureaus can improve their offerings for financial institutions (which leverage consumer data), thereby achieving greater cross-product economies of scope. While that alone might be valuable, credit bureaus could create and capture even more value by linking the two kinds of products to facilitate interactions between consumers and financial institutions (as described above). This would create an MSP and generate network effects: If more consumers use the credit and identity-theft-protection products, that increases the value of the offerings for financial institutions, which can then transact with more consumers more effectively and vice versa.

Two risks are associated with this strategy. First, as with scenario number two, you may waste resources on a feature that ultimately creates little value for your customers or your company relative to the underlying product or service. Second, optimizing for interactions between customers of different products may lead to design choices that limit the growth potential of one or the other product on its own. Once again, it is imperative to use market research and experiments to answer a few questions: Would considerable proportions of your offerings' respective customers derive significantly greater benefits from interacting or transacting through you? If yes, can your offerings substantially enhance those interactions? How will the customers of your two offerings react to the addition of an MSP feature? How will that feature affect the way customers interact with the original products?

4. Supplying to a Multisided Platform

In this scenario you become an MSP by creating an offering for your customers' customers that enhances the value of the product or service they buy from your customers. (Although this strategy is logically possible, we are not yet aware of examples of its successful implementation.)

It is important to emphasize that this strategy goes beyond the more traditional "ingredient brand" strategy, which is also a "customers' customers" approach. Indeed, some (essential) ingredient suppliers have created brands in the eyes of their customers' customers (for example, Intel's "Intel Inside") that allow them to extract more value from their customers. But because these ingredient suppliers offer no products or services directly to their customers' customers, they are not MSPs.

The major pitfall with this scenario is that your customers are likely to react negatively to any attempt to go after their customers. Nevertheless, we believe this strategy could work under certain circumstances. The key is to convince your customers that the product or service you provide to their customers is truly complementary to—rather than competitive with—their own offerings.

Shopify is a leading provider of e-commerce tools to online and retail merchants. Currently the company has no direct connection with its customers' users. It could, however, start offering a common log-in or loyalty program to users of its customers' sites. Whether such an initiative would be successful would hinge on whether Shopify could persuade its merchant customers that the offering was a valuable added service rather than simply an attempt to take control of their customer relationships.

The decision whether and how to convert an offering into an MSP should be informed by who your current customers are, how you currently interact with them, and how they interact with one another. The most fundamental challenge associated with this endeavor is transitioning from a world in which you have 100% control over what your customers are offered to one in which you can only influence the value that is created for them (by third parties or by interactions among themselves).

A final consideration is organizational and leadership challenges. If a company has a solid reputation that is rooted in creating and offering products, shifting to an MSP-focused strategy might be difficult for employees who deeply identify with those products. And companies that sell successful products or services often have strong research and development operations and many engineers in leadership roles; shifting to an MSP strategy that depends on the adept management of third-party relationships might require putting business-development and marketing professionals in significant leadership roles, generating internal conflict. Furthermore, as a company's strategy moves from a product or service orientation to being more MSP-centric, boards, CEOs and senior management teams may find it difficult to deal with multiple or hybrid strategies, adopt and track new performance metrics, and enforce some degree of technological or customer experience consistency between previously separate products and services.

Nevertheless, if you decide that creating a platform will provide great opportunities for growth and increased profitability and thwart potential competitive threats, the effort to make the transformation may well be worthwhile.

Words and Expressions

associate	n.	联合,同事
scenario	n.	情节,剧本,方案
pitfall	n.	(捕猎野兽用的)陷阱,意想不到的困难,易犯的错误
emulate	vt.	与……竞争,努力赶上
articulate	adj.	表达能力强的,口齿清楚的,发音清晰的
	vt. & vi.	清楚地表达
module	n.	模块,登月舱,指令舱
interface	n.	(人机)界面(尤指屏幕布局和菜单),接口
utility bills		水电用费
backlash	n.	(对社会变动等的)强烈抵制,集体反对
endorse	v.	在(票据)背面签名,签注(文件),认可,签署
curate	n.	助理牧师,副牧师

	vt.	组织(展览)
cannibalize	v.	吃同类的肉,拆用……的配件,调拨……的人员
coopt	vt.	由现会员选举,增补……为新成员
cede	vt.	让给,割让,放弃
matchmaking	n.	做媒,保媒,牵线搭桥
wearable	adj.	可穿用的,可佩带的,耐用的
	n.	衣服
detriment	n.	损害,损害物
perverse	adj.	任性的,固执的,错误的,荒谬的,反常的
loot	n.	掠夺品,战利品,抢劫
	vt. & vi.	抢劫,洗劫,强夺
leverage	n.	杠杆系结构,杠杆率,杠杆传动,杠杆作用
cross-product	n.	交叉乘积,向量积
hinge	n.	(门、盖等的)铰链,枢纽,关键
	vt.	装铰链
metrics	n.	衡量标准
thwart	vt.	反对,阻碍,挫败

Notes to the Text

1. Airbnb(AirBed and Breakfast):爱彼迎。爱彼迎是一家联系旅游人士和家有空房出租的房主的服务型网站,它可以为用户提供多样的住宿信息。

2. Marriott:万豪国际集团,全球首屈一指的酒店管理公司,业务遍及美国及其他67个国家和地区。该公司的名称来自万豪国际集团董事长兼首席执行官 J. W. Marriott, Jr。

3. Alibaba:阿里巴巴网络技术有限公司(简称"阿里巴巴集团"),1999年以马云为首的18人在浙江杭州创立。阿里巴巴集团经营多项业务,也从关联公司的业务和服务中取得经营商业生态系统上的支援。业务和关联公司的业务包括:淘宝网、天猫、聚划算、全球速卖通、阿里巴巴国际交易市场、1688、阿里妈妈、阿里云、蚂蚁金服、菜鸟网络等。

4. Facebook:脸书,是美国的一个社交网络服务网站,创立于2004年2月4日,总部位于美国加利福尼亚州帕拉阿图,2012年3月6日发布Windows版桌面聊天软件Facebook Messenger。主要创始人是马克·扎克伯格。

5. Uber(Uber Technologies, Inc.):优步,是一家美国硅谷的科技公司。Uber在2009年由特拉维斯·卡兰尼克和好友加雷特·坎普创立,因旗下同名打车app而名声大噪。

The Science of Pep Talks

To fire up your team, draw on a research-proven, three-part formula

Daniel Mcginn

July – August, 2017, *Harvard Business Reviw*

Daniel Mcginn is a senior editor at *Harvard Business Review* and the author of *Psyched Up: How the Science of Mental Preparation Can Help You Succeed* (Portfolio, 2017), from which this article is adapted.

> Erica Galos Alioto stands in front of 650 sales reps in the New York office of Yelp, the online review company, wearing a pair of shiny gold pants that she calls her lucky LDOM pants. LDOM is Yelp's acronym for "last day of the month", and for Alioto, senior vice president for local sales, it means giving a speech that will motivate her sales force to cold-call 70 potential customers each and close deals before the accountants finalize that month's books.
>
> She speaks for 20 minutes, extolling the group for being Yelp's top sales producer. She namechecks the best performers on the team and suggests ways for everyone else to adopt the same mentality. She tells stories. She asks questions.
>
> "This office is currently $1.5 million away from target this month ... We have an action plan here. Are we going to execute?" There's moderate applause. She asks again, in a louder voice: "Are we going to execute?" Big applause.
>
> Alioto has worked hard to perfect these speeches because she knows her success depends on them. Indeed, the ability to deliver an energizing pep talk that spurs employees to better performance is a prerequisite for any business leader. And yet few managers receive formal training in how to do it. Instead, they learn mostly from mimicry-emulating inspirational bosses, coaches they had in school, or even characters from films such as *Glengarry Glen Ross* and *The Wolf of Wall Street*. Some people lean on executive coaches for help, but often the advice rests on the coaches' personal experience, not research.

There is, however, a science to motivating people in this way. To better understand the various tools that help people get psyched up in the moments before important performances, I talked extensively with academics and practitioners in business and a variety of other fields. I discovered that while every individual has his or her own tips and tricks, according to the science, most winning formulas include three key elements: direction giving, expressions of empathy, and meaning making. The most extensive research in this field—dubbed motivating language theory, or MLT—comes from Jacqueline and Milton Mayfield, a husband-and-wife team at Texas A&M International University who have studied its applications in the corporate world for nearly three decades. Their findings are backed by studies from sports psychologists and military historians. And all the evidence suggests that once leaders understand these three elements, they can learn to use them more skillfully.

Three Elements, Carefully Balanced

The Mayfields describe direction giving as the use of "uncertainty-reducing language". This is when leaders provide information about precisely how to do the task at hand by, for example, giving easily understandable instructions, good definitions of tasks, and detail on how performance will be evaluated.

"Empathetic language" shows concern for the performer as a human being. It can include praise, encouragement, gratitude, and acknowledgment of a task's difficulty. Phrases like "How are we all doing?" "I know this is a challenge, but I trust you can do it", and "Your well-being is one of my top priorities" all fit into this category.

"Meaning-making language" explains why a task is important. This involves linking the organization's purpose or mission to listeners' goals. Often, meaning making language includes the use of stories—about people who've worked hard or succeeded in the company, or about how the work has made a real difference in the lives of customers or the community.

A good pep talk—whether delivered to one person or many—should include all three elements, but the right mix will depend on the context and the audience. Experienced workers who are doing a familiar task may not require much direction. Followers who are already tightly bonded with a leader may require less empathetic language. Meaning making is useful in most situations, but may need less emphasis if the end goals of the work are obvious.

For example, the Mayfields studied the CEO of a California pharmaceutical start-up focused on drugs to alleviate heart disease and amyotrophic lateral sclerosis (ALS). Many of the company's employees have lost loved ones to these ailments, so they bring an unusual sense of purpose to their work. As a result, at all-hands meetings, the CEO can easily make statements like this: "I know everybody here wants to help save lives and make people's lives better. That's what our work is all about."

In contrast, the supervisor of a fast-food restaurant speaking to part-time teenage employees will need to work harder to incorporate all three elements of motivating language theory into his chats with staff, but he can't rely solely on direction giving. Milton Mayfield suggests empathetic lines: "I know this work is difficult; you go home every night smelling of grease, and you're working so late that you're up until midnight finishing your homework." Or, to creatively link labor to purpose, the supervisor might say: "Our goal as a company isn't just to provide people with fast, satisfying meals; it's also to provide good, stable jobs so that employees like you have money to help your families, to save for college, or to enjoy yourselves when you're not at work. The more you help this restaurant meet its goals, the better we'll be able to continue doing that." According to the Mayfields' research, meaning making is almost always the most difficult of the three elements to deliver.

Research from other fields offers additional insight into what gives the best pep talks their power. Tiffanye Vargas, a sports psychology professor at California State University at Long Beach, has published a half-dozen lab and field studies exploring which types of speeches best motivate athletes in different situations, some of which may also be applicable to business contexts. Her research suggests that across a variety of sports, coaches' pre-game remarks do matter: 90% of players say they enjoy listening, and 65% say the speeches affect the way they play. She's found that people prefer an information-rich (uncertainty-reducing) speech if they're playing an unknown opponent or a team to which they've narrowly lost in the past. (For example: "We're going to beat this team with tough man-to-man coverage. Joe, your job is to neutralize that shooting guard; Jimmy, you box out that star rebounder on every play.") If a team is an underdog or playing in a high-stakes game, a more emotional pep talk (with more empathetic and meaning-making language) is more effective. (For example: "We've exceeded all expectations in this tournament. No one expects us to win. But I expect you to win. I know you can win. You have to win. For your teammates, for the fans—because you deserve this victory.")

Military speeches also tend to use the three elements of MLT in varying proportions, even if the terminology is different. When Keith Yellin, a former officer in the US Marine Corps and the author of *Battle Exhortation: The Rhetoric of Combat Leadership*, analyzed pre-combat speeches dating back to the ancient Greeks and Romans (including literary accounts, such as the "Once more unto the breach" oratory in Shakespeare's *Henry V*), he found 23 "common topics" that generals call on. These include language that qualifies as direction giving ("Follow the plan"), but most of the themes appeal to soldiers' reason (by comparing their superior army to opponents' weaker forces) or emotions (by saying God is on their side or by highlighting the evilness of the enemy). Since the soldiers are about to risk their lives, it makes sense that a commander would focus on the larger purpose of the battle and why the risk is worthwhile.

At the same time, Yellin acknowledges that pre-combat oratory is less common today than in earlier wars, and its balance of elements has shifted. That's partly because today's armies are stealthy (limiting opportunities for speeches), but it's also because they're now more professionalized, made up mostly of career soldiers who voluntarily enlisted, rather than civilian soldiers or draftees. While new recruits might still benefit from rah-rah pep talks, seasoned soldiers already know their purpose and don't need as much empathy.

Stanley McChrystal, the retired four-star general who oversaw special operations in Iraq and Afghanistan, echoes this view. "If you went out with Delta Force or the Rangers or the SEALS in this last war, we were fighting every night," he says. "Stuff is happening so fast, they're all business." Earlier in his career, however, when he was leading younger soldiers, he relied more on emotion and meaning: "During the last 30 minutes or so [before a mission], it was more about building the confidence and the commitment to each other." He says he tended to start with direction giving ("Here's what I'm asking you to do") but quickly shifted to meaning making ("Here's why it's important") and empathy ("Here's why I know you can do it" and "Think about what you've done together before"), and then ended with a recap ("Now let's go and do it").

The upshot of all this research and anecdotal evidence is that leaders in any context need to understand each element of motivating language theory and be conscious of emphasizing the right one at the right time.

Putting Theory into Practice

Alioto, the Yelp sales leader, has never studied the Mayfields' work, but she seems to have adopted the framework on her own. She leads with empathy—thanking the entire team for its hard work, singling out people or small teams who've been crushing it, and emphasizing that if one Yelp salesperson can put up spectacular numbers, all the reps are capable of it, since they have similar skills and training. After reading a transcript of her talk, the Mayfields point to this line in particular: "No matter what's happened to you up to this point in the month, you can make it a successful day." Then she shifts to direction giving, offering insight on a basic informational concept—often dealing with having the right mindset or a commitment to act. For example, she tells the reps to write one goal for the day on a post-it and stick it on their computer.

Alioto ends with meaning making—an emotional rallying cry that connects LDOM to a bigger goal and leaves the group energized: "Every time you win the heart and mind of a business owner, you're not only helping yourself—you're helping your team, you're helping your office, you're helping your company, and you're helping Yelp get where it wants to be." The Mayfields note that she could have gone a step further by connecting sales reps' work to how Yelp improves end users' lives by giving them access to recommendations and reviews of restaurants and other businesses. But on the whole, they give high marks to Alioto's use of rhetoric to motivate a sales team.

It's important to note, however, that Alioto's instruction, empathy, and meaning making don't stop when the salespeople file back to their desks. After her speech, she walks the sales floor, talking individually with more than a hundred reps and continuing to employ the different elements from motivating language theory. In one conversation, she talks to a rep about how to more forcefully close an ambivalent prospect. With a salesperson about to call an automobile mechanic, she talks about the specifics of that category. In other conversations, she tries to boost reps' confidence or emphasize the team's goals.

By day's end, the *New York Yelpers* have sold $1.45 million in new ads, meeting their quota and falling just $50,000 short of that month's stretch target. Many individual reps achieve their BME, Yelp-speak for "best month ever".

It's impossible to say how much her morning remarks and one-on-one talks influenced those results, but Alioto felt the day was successful. "My speech wasn't anything groundbreaking, but it helped them think about where they are and what they are capable of in a different way," she says. "I try to make everyone understand that they have the power to control their day."

Words and Expressions

draw on		凭借,利用,动用
psych up		自我暗示,激励,使兴奋起来,使(为比赛、表演等)做好精神准备
adapt	vt.	改编,改写
reps	n.	(representative)销售代表,销售专员
cold-call	vt.	打电话给陌生人,联系完全陌生的人
close deal		完成交易
finalize	vt.	最后确定,最终敲定
extol	vt.	赞扬,颂扬
namecheck	vt.	指名道姓地提及(某人)
energize	vt.	使充满热情,给(某人)增添能量(或精力、活力、干劲)
spur	vt.	鞭策,激励
prerequisite	n.	先决条件,前提,必要条件
mimicry	n.	模仿,模仿的技巧
inspirational	adj.	启发灵感的,鼓舞人心的
lean on		依赖,依靠
rest on		根据,基于
practitioner	n.	从业者,执业医生,习艺者,专门人才
winning	adj.	获胜的,赢的,吸引人的
formula	n.	方案,方法,公式,方程式,计算式,分子式

dub	vt.	给……起绰号,把……称为
motivating language theory		激励语言理论
military	adj.	军事的,军队的
skillfully	adv.	巧妙地
gratitude	n.	感激之情,感谢
fit into		归属,适于(特定情形或体系),融入,与……相处融洽
bond	vt.	使结合,建立互信关系,与……紧密联系
pharmaceutical	adj.	制药的,配药的,卖药的
	n.	药物
start-up	n.	刚成立的公司,新企业(尤指互联网公司)
	adj.	(新企业或工程)开办阶段的
alleviate	vt.	减轻,缓和,缓解
amyotrophic lateral sclerosis (ALS)		肌萎缩侧索硬化症
ailment	n.	疾病(尤指微恙),不安
all-hands meeting		全体员工大会
incorporate into		使……成为……的一部分
solely	adv.	仅,只,唯,单独地
grease	n.	(炼过的)动物油脂,润滑油
be up		熬夜
athlete	n.	运动员,田径运动员
narrowly	adv.	勉强地,以毫厘之差
coverage	n.	覆盖范围(或方式)
neutralize	vt.	使无效,(化学)中和,使成为中性,使中立
shooting guard		得分后卫
box out		卡位抢篮板
rebounder	n.	善于抢篮板球之球员
underdog	n.	失败者,退居下风的人,受压迫者,打败了的选手
high-stakes	adj.	高风险的
tournament	n.	锦标赛
terminology	n.	(某学科的)术语,有特别含义的用语,专门用语
Marine Corps		海军陆战队
exhortation	n.	讲道词,训导,劝告
rhetoric	n.	华而不实的言语,花言巧语,修辞技巧
combat	n.	搏斗,打仗,战斗

Unit Fourteen Product Promotion

qualify	vt.	符合,配得上(某称号、名称等)
evilness	n.	邪恶
oratory	n.	演讲术,(用长词或正式词语的)辞藻华丽的言辞
stealthy	adj.	悄悄的,鬼鬼祟祟的
professionalize	vt.	使专业化,使职业化
career soldiers		职业军人
voluntarily	adv.	自愿地,自动地,主动地,无偿地,义务地
enlist	vt.	(使)入伍,征募,从军,争取,谋取(帮助、支持或参与)
civilian	n.	平民,老百姓
draftee	n.	被征召入伍者(等同于 conscript)
rah-rah	adj.	<美口>(大学生体育比赛中的)为己方大声叫好的
seasoned	adj.	富有经验的,老于此道的
stuff	n.	(事物名称不详、无关紧要或所指事物明显时)东西,物品,玩意儿
commitment	n.	承诺,许诺,委任,委托,致力,献身,承担义务
recap(= recapitulate)	vt. & vi.	扼要重述,概括
upshot	n.	结果
anecdotal	adj.	轶事的,趣闻的,多轶事的,含轶事的
put up		赢得,达到
mindset	n.	观念模式,思维倾向,心态
post-it	n.	报事贴(注册商标),一种边缘带有贴纸的便笺纸
rally	vi.	聚集,集合,反弹,反败为胜,恢复(元气等)
file	vi.	排成一行行走
ambivalent	adj.	矛盾的,摇摆不定的,犹豫不决的
prospect	n.	可能性,希望,前景,成功的机会
stretch target		伸张指标,伸张性目标
groundbreaking	adj.	开创性的,突破性的

 Notes to the Text

1. *Glengarry Glen Ross*:《拜金一族》,是亚提森娱乐出品的剧情片,由詹姆斯·福雷执导,杰克·莱蒙、凯文·史派西等人主演,于1992年10月2日在美国上映。影片讲述了一个房地产中介公司,为了打开销售局面制定销售奖励政策,四位推销员为了奖励想尽办法拉生意的故事。

2. *The Wolf of Wall Street*:《华尔街之狼》,是马丁·斯科塞斯执导的一部喜剧电影,莱昂纳多·迪卡普里奥、玛格特·罗比、乔纳·希尔领衔主演。影片讲述的是华尔街传奇人物乔丹·贝尔福特的故事,这位股票经纪人曾在 3 分钟内赚取 1200 万美元,31 岁时就拥有亿万家产。影片根据乔丹的个人回忆录改编,讲述了他游走在法律边缘的发家生涯以及迷失于性和毒品的沉沦生活。

3. Texas A&M University:得克萨斯 A&M 大学,简称 TAMU。该校建立于 1876 年,位于美国得克萨斯州的卡城,是世界百强名校,北美顶尖研究型大学联盟"美国大学协会"(AAU)成员,全美第六大公立高校,拥有极高的学术成就和教学水准。该校建校之初为德州农机学院(Texas College of Agriculture and Mechanics),留下 A 和 M 的缩写,只是为了不忘历史。

4. California State University:加利福尼亚州立大学(简称为"加州州立大学",缩写为 CSU 或 Cal State),是美国加州的一个公立大学系统。它是组成加州公立高等教育体系的三个大学系统之一,另外两部分分别是加利福尼亚大学系统(UC 系统,10 个校区)和加州社区大学系统(123 所)。加州州立大学是全美规模最大的公立大学。与科研型大学加州大学(UC)不同的是,加州州立大学(CSU)是教学型大学。这两所大学都没有所谓"主校区"的概念,每个分校都有自己独立的教学、招生、财政、管理体系。加州州立大学长滩分校〔California State University, Long Beach(CSULB)〕成立于 1949 年。

5. Delta Force, Combat Applications Group(CAG):美国三角洲部队,由曾在英国空降特勤队中服役的美国陆军上校贝克卫斯建立,成立于 1977 年 11 月,名为"第一特种部队作战分队",简称"三角洲部队",是美国最为神秘的特种部队,也是当今世界上规模最大、装备最齐全、资金最雄厚的部队。三角洲部队初期深受英国空降特勤队的影响,其组织、构想和功能都和空降特勤队类似,划分为几个中队,每个中队再分为几个小组,他们可以 16 个人一组行动,也可以 8 人一组分两组行动。它的主要任务是要对付影响美国利益的恐怖事件。

6. SEALS:海豹,是美军三栖突击队的别名,SEAL 取 Sea(海)、Air(空)、Land(陆)之意。突击队正式成立于 1962 年,前身是美国海军水下爆破队,到 1988 年时已经扩大到两个战斗群,共有 7 个中队,人数约 1600 人。海豹突击队现已成为美国实施局部战争、应付突发事件的撒手锏。

Grading a Sales Leader's Pep Talk

July – August, 2017, *Harvard Business Review*

  HBR asked Milton and Jacqueline Mayfield to evaluate how well Yelp sales leader Erica Galos Alioto used motivating language theory with her team. They highlighted the three elements—direction-giving language, empathetic language, and meaning-making language—and offered comments on her approach. Edited excerpts follow.

Let me just say how impressed I am with this group ... Thank you for being the top office in Yelp right now, and for welcoming me with such incredible energy.

Right now the New York office is leading the company with 104% of quota, and there are two days left in the month. That's absolutely insane ... Colleen is at $80,000. I tried to say hello to her yesterday, but she was on the phone, pitching like a mad woman, so I couldn't .... (*Praising the Group and Individual Contributions*)

Everybody knows how amazing the last day of the month is in the New York office. But LDOM isn't really about the day of the month. It's about how we approach that day. There's something about that particular day that makes us come in with the ridiculous amount of grit and determination, the ability to make the unthinkable happen, (*Portraying Ldom as a Transcendent Event and Connecting the Reps' Actions to a Larger Goal*) the energy to achieve just about anything so that no matter where we are in relation to quota, we're going to win. All those people who've been telling us no all month long—we're going to turn that around and get a yes ... (*Acknowledging That Some People Are Lagging, but Emphasizing Their Self-efficacy and Resilience*)

Hopefully everybody has a pen and paper. I want you all to take a moment and write down what success looks like for you today. It may be how many business owners you talked to, or how many hearts and minds you won ... Write it down. (*Offering Specific Guidance on How to Approach the Day's Task*)

When you woke up this morning, what was your mentality? Sometimes we get into negative self-talk. Sometimes it may sound like this: "Why is Jon at target today? He must have a really great territory." Sometimes we believe if somebody is achieving something that we're not, it must be because the other person has some advantage. (*Recognizing Employees' Tendency to Get Discouraged, Rather Than Be Emboldened, by Colleagues' Success*)

Guess what? We also have plenty of examples of what people think of as a bad territory, and we put somebody new on it, and they go out and absolutely crush it.

If there's anything negative in your thinking, I encourage you to turn that thinking on its head. Instead of looking at the differences between you and somebody else with a lot of success, look for similarities. (*Instructing Reps to Avoid Negativity*)

We've got two days to make it happen. Everything you do today, every action you take to make that successful outcome, every time you pitch, every business owner you talk to, every time you encourage a teammate to be better, every time you win the heart and mind of a business owner, you're not only helping yourself—you're helping your team, you're helping your office, you're helping your company, and you're helping Yelp get where it wants to be. (*Connecting Today's Work to the Company's Larger Goal*)

Words and Expressions

pep talk		鼓舞士气的讲话
pep	n.	活力,锐气,劲头
motivating	adj.	激励的,激发的
empathetic	adj.	移情的,有同感的,能产生共鸣的
excerpt	n.	摘录,节选
incredible	adj.	不能相信的,难以置信的,极好的,极大的
quota	n.	定额,限额,配额,定量,指标
pitch		~ sth(at sb)	~ sth(as sth)(使产品或服务)针对,面向,确定销售对象(或目标市场)
insane	adj.	疯狂的
come in		加入,参与(讨论、安排或任务)
ridiculous	adj.	愚蠢的,荒谬的,荒唐的
grit	n.	勇气,决心
transcendent	adj.	卓越的,杰出的,极其伟大的
turn around		(使)调转方向,(使)转向
self-efficacy	n.	自我效能,自我效能感,自我成效感
resilience	n.	快速恢复的能力,适应力
mentality	n.	心态,思想状况,思想方法
self-talk	n.	自我对话,自言自语
territory	n.	领域,管区,地盘
embolden	vt.	使增加勇气,使更有胆量,使更有信心
crush	vt.	破坏,毁坏(某人的信心或幸福)

Notes to the Text

1. Yelp:美国最大点评网站,2004 年 7 月在旧金山成立,至今已扎根于 32 个国家的主要城市,是当地商家信息最全面的平台。2012 年 3 月 2 日登陆纽交所,股票代码为 YELP,共发行 715 万股普通股。2017 年 8 月 16 日,支付宝"发现"平台宣布接入全球最大点评网站 Yelp。

Unit Fifteen

Enterprise Data Management

What's Your Data Strategy?

The key is to balance offense and defense
Leandro Dalle Mule and Thomas H. Davenport
May – June, 2017, *Harvard Business Review*

Leandro Dalle Mule is the chief data officer at AIG. Thomas H. Davenport is the President's Distinguished Professor of Information Technology and Management at Babson College, a fellow at the MIT Initiative on the Digital Economy, and a senior adviser at Deloitte Analytics.

More than ever, the ability to manage torrents of data is critical to a company's success. But even with the emergence of data-management functions and chief data officers (CDOs), most companies remain badly behind the curve. Cross-industry studies show that on average, less than half of an organization's structured data is actively used in making decisions and less than 1% of its unstructured data is analyzed or used at all. More than 70% of employees have access to data they should not, and 80% of analysts' time is spent simply discovering and preparing data. Data breaches are common, rogue data sets propagate in silos, and companies' data technology often isn't up to the demands put on it.

> **IN BRIEF**
> **The Challenge**
> To remain competitive, companies must wisely manage quantities of data. But data theft is common, flawed or duplicate data sets exist within organizations, and IT is often behind the curve.
> **The Solution**
> Companies need a coherent strategy that strikes the proper balance between two types of data management: defensive, such as security and governance, and offensive, such as predictive analytics.
> **The Execution**
> Regardless of its industry, a company's data strategy is rarely static; typically, a chief data officer is in charge of ensuring that it dynamically adjusts as competitive pressures and overall corporate strategy shift.

Having a CDO and a data-management function is a start, but neither can be fully effective in the absence of a coherent strategy for organizing, governing, analyzing, and deploying an organization's information assets. Indeed, without such strategic management many companies struggle to protect and leverage their data—and CDOs' tenures are often difficult and short (just 2.4 years on average, according to Gartner). In this article we describe a new framework for building a robust data strategy that can be applied across industries and levels of data maturity. The framework draws on our implementation experience at the global insurer AIG (where DalleMule is the CDO) and our study of half a dozen other large companies where its elements have been applied. The strategy enables superior data management and analytics—essential capabilities that support managerial decision making and ultimately enhance financial performance.

The "plumbing" aspects of data management may not be as sexy as the predictive models and colorful dashboards they produce, but they're vital to high performance. As such, they're not just the concern of the CIO and the CDO; ensuring smart data management is the responsibility of all C-suite executives, starting with the CEO.

Defense versus Offense

Our framework addresses two key issues: It helps companies clarify the primary purpose of their data, and it guides them in strategic data management. Unlike other approaches we've seen, ours requires companies to make considered trade-offs between "defensive" and "offensive" uses of data and between control and flexibility in its use, as we describe below. Although information on enterprise data management is abundant, much of it is technical and focused on governance, best practices, tools, and the like. Few if any data-management frameworks are as business focused as ours: It not only promotes the efficient use of data and allocation of resources but also helps companies design their data-management activities to support their overall strategy. Data defense and offense are differentiated by distinct business objectives and the activities designed to address them.

Data defense is about minimizing downside risk. Activities include ensuring compliance with regulations (such as rules governing data privacy and the integrity of financial reports), using analytics to detect and limit fraud, and building systems to prevent theft. Defensive efforts also ensure the integrity of data flowing through a company's internal systems by identifying, standardizing, and governing authoritative data sources, such as fundamental customer and supplier information or sales data, in a "single source of truth". Data offense focuses on supporting business objectives such as increasing revenue, profitability, and customer satisfaction. It typically includes activities that generate customer insights (data analysis and modeling, for example) or integrate disparate customer and market data to support managerial decision making through, for instance, interactive dashboards.

Offensive activities tend to be most relevant for customer-focused business functions such as sales and marketing and are often more real-time than is defensive work, with its concentration on legal, financial, compliance, and IT concerns. (An exception would be data fraud protection, in which seconds count and real-time analytics smarts are critical.) Every company needs both offense and defense to succeed, but getting the balance right is tricky. In every organization we've talked with, the two compete fiercely for finite resources, funding, and people. As we shall see, putting equal emphasis on the two is optimal for some companies. But for many others it's wiser to favor one or the other.

Some company or environmental factors may influence the direction of data strategy: Strong regulation in an industry (financial services or health care, for example) would move the organization toward defense; strong competition for customers would shift it toward offense. The challenge for CDOs and the rest of the C-suite is to establish the appropriate trade-offs between defense and offense and to ensure the best balance in support of the company's overall strategy.

Decisions about these trade-offs are rooted in the fundamental dichotomy between standardizing data and keeping it more flexible. The more uniform data is, the easier it becomes to execute defensive processes, such as complying with regulatory requirements and implementing data-access controls. The more flexible data is—that is, the more readily it can be transformed or interpreted to meet specific business needs—the more useful it is in offense. Balancing offense and defense, then, requires balancing data control and flexibility, as we will describe.

Single Source, Multiple Versions

Before we explore the framework, it's important to distinguish between information and data and to differentiate information architecture from data architecture. According to Peter Drucker, information is "data endowed with relevance and purpose". Raw data, such as customer retention rates, sales figures and supply costs, is of limited value until it has been integrated with other data and transformed into information that can guide decision making. Sales figures put into a historical or a market context suddenly have meaning—they may be climbing or falling relative to benchmarks or in response to a specific strategy.

A company's data architecture describes how data is collected, stored, transformed, distributed, and consumed. It includes the rules governing structured formats, such as databases and file systems, and the systems for connecting data with the business processes that consume it. Information architecture governs the processes and rules that convert data into useful information. For example, data architecture might feed raw daily advertising and sales data into information architecture systems, such as marketing dashboards, where it is integrated and analyzed to reveal relationships between ad spend and sales by channel and region.

Many organizations have attempted to create highly centralized, control-oriented approaches to data and information architectures. Previously known as information engineering and now as master data management, these top-down approaches are often not well suited to supporting a broad data strategy. Although they are effective for standardizing enterprise data, they can inhibit flexibility, making it harder to customize data or transform it into information that can be applied strategically. In our experience, a more flexible and realistic approach to data and information architectures involves both a single source of truth (SSOT) and multiple versions of the truth (MVOTs). The SSOT works at the data level; MVOTs support the management of information.

In the organizations we've studied, the concept of a single version of truth—for example, one inviolable primary source of revenue data—is fully grasped and accepted by IT and across the business. However, the idea that a single source can feed multiple versions of the truth (such as revenue figures that differ according to users' needs) is not well understood, commonly articulated, or, in general, properly executed.

The key innovation of our framework is this: It requires flexible data and information architectures that permit both single and multiple versions of the truth to support a defensive-offensive approach to data strategy.

OK. Let's parse that.

The SSOT is a logical, often virtual and cloud-based repository that contains one authoritative copy of all crucial data, such as customer, supplier and product details. It must have robust data provenance and governance controls to ensure that the data can be relied on in defensive and offensive activities, and it must use a common language—not one that is specific to a particular business unit or function. Thus, for example, revenue is reported, customers are defined, and products are classified in a single, unchanging, agreed upon way within the SSOT.

THE ELEMENTS OF DATA STRATEGY

	DEFENSE	OFFENSE
KEY OBJECTIVES	Ensure data security, privacy, integrity, quality, regulatory compliance, and governance	Improve competitive position and profitability
CORE ACTIVITIES	Optimize data extraction, standardization, storage, and access	Optimize data analytics, modeling, visualization, transformation, and enrichment
DATA-MANAGEMENT ORIENTATION	Control	Flexibility
ENABLING ARCHITECTURE	SSOT (Single source of truth)	MVOTs (Multiple versions of the truth)

Not having an SSOT can lead to chaos. One large industrial company we studied had more than a dozen data sources containing similar supplier information, such as name and address. But the content was slightly different in each source. For example, one source identified a supplier as Acme; another called it Acme, Inc.; and a third labeled it ACME Corp. Meanwhile, various functions within the company were relying on differing data sources; often the functions weren't even aware that alternative sources existed. Human beings might be able to untangle such problems (though it would be labor-intensive), but traditional IT systems can't, so the company couldn't truly understand its relationship with the supplier. Fortunately, artificial intelligence tools that can sift through such data chaos to assemble an SSOT are becoming available. The industrial company ultimately tapped one and saved substantial IT costs by shutting down redundant systems. The SSOT allowed managers to identify suppliers that were selling to multiple business units within the company and to negotiate discounts. In the first year, having an SSOT yielded $75 million in benefits.

An SSOT is the source from which multiple versions of the truth are developed. MVOTs result from the business-specific transformation of data into information—data imbued with "relevance and purpose". Thus, as various groups within units or functions transform, label, and report data, they create distinct, controlled versions of the truth that, when queried, yield consistent, customized responses according to the groups' predetermined requirements.

Consider how a supplier might classify its clients Bayer and Apple according to industry. At the SSOT level these companies belong, respectively, to chemicals/pharmaceuticals and consumer electronics, and all data about the supplier's relationship with them, such as commercial transactions and market information, would be mapped accordingly. In the absence of MVOTs, the same would be true for all organizational purposes. But such broad industry classifications may be of little use to sales, for example, where a more practical version of the truth would classify Apple as a mobile phone or a laptop company, depending on which division sales was interacting with. Similarly, Bayer might be more usefully classified as a drug or a pesticide company for the purposes of competitive analysis. In short, multiple versions of the truth, derived from a common SSOT, support superior decision making.

At a global asset management company we studied, the marketing and finance departments both produced monthly reports on television ad spending—MVOTs derived from a common SSOT. Marketing, interested in analyzing advertising effectiveness, reported on spending after ads had aired. Finance, focusing on cash flow, captured spending when invoices were paid. The reports therefore contained different numbers, but each represented an accurate version of the truth.

Procter & Gamble has adopted a similar approach to data management. The company long had a centralized SSOT for all product and customer data, and other versions of data weren't allowed. But CDO Guy Peri and his team realized that the various business units had valid needs for customized interpretations of the data. The units are now permitted to create controlled data transformations for reporting that can be reliably mapped back to the SSOT. Thus the MVOTs diverge from the SSOT in consistent ways, and their provenance is clear.

In its application of the SSOT-MVOTs model, the Canadian Imperial Bank of Commerce (CIBC) automated processes to ensure that enterprise source data and data transformations remained aligned. CIBC's CDO, Jose Ribau, explains that the company's SSOT contains all basic client profile and preference data; MVOTs for loan origination and customer relationship management transform the source data into information that supports regulatory reporting and improved customer experience. Automated synchronization programs connect SSOT and MVOTs data, with nightly "exception handling" to identify and address data integrity issues such as inconsistent customer profiles.

Although the SSOT-MVOTs model is conceptually straightforward, it requires robust data controls, standards, governance, and technology. Ideally, senior executives will actively participate on data governance boards and committees. But data governance isn't particularly fun. Typically, enterprise CDOs and CTOs lead data and technology governance processes, and business and technology managers in functions and units are the primary participants. What's critical is that single sources of the truth remain unique and valid, and that multiple versions of the truth diverge from the original source only in carefully controlled ways. (For more on data governance and technology, see the sidebars "Good Governance, Good Data" and "A Lake of Data".)

Striking a Balance

Let's return now to data strategy—striking the best balance between defense and offense and between control and flexibility. Whereas the CEO—often with the CIO—is ultimately responsible for a company's data strategy, the CDO commonly conceives it and leads its development and execution. The CDO must determine the right trade-offs while dynamically adjusting the balance by leveraging the SSOT and MVOTs architectures.

It's rare to find an organization—especially a large, complex one—in which data is both tightly controlled and flexibly used. With few exceptions, CDOs find that their best data strategy emphasizes either defense and control (which depends on a robust SSOT) or offense and flexibility (enabled by MVOTs). Devoting equal attention to offense and defense is sometimes optimal, but in general it's unwise to default to a 50 / 50 split rather than making considered, strategic tradeoffs. To determine a company's current and desired positions on the offense-defense spectrum, the CDO must bear in mind, among other things, the company's overall strategy, its regulatory environment, the data capabilities of its competitors, the maturity of its data-management practices, and the size of its data budget. For example, insurance and financial services companies typically operate in heavily regulated environments, which argues for an emphasis on data defense. (That is the case at AIG.) Retailers, operating in a less-regulated environment where intense competition requires robust customer analytics, might emphasize offense. (See the exhibit "The Data-Strategy Spectrum".)

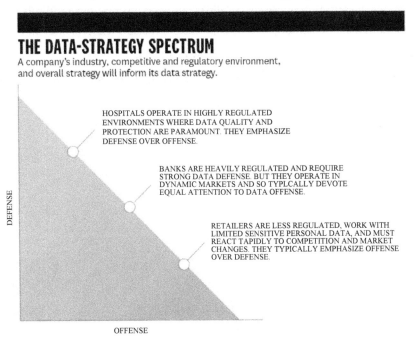

THE DATA-STRATEGY SPECTRUM
A company's industry, competitive and regulatory environment, and overall strategy will inform its data strategy.

HOSPITALS OPERATE IN HIGHLY REGULATED ENVIRONMENTS WHERE DATA QUALITY AND PROTECTION ARE PARAMOUNT. THEY EMPHASIZE DEFENSE OVER OFFENSE.

BANKS ARE HEAVILY REGULATED AND REQUIRE STRONG DATA DEFENSE. BUT THEY OPERATE IN DYNAMIC MARKETS AND SO TYPLCALLY DEVOTE EQUAL ATTENTION TO DATA OFFENSE.

RETAILERS ARE LESS REGULATED, WORK WITH LIMITED SENSITIVE PERSONAL DATA, AND MUST REACT TAPIDLY TO COMPETITION AND MARKET CHANGES. THEY TYPICALLY EMPHASIZE OFFENSE OVER DEFENSE.

DEFENSE

OFFENSE

As Peri points out, defense and offense often require differing approaches from IT and the data management organization. Defense, he argues, is day-to-day and operational, and at P&G is largely overseen by permanent IT teams focused on master data management, information security, and so forth. Offense involves partnering with business leaders on tactical and strategic initiatives. Leaders may be reluctant to engage with master data management, but they are happy to collaborate on optimizing marketing and trade promotion spending.

Of course, plenty of cases don't fall neatly into either the offense or the defense category: The CDO of a large hedge fund told us that he was less concerned with data protection than with rapidly gathering and using new data. The most valuable data for his fund is primarily external, publicly or commercially available, captured in real time, and already of good quality, structured, and cleansed. Additionally, although his business is in financial services, it's not heavily regulated. Thus he focuses primarily on data offense. Wells Fargo's CDO, A. Charles Thomas, has enterprise responsibility for customer-related analytics, an offensive activity, and strives to keep the balance between offensive and defensive activities around 50/50, even structuring meeting agendas to focus equally on the two.

The tool "Assess Your Strategy Position" offers diagnostic questions that can help CDOs place their companies on the offense-defense spectrum and gauge whether their data strategy aligns with their corporate strategy. Determining an organization's current and desired positions on the spectrum will force executives to make trade-offs between offensive and defensive investments. Of course, this tool is not a precise measure. CDOs should use the results to inform data strategy and discussions with other C-level executives.

ASSESS YOUR STRATEGY POSITION

Choose from among the following 16 objectives the eight that are *most important* to your business. Selecting that subset will require considered trade-offs that reveal your offense-defense orientation.

#	Objective	CHECK THE EIGHT THAT QUALIFY.	TOTAL NUMBER OF CHECKED BOXES
1	Reduce general operating expenses		
2	Meet industry regulatory requirements		
3	Prevent cyberattacks and data breaches		
4	Mitigate operational risks such as poor access controls and data losses		
5	Improve IT infrastructure and reduce data-related costs		
6	Streamline back-office systems and processes		
7	Improve data quality (completeness, accuracy, timeliness)		
8	Rationalize multiple sources of data and information (consolidate and eliminate redundancy)		
9	Improve revenue through cross-selling, strategic pricing, and customer acquisition		
10	Create new products and services		
11	Respond rapidly to competitors and market changes		
12	Use sophisticated customer analytics to drive business results		
13	Leverage new sources of internal and external data		
14	Monetize company data (sell as a product or a service)		
15	Optimize existing strong bench of analysts and data scientists		
16	Generate return on investments in big data and analytics infrastructure		

Data Defense: Strong defense is characterized by single source of truth (SSOT) architecture, robust data governance and controls, and a more centralized data-management organization.

Data Offense: Strong offense is characterized by multiple versions of the truth (MVOTs) architecture, high data flexibility, and a more decentralized data-management organization.

We find that companies with the most-advanced data strategies started at one point and gradually migrated to a new, stable position. For example, they may have shifted their focus from defense and data control toward offense as their data defense matured or competition heated up. The opposite path—from offense toward defense, and from flexible toward controlled—is possible but usually more difficult.

Consider how data strategy has shifted at CIBC. The bank established the chief data officer role a few years ago and for the first 18 months maintained a 90% defensive orientation, focusing on governance, data standardization, and building new data-storage capabilities. When Jose Ribau took over as CDO, in 2015, he determined that CIBC's defense was sufficiently solid that he could shift toward offense, including more advanced data modeling and data science work. Today CIBC's data strategy strikes a 50/50 balance. Ribau expects that the new attention to offense will drive increased ROI from data products and services and nurture analytical talent for the future.

Regardless of what industry a company is in, its position on the offense-defense spectrum is rarely static. As competitive pressure mounts, an insurer may decide to increase its focus on offensive activities. A hedge fund may find itself in a tougher regulatory environment that requires rebalancing its data strategy toward defense. How a company's data strategy changes in direction and velocity will be a function of its overall strategy, culture, competition, and market.

Organizing Data Management

As with most organizational design, data-management functions can be built centrally or decentralized by function or business unit. The optimal design will depend on a company's position on the offense-defense spectrum. A centralized data function typically has a single CDO with accountability across the entire organization, ensuring that data policies, governance and standards are applied consistently. This design is most suitable for businesses that focus on data defense.

Conversely, several companies we studied found that data offense can be better executed through decentralized data management, typically with a CDO for each business unit and most corporate functions. "Unit CDOs" tend to report directly to their business but have a matrix reporting relationship to the enterprise CDO. That helps prevent the development of data silos (which can lead to redundant systems and duplicate work) and ensures that best practices are shared and standards are followed. Generally speaking, unit CDOs own their respective versions of the truth, while the enterprise CDO owns the SSOT. A decentralized approach is well suited to offensive strategies because it can increase the agility and customization of data reporting and analytics. In many companies, among them Wells Fargo, CIBC and P&G, the CDO is responsible for both analytics and data management, facilitating the ability to balance offense and defense.

Finally, in choosing between a centralized and a decentralized data function, it's important to consider how funding will be determined, allocated and spent. The budget may appear larger for a centralized function than for a decentralized one simply because it's concentrated under one CDO. Decentralized budgets are typically more focused on offensive investments, are closer to the business users, and have more tangible ROIs, whereas centralized budgets are more often focused on minimizing risk, reducing costs, and providing better data controls and regulatory oversight—activities that are less close to business users and usually have a less-tangible ROI. Thus creating a business case to justify the latter is usually trickier. The importance of investing in data governance and control—even if the payoff is abstract—is more easily understood and accepted if a company has suffered from a major regulatory challenge, a data breach, or some other serious defense-related issue. Absent a traumatic event, enterprise CDOs should spend time educating senior executives and their teams about data-defense principles and how they create value.

> Emerging technologies may enable a next generation of data-management capabilities, potentially simplifying the implementation of defensive and offensive strategies. Machine learning, for example, is already facilitating the creation of a single source of truth in many companies we studied. The promise is more dynamic, less-costly SSOTs and MVOTs. However, no new technology will obviate an effective, well-run data-management function. Our framework will become even more relevant as distributed technology solutions—block chain, for example—come into play. Data was once critical to only a few back-office processes, such as payroll and accounting. Today it is central to any business, and the importance of managing it strategically is only growing. In September 2016, according to the technology conglomerate Cisco, global annual Internet traic surpassed one zettabyte (1,021 bytes) the equivalent, by one calculation, of 150 million years of high-definition video. It took 40 years to get to this point, but in the next four, data traffic will double. There is no avoiding the implications: Companies that have not yet built a data strategy and a strong data management function need to catch up very fast or start planning for their exit.

Extended Reading:

1. A New Data Architecture Can Pay for Itself

When companies lack a robust SSOT-MVOTs data architecture, teams across the organization may create and store the data they need in siloed repositories that vary in depth, breadth, and formatting. Their data management is often done in isolation with inconsistent requirements. The process is inefficient and expensive and can result in the proliferation of multiple uncontrolled versions of the truth that aren't effectively reused. Because SSOTs and MVOTs concentrate, standardize, and streamline data-sourcing activities, they can dramatically cut operational costs.

One large financial services company doing business in more than 200 countries consolidated nearly 130 authoritative data sources, with trillions of records, into an SSOT. This allowed the company to rationalize its key data systems; eliminate much supporting IT infrastructure, such as databases and servers; and cut operating expenses by automating previously manual data consolidation. The automation alone yielded a 190% return on investment with a two-year payback time. Many companies will find that they can fund their entire data management programs, including staff salaries and technology costs, from the savings realized by consolidating data sources and decommissioning legacy systems.

The CDO and the data-management function should be fully responsible for building and operating the SSOT structure and using the savings it generates to fund the company's data program. Most important is to ensure at the outset that the SSOT addresses broad, high-priority business needs, such as applications that benefit customers or generate revenue, so that the project quickly yields results and savings—which encourages organization-wide buy-in.

2. Good Governance, Good Data

A sound data strategy requires that the data contained in a company's single source of truth (SSOT) is of high quality, granular, and standardized, and that multiple versions of the truth (MVOTs) are carefully controlled and derived from the same SSOT. This necessitates good governance for both data and technology. In the absence of proper governance, some common problems arise:

Data definitions may be ambiguous and mutable. With no concrete definition at the outset of what constitutes the "truth" (whether an SSOT or MVOTs), stakeholders will squander time and resources as they try to manage non-standardized data.

Data rules are vague or inconsistently applied. If rules for aggregating, integrating, and transforming data are unclear, misunderstood, or simply not followed—particularly when data transformation involves multiple poorly defined steps—it's difficult to reliably replicate transformations and leverage information across the organization.

Feedback loops for improving data transformation are absent. Complex data analyses such as predictive modeling may be undertaken by one group but prove useful across an organization. Without mechanisms for making these outputs available to others (by, for example, integrating them into appropriate MVOTs), stakeholders may needlessly duplicate work or miss opportunities.

Strong data governance usually involves standing committees or review boards composed of business and technology executives, but it relies heavily on robust technology oversight. If technology rules prevent a marketing executive from buying a server on his or her corporate purchasing card, it's much less likely that marketing will, for instance, create unregulated "shadow" MVOTs or a marketing analytic that duplicates an existing one.

3. A Lake of Data

Until a few years ago, technological limitations made it hard to build the SSOT-MVOTs data architecture needed to support a robust data strategy. Companies depended on traditional data warehouses that stored structured enterprise data in hierarchical files and folders, but these were not always suited to managing vast and growing volumes of data and new formats. To meet the need for a cheaper, more agile and scalable architecture, Silicon Valley engineers devised the "data lake", which can store virtually unlimited amounts of structured and unstructured data, from databases to spreadsheets to free text and image files. Data lakes are an ideal platform for SSOT-MVOTs architecture. A lake can house the SSOT, extracting, storing, and providing access to the organization's most granular data down to the level of individual transactions. And it can support the aggregation of SSOT data in nearly infinite ways in MVOTs that also reside in the lake. Data warehouses still have their uses: They store data for production applications (such as general ledger and order-management systems) that require tight security and access controls, which few data lakes can do. Many companies have both data lakes and warehouses, but the trend is for more and more data to reside in a lake.

Words and Expressions

silo	n.	筒仓
siloed	adj.	孤岛式的,筒仓式的
repository	n.	仓库,贮藏室,存放处
proliferation	n.	激增,涌现,增殖
multiple versions of the truth (MVOT)		多重事实版本
streamline	vt.	使(系统、机构等)效率更高,(尤指)使增产节约
consolidate	vt.	(使)结成一体,合并
rationalize	vt.	使合理化,进行合理化改革,使有经济效益
decommission	vt.	正式停止使用
authoritative	adj.	权威的,可信的
legacy system		遗留系统,原有系统,传统系统
at the outset		从一开始

buy-in	n.	认可, 买账
granular	adj.	分析需要更为细致的
derive	vt.	获得, 取得, (使)起源, (使)产生
necessitate	vt.	使成为必要
mutable	adj.	可变的, 会变的
replicate	vt.	复制, (精确地)仿制, 再造
predictive modeling		预测模型, 预测建模
duplicate	vt.	(尤指不必要时)重复, 再做一次, 复制, 复印
standing committee		常务委员会, 常设委员会
review board		评审委员会, 评审组
oversight	n.	负责, 照管
server	n.	电脑服务器
Corporate Purchasing Card		企业采购卡
unregulated	adj.	无序的, 无原则的
marketing analytics		营销分析, 市场分析
rogue	adj.	离群的, 行为失常的, 暴戾的
	n.	无赖, 捣蛋鬼
coherent	adj.	连贯的, 一致的, 明了的
robust	adj.	强健的, 健康的, 粗野的, 粗鲁的
maturity	n.	成熟, 到期, 完备
fraud	n.	欺骗, 骗子, 诡计
integrity	n.	完整, 正直, 诚实, 廉正
parse	vt.	解析, 从语法上分析
redundant	adj.	多余的, 过剩的, 被解雇的, 失业的, 冗长的, 累赘的
pesticide	n.	杀虫剂
diverge	vi.	分歧, 偏离, 分叉, 离题
	vt.	使偏离, 使分叉
provenance	n.	出处, 起源
spectrum	n.	光谱, 频谱, 范围
velocity	n.	速度
conversely	adv.	相反地
matrix	n.	矩阵, 模型, 社会环境, 政治局势

Notes to the Text

1. SSOT (single source of truth)：单一（身份）信息源，在来自不同信息源的同一属性信息中，作为唯一的标准数据存在。由 HR 管理的 HR 系统中存储了人员的姓名、邮箱、手机号三个属性信息；由 IT 人员管理的 OA 系统中存储了姓名、生日、手机号三个属性信息。某员工只告知 IT 人员需更换手机号码，IT 人员在 OA 系统中进行了更新。所以，当使用以手机号为准的应用时，OA 所提供的手机号信息就是 SSOT。企业应当确认针对每一个属性信息的 SSOT。接下来，需要找到一个可以统一所有信息源的目录，汇集并梳理出所有标准数据，清除无效数据形成一个完整可用的 SSOT，并作为身份管理服务的 SSOT。

2. feedback loop：反馈环系统，在输出端通过一定通道反送到输入端，形成闭合的回路，分为正反馈环和负反馈环。正反馈环是指市场中的投资者受到分析师乐观的收益预测、通货膨胀回落、"货币幻觉"的影响等，导致了投机性价格上升，最初的投资者取得了成功，从而吸引了公众的注意力，导致了价格的进一步上涨，因为通过投资者需求的上升，最初的价格上涨又反馈到了更高的价格中。负反馈环则与之相反。

3. Data Lake：数据湖，是一个集中式存储库，允许以任意规模存储所有结构化和非结构化数据。可以按原样存储数据（无须先对数据进行结构化处理），并运行不同类型的分析——从控制面板和可视化到大数据处理、实时分析和机器学习，以指导做出更好的决策。

4. Babson College：巴布森学院，位于美国马萨诸塞州的巴布森公园，建成于 1919 年，是全美最著名商学院之一。该校主要致力于商科教育与企业家培养，因而不参与 US News 综合大学排名，然而该校的创业学课程连续 25 年位列 US News 全美第一，超过哈佛、宾夕法尼亚等顶尖商学院。其创新实践的企业家精神作为巴布森学院的核心价值贯彻到学校开设的所有商科及文理通识课程上。

5. ROI：投资回报率，是指通过投资而应返回的价值，即企业从一项投资活动中得到的经济回报。它涵盖了企业的获利目标。利润和投入经营所必备的财产相关，因为管理人员必须通过投资和现有财产获得利润。投资可分为实业投资和金融投资两大类，人们平常所说的金融投资主要是指证券投资。